A WORLD BANK COUNTRY STUDY

Mongolia

Toward a Market Economy

The World Bank
Washington, D.C.

First printing September 1992

World Bank Country Studies are among the many reports originally prepared for internal use as part of the continuing analysis by the Bank of the economic and related conditions of its developing member countries and of its dialogues with the governments. Some of the reports are published in this series with the least possible delay for the use of governments and the academic, business and financial, and development communities. The typescript of this paper therefore has not been prepared in accordance with the procedures appropriate to formal printed texts, and the World Bank accepts no responsibility for errors.

The World Bank does not guarantee the accuracy of the data included in this publication and accepts no responsibility whatsoever for any consequence of their use. Any maps that accompany the text have been prepared solely for the convenience of readers; the designations and presentation of material in them do not imply the expression of any opinion whatsoever on the part of the World Bank, its affiliates, or its Board or member countries concerning the legal status of any country, territory, city, or area or of the authorities thereof or concerning the delimitation of its boundaries or its national affiliation.

The complete backlist of publications from the World Bank is shown in the annual *Index of Publications,* which contains an alphabetical title list (with full ordering information) and indexes of subjects, authors, and countries and regions. The latest edition is available free of charge from the Distribution Unit, Office of the Publisher, Department F, The World Bank, 1818 H Street, N.W., Washington, D.C. 20433, U.S.A., or from Publications, The World Bank, 66, avenue d'Iéna, 75116 Paris, France.

ISSN: 0253-2123
ISBN: 0-8213-2247-8

Abstract

This report, the World Bank's first overall review of the Mongolian economy, describes the economic pressures that surfaced in 1991 and the various measures taken by the government since then. After an introductory background, Chapters 2, 3 and 4 assess recent economic developments, the key reform and policy issues, and the country's development prospects in the medium term. Annex 1 provides background notes on the main sectors and selected issues. A statistical appendix is contained in Annex 2.

The report was originally presented to the Bank's Board of Executive Directors in December 1991. Although this version has been updated, the revisions have been limited. While the economy is changing rapidly and most recent data and policy developments have not been included, this analysis of structure and past trends of the economy is expected to be of interest to those working on reforming socialist economies in general, and Mongolia in particular.

CURRENCY EQUIVALENTS
(As of June 30, 1992)

Currency unit = tugrik (Tug)

$1.00	=	Tug 40	(for official commercial transactions)
Tug 1	=	$0.025	
$1.00	=	Tug 250	(for free market transactions)
Tug 1	=	$0.0004	

FISCAL YEAR

January 1 to December 31

WEIGHTS AND MEASURES

Metric System

Preface

Mongolia became a member of the World Bank Group (IBRD, IDA and IFC) on February 14, 1991. A World Bank economic mission visited Mongolia from June 21 to July 5, 1991. It was led by Mete Durdag, and its members included Alan Gelb, Frida Johansen, Kathy Ogawa (all IBRD); John Leimone (IMF); and Cevdet Denizer and Victor Gabor (Consultants). Ramesh Chander and Shahid Yusuf participated in the latter part of the mission's work and Peter Harrold contributed to the drafting of the report. The mission wishes to thank the Mongolian authorities, and in particular the Ministry of Finance, the Bank of Mongolia and the Ministry of National Development, for their support and cooperation in providing the information and data used in this report. It also wishes to acknowledge the cooperation received and the benefit derived from recent work undertaken inter alia by the IMF, the Asian Development Bank (ADB), the United Nations Development Programme (UNDP), and by several United Nations Specialized Agencies.

This report, the World Bank's first review of the Mongolian economy, analyzes the country's economic policies and development prospects at the time of membership. Statistics for 1991 were updated in July 1992 prior to publication.

ACRONYMS

ADB	Asian Development Bank
Aimag	Province/Provincial Government
BOM	Bank of Mongolia (*Mongolbank*) (the central bank)
CCA	Convertible Currency Area
CIS	Commonwealth of Independent States
CMEA (COMECON)	Council for Mutual Economic Assistance
EEC	European Economic Community
ESCAP	Economic and Social Commission for Asia and the Pacific
FDI	Foreign Direct Investment
FTC	Foreign Trade Corporation
GATT	General Agreements on Tariff and Trade
IBEC	International Bank for Economic Cooperation
IDA	International Development Association
IMF	International Monetary Fund
MCC	Mongolian Coal Corporation (*Mongol Nuurs*)
MFE	Ministry of Fuel and Energy
MFN	Most Favored Nation
MIAT	Mongolian International Air Transport
MND	Ministry of National Development
MOF	Ministry of Finance
MOL	Ministry of Labor
MPC	Mongolian Petroleum Company
MPR	Mongolian People's Republic
MPRP	Mongolian People's Revolutionary Party
MTI	Ministry of Trade and Industry
NMP	Net Material Products
PSIP	Public Sector Investment Program
PISC	Petroleum Import and Supply Corporation
REER	Real Effective Exchange Rate
SBA	(IMF) Stand-By Agreement
SNA	System of National Accounts
Somon	County/County Government
SSO	State Statistical Office
UNDP	United Nations Development Programme
USSR	Union of Soviet Socialist Republics

Table of Contents

Page No.

BOXES IN TEXT

TABLES IN TEXT

ANNEXES

MAP

Executive Summary

Background

i. For most of its 70-year history as an independent state, Mongolia has been a centrally planned economy with extremely close ties to the Soviet Union, particularly since 1946. During this period, the country has been gradually transformed from a rural, essentially nomadic economy to one with a large industrial sector, mainly for the production of semiprocessed raw materials. Industrialization was made possible by large investments and loans from the Soviet Union, particularly in the early 1980s, which permitted Mongolia to run large fiscal and external deficits and to enjoy relatively high rates of growth.

ii. This situation began to change in the mid-1980s as Mongolians became increasingly dissatisfied with the rigidities of the centrally planned system. Some reforms were initiated as early as 1986 but did not improve the situation dramatically. After popular demonstrations in March 1990 and the country's first multiparty elections in July 1990, a new coalition government was formed that pledged to "construct a market-oriented economy." Since then, the government has embarked upon a comprehensive program of reforms covering the entire spectrum of economic policies, including privatization, price liberalization, and the establishment of new institutions for macroeconomic management.

iii. The new policy framework coincided with two major external shocks that have seriously affected the economy. First, owing to its own economic difficulties, the Soviet Union terminated its financial and technical assistance to Mongolia in 1991, except for the completion of ongoing turnkey projects; it has also found it difficult to maintain regular supplies to Mongolia of essential commodities such as cement, fertilizers, petroleum and spare parts. Second, the collapse of the Council for Mutual Economic Assistance (CMEA) system in 1991 has seriously disrupted Mongolia's external trade.

iv. Thus, Mongolia's economic reform process has begun under adverse circumstances. The external shocks have had two major effects. In the short term, they have necessitated strong stabilization measures to reduce large structural deficits in Mongolia's fiscal and external accounts. For the longer haul, they have emphasized the need for immediate policy changes to reorient and restructure the economy, so that efficient, self-sustaining growth can be resumed as soon as possible.

Recent Developments

v. The impact of the rapidly changing external environment was first felt in 1990, when GDP fell by 2.1 percent, the first decline in many years. A steeper drop occurred in 1991, estimated at over 16 percent. Among the major sectors, the most rapid decline occurred in the construction sector, as investment decreased dramatically following the abrupt termination of external assistance. This has already created a rapid increase in unemployment, despite the moderating effect of the development of the private sector, which has been creating new jobs in response to economic liberalization.

vi. The reduction in foreign savings is leading to problems in financing the fiscal deficit, equivalent to about 17 percent of GDP in recent years. In 1991 the government resorted to heavy indirect borrowing from the central bank. Reforms under way, such as the conversion of enterprise profit remittances to taxes and changes in the price structure, have reduced old sources of fiscal revenue, while new ones are not yet fully effective. Credit to government and state enterprises together increased in 1991 by almost 50 percent. Credit to private enterprises also grew, fourfold. Estimating the impact of this credit expansion on inflation is not easy, because data are few and because the administrative doubling of most prices in January 1991 makes comparisons with earlier years unreliable. In addition, prices increased further, by an estimated 120 percent in 1991. The rapid growth of money supply in the face of declining production thus raises the specter of hyperinflation. This is why stabilization measures are being given top priority.

vii. Perhaps the most serious impact is visible in the foreign trade sector. In 1986-89, Mongolia's current account deficit was equal to about 30 percent of GDP. The deficit declined sharply in 1991, as imports and exports of goods and services fell by about 75 percent and 45 percent, respectively, from their 1989 levels in the face of the CMEA and USSR difficulties. Reserves became negative as Mongolia turned to hard currency imports to supplement declining CMEA supplies. All this has been compounded by recently poor prospects for some of Mongolia's main hard currency exports--cashmere, wool, and leather products.

viii. Thus, a wide range of measures is needed, both to arrest this serious economic decline and to stimulate efficiency gains and create new sources of growth.

Stabilization and Macroeconomic Reforms

ix. Mongolia has moved swiftly to remove its old central planning system, and new institutions and policy instruments are being put in place. In May 1991, a new central bank was created and the commercial functions of the old monobanking system are being privatized. Now that the central bank is operational, it has begun to tighten monetary policy, and strict money and credit targets have been adopted as part of Mongolia's stand-by program with the International Monetary Fund (IMF). Clearly, with recent runaway money growth and rapid inflation, reimposing monetary discipline is the central bank's most important and immediate task. Beyond this, its main priority will be to establish itself and train its staff to regulate and supervise a private banking system, and to complete the privatization of its commercial banking functions. Privatization has not proceeded as fast as had been expected, not least because of the many bad loans on the books of these banks as a result of past directed credit. While it is necessary to remove nonperforming loans from the banks' portfolios before privatization, it will also be necessary to avoid monetizing such debts.

x. Among the first measures that the government instituted were reforms of the taxation system, recognizing that old sources of finance would fast disappear. Indeed, continued adjustment of public finances remains at the heart of the stabilization effort and of the program to create a new economic system. Already, new corporate and personal income taxes have been instituted, and a new customs tax has replaced the old import price differential system. New indirect taxes have been imposed to fill the large revenue gap.

xi. The authorities have begun to reduce public expenditures, primarily by postponing or eliminating investment expenditures and by cutting the size of the civil service. In addition, cost recovery measures are planned to reduce net outlays in health and education. The major area still needing effort is reducing subsidies, which account for a quarter of public expenditure. Industrial and trade subsidies should be eliminated rapidly, as part of the transition to a market economy.

xii. On the external side, Mongolia has relied heavily on exchange rate measures and barter trade to adjust its external accounts. The rate moved from Tug 3 = $1 in June 1990 to Tug 40 = $1 today. However, a special rate of Tug 7 = $1 was maintained until November 1991 and then Tug 75 = $1 until March 1992 for barter trade with the Soviet Union. Foreign exchange retention is permitted (to differentiated ceilings) and can be exchanged in a third, parallel exchange market, at higher rates. However, nothing similar to the liberalization of foreign exchange has taken place in trade, which is still dominated by the old trade corporations and by compulsory state orders. Removal of this monopsony situation is urgently needed to improve incentives for nonstate corporations to increase export efforts.

xiii. Finally, the authorities have yet to define clear policy coordination mechanisms with regard to macroeconomic issues. The old central planning system has been formally discarded but has not yet been fully replaced by new institutions and processes. Despite help from international agencies, these mechanisms are only slowly emerging.

Policies for Structural Change

xiv. Mongolia has also moved to institute a wide range of policies to improve efficiency in its industrial, agricultural, and service sectors. These will need to be supplemented by medium-term development strategies and accompanied by a reorientation of the role of government. Price reform has been given a central role. Already prices accounting for some 70 percent of all transactions have been liberalized, and some of the remaining 30 percent (excluding some public services) are scheduled to be freed by the end of 1992. While this is encouraging, price liberalization needs to be accompanied by the abolition of the state order system, especially the state marketing organizations in the agricultural sector. Instead, such organizations may offer in some cases minimum support prices to ensure some stability to farmers as new mechanisms are developed. For the remaining public services, appropriate pricing policies will be necessary, especially passing through the full cost of imported products, where the highly overvalued barter exchange rate has caused severe distortions.

xv. The government has placed privatization of state-owned enterprises at the center of its reform program. Over 2,000 enterprises, including 340 large ones, are to be privatized through a voucher system. Originally, the government hoped to achieve this over a twelve-month period, but has since adopted a more realistic three-year timetable. It will be important to link the pace and sequencing of the privatization program to reforms in other areas, in particular price and marketing reforms. Marketing reforms must precede privatization, not follow it. A particularly difficult issue is how to treat the enterprises' Tug 10 billion of domestic debt. Clearly, enterprises will have to be valued on a net basis, and debt may have to be converted into long-term bonds. Care will also be needed in addressing the possible macroeconomic impact of privatization, especially the distributional effects of the ownership transfer.

xvi. Considerable effort has gone into the price reform and privatization programs, but less attention has been given to promoting new private sector activities. Good progress has been made on the enabling environment, but this will need to be backed by supportive institutions. Sufficient credit, for example, must be available for new private enterprises so that they do not get squeezed out of the market by state-owned ones. Similarly, a significant number of enterprises (in terms of asset value) will remain in public hands indefinitely and others for some time prior to their privatization; early thought will need to be given to how such enterprises will be managed and regulated and how the state's ownership role will be exercised.

xvii. These reform issues--especially price reform and privatization--will be crucial for medium-term sectoral development. In agriculture, privatization of the herds and a full role for market forces are the main issues. Industry is hampered in particular by inefficiency and locational issues deriving from the central planning system. The energy sector has suffered from poor pricing policies, and from lack of access to modern technology, which has had an adverse impact on the urban environment.

xviii. As reforms take hold, government will have to assume new roles. Preparation for this shift needs to start soon. For example, the government will continue to have a role in providing agricultural services; industrial retraining, and especially management development, will be required; and public investment will need to be refocused away from production and toward financing essential economic infrastructure. The latter is especially important in transport and energy, where capacity constraints could pose serious obstacles to economic diversification, especially in terms of external trade. There are perhaps two key roles for government. First is to reorient the government itself and the civil service to managing an economy _indirectly_ instead of by the old administrative means. It is evident, for example, in the program to promote small business, that the government still thinks in terms of direct actions rather than enabling policies.

xix. The second is to focus resources on the social safety net. The socialist system made notable achievements in terms of health, education, housing, and poverty alleviation. In the rush to discard the old structure, these functions of government should not be forgotten. During stabilization, special efforts need to be made to protect the most vulnerable groups from the effect of output declines and relative price shifts. At the same time, long-term gains in human resource development need to be maintained and improved.

Development Prospects

xx. Mongolia's medium-term development prospects include its well-educated labor force, abundant agricultural and natural resources, and the traditional resilience of its rural economy. However, the country also faces a number of basic developmental constraints, in addition to its serious short-term problems. In 1991, the economy was hit by severe external shocks, and the authorities responded with a strong stabilization program and simultaneous structural reforms. The program was designed to limit the decline in GDP to 5 percent in 1992 and, after a year of zero growth in 1993, to resume average growth of 3 percent annually thereafter. [As in other socialist economies in transition, GDP growth rates can be seriously understated during reforms because of large relative price shifts and unmeasured activity.]

xxi. This scenario was based on two critical assumptions: that Mongolia's external environment would not deteriorate further; and that the government's reform program and policies would be effectively implemented on schedule. The greatest risk to the government's program is the prospect of a further collapse in trade with Russia and other former Soviet republics. Given Mongolia's high import dependence and harsh climate, this breakdown in trade could have potentially devastating consequences on its economy and people, although its rural sector may provide some resilience and security. Even in the absence of further external deterioration, the government's targets may not be achieved because of policy failures, either in design or implementation. The program's realization may therefore require bolder and firmer reform measures by government and a strong response from the private sector.

xxii. Throughout the period of stabilization, Mongolia will have to rely heavily on external financing if it is to have an acceptable minimum level of imports to maintain production and begin a modest recovery. Nevertheless, the balance of payments is subject to considerable risk, implying that Mongolia should obtain external financing primarily on concessional terms, with restricted access to commercial sources. If such terms can be achieved, related debt service should not be a problem, provided that the servicing of Mongolia's debt to the former Soviet republics remains manageable.

I. GEOGRAPHY, DEMOGRAPHY AND HISTORY

Geography

1.1 Mongolia is a large but sparsely populated country, landlocked between the Commonwealth of Independent States (CIS) to the north and China to the east, west, and south.1/ Its total land area (1.6 million km^2) is about half the size of India and four times larger than Japan. It is 2,400 km long from west to east and 1,250 km from north to south. With an average elevation about 1,600 meters above sea level, the climate is semiarid continental. Mongolia's winters are long and severe, with average temperatures below freezing from October to March. The average temperature in January is about -25°C, with lows often below -40°C.

Natural Resources

1.2 Mongolia has abundant agricultural land and is rich in mineral resources, including coal, copper, molybdenum, fluorite, gold, iron ore, lead, oil, phosphates, tin, uranium, and wolfram, of which the first three are the most important. Coal reserves total an estimated 20 billion tons. The main copper and molybdenum mines, at Erdenet, are managed as a joint venture between Mongolia and the former Soviet Union. The Erdenet mine produces copper concentrate for export to the former Soviet Union and is by far the country's largest export earner. Thermal power, generated from domestic coal and imported diesel oil, is supplemented by electricity imports from the Russian grid, especially for the Erdenet copper plant.

1.3 About 80 percent of the land is suitable mainly for animal husbandry. Mongolia's 26 million head of livestock (1989) include: sheep (58 percent), goats (20 percent), cattle (11 percent), horses (9 percent) and camels (2 percent). Crop cultivation began on a significant scale only in the 1950s with the development of virgin land. Agriculture is constrained by the severe climate, which permits only a 90-day growing and harvesting season and causes large crop losses because of sharp fluctuations in temperature (as much as 30°C in a day). Most crops are cultivated on large state farms. Forests cover about 10 percent of the territory (15 million ha).

Demography

1.4 With a total population estimated at 2.1 million in July 1989, Mongolia's population density, at 1.3 persons per km^2, is one of the lowest in the world. About 58 percent of the population lives in urban areas, a quarter of it in the capital city of Ulaanbaatar. Nearly 90 percent are Mongols, of which the Khalkha-Mongols comprise the largest subgroup (about 75 percent of the total). Other ethnic groups include Kazakhs (5.3 percent), Chinese (2 percent), Russians (2 percent), Tuvins, Uzbeks, Uighurs, and others (1.5 percent). The official language is Khalkha Mongol.

1/ This chapter draws extensively on: Mongolia: A Country Study, Federal Research Division, Library of Congress, Robert L. Worden and Andrea Matles (eds.), 1991, and IMF Occasional Paper No. 79.

1.5 With an estimated birth rate of 35.1 per 1,000 and an estimated death rate of 7.6 per 1,000 in July 1989, Mongolia's 2.8 percent rate of population growth is one of the highest in Asia. Its population has more than doubled since 1960 owing, until recently, to the government's pro-natalist policy. The infant mortality rate was about 70 per 1,000 live births. Life expectancy was 60 for males and 62.5 for females.

Political and Economic History

1.6 After the collapse of the Mongol Empire (established by Genghis Khan in 1291), Mongolia was a frontier province of China from 1691 until early this century and became an independent state on July 11, 1921. Following three years of constitutional monarchy, nominally headed by Buddhist leaders, the Mongolian People's Republic (MPR) was founded in 1924. Its capital was renamed Ulaanbaatar (Red Hero).

1.7 After World War II, Mongolia became a centrally planned command economy, characterized by five-year plans that emphasized the development of industry and energy. Mongolia began an increasingly close association with the Soviet Union with the signing of a Treaty of Friendship and Mutual Assistance in 1946. After joining COMECON in 1962, Mongolia's trade expanded, and its partner nations became involved in building Mongolia's infrastructure and developing some of its large productive enterprises and mining complexes, in effect laying the foundation of a modern industrial sector (Box 1.1).

1.8 Tsedenbahl was Mongolia's leader during much of this period. His removal from power in August 1984 marked the beginning of the economic and political reforms now under way. Dissatisfaction with the rigidity of the centrally planned economy was mounting and, partly influenced by the Soviet Union's "glasnost" and "perestroika" policies, Mongolia launched its own program of political openness and economic restructuring in 1986. The economic reform program had five goals: (a) acceleration of development; (b) application of science and technology to production; (c) reform of management and planning; (d) greater independence of enterprises; and (e) balance of individual, collective, and societal interests. Accelerated development was to result from the attainment of the other four goals. Scientific research was to be redirected so that it would be better linked to economic development objectives. Reform of management and planning started with the streamlining of government agencies in charge of the economy, and the duties of the State Planning and Economic Committee were limited to overseeing capital investment policy. The number of indicators specified in the five-year development plan and annual economic plans was also reduced. Enterprises were granted more financial autonomy, first for a limited number of enterprises, and later more widely. Enterprises were made accountable for their own losses--previously they would receive state subsidies--and for fulfilling sales contracts and export orders; output above state orders could be sold at the enterprises' discretion.

Box 1.1: MONGOLIA'S RELATIONSHIP WITH COMECON

Mongolia joined Council for Mutual Economic Assistance (COMECON) in 1962 and until 1991, when COMECON was dissolved, its foreign economic relations were predominantly with this group. Bilateral foreign economic relations with COMECON members were conducted mainly through the various joint intergovernmental commissions on economic, scientific, and technical cooperation. Intergovernmental commissions met annually or semiannually to coordinate planning and to discuss annual and five-year agreements on trade and technical and financial assistance. Mongolia coordinated its five-year plans with COMECON's five-year multilateral cooperation plans.

Participation in COMECON provided the following trade advantages: it ensured markets for Mongolia's exports and helped satisfy most of its import requirements; it offered "incentive prices" for some imports (e.g., fuel) that were lower than prices charged to the more developed COMECON nations; and it financed Mongolia's trade deficit with the Soviet Union--by grant until 1980 and thereafter on concessional loan terms.

As a member of COMECON's International Bank for Economic Cooperation and International Investment, Mongolia was able to secure loans at preferential rates. Most financial assistance came from the Soviet Union in the form of grants or concessional credits (2 percent per annum). Soviet credits to Mongolia totaled an estimated R 450 million for the Third Five-Year Plan period (1961-65), R 470 million for the Fourth Plan (1966-70), R 550 million for the Fifth Plan (1971-75), and about R 1.1 billion for the Sixth Plan (1976-80). These credits were used for capital investment (estimated at 32.2 percent from 1958-60; 47 percent from 1961-65; and 59 percent from 1976-79), technical assistance, and trade financing. Soviet grant assistance to Mongolia is estimated at R 50 million from 1966-75; and R 40 million from 1976-80.

Turnkey projects, financed by loans mainly (but not exclusively) from the Soviet Union, were Mongolia's main form of external assistance in the 1980s. The Soviet Union helped construct or modernize over 500 facilities during 1961-80 and by 1981, these accounted for more than half of Mongolia's total industrial output; 90 percent of thermal power generation; 80 percent of coal production; 70 percent of confectionery and bakery products; and 100 percent of woolen cloth, felt, formula food, copper and molybdenum concentrate, and fluorite output.

Other turnkey projects constructed in Mongolia during the 1980s include a woodworking combine, a glue factory, and two distilleries built by Poland; a clothing mill and flour mill by Hungary; a tannery and a cement works by Czechoslovakia; a furniture and a cardboard combine by Romania; a meat combine by the former German Democratic Republic; a sheepskin coat factory and the Sharin Gol state farm's fruit and vegetable processing factories by Bulgaria; and a house-building combine and spinning mill by the Soviet Union. Turnkey projects were often part of larger joint Soviet-Mongolian development programs, such as those at Baga Nuur, Choibalsan, Darhan, and Erdenet.

Joint-stock companies and joint ventures between Mongolia and the Soviet Union and other COMECON members have been important in securing foreign investment and technical assistance as well as building infrastructure, developing the mining sector, and founding financial and trading institutions. Examples include Mongolbank, Mongoltrans (Mongolian Transportation), the Ulaanbaatar Railroad, and the Erdenet Mining and Concentrating Combine. Many joint-stock companies were eventually handed over to sole Mongolian ownership by the Soviets. Major joint ventures that had not been turned over to sole Mongolian ownership as of late 1991 were the following:

- Erdenet Mining and Concentrating Combine--Soviet Union
- Mongolbolgarmetall--Bulgaria--mining
- Mongolcheckhoslovakmetall--Czechoslovakia--exploitation of fluorite and tin
- Mongolsovtsvetmet--Soviet Union--exploitation of nonferrous metals
- Sovmongolpromstroy--Soviet Union--construction

1.9 Since independence in 1921, Mongolia has evolved from an underdeveloped, primarily pastoral economy to one with a large industrial sector. Its main but not sole exports are agricultural products and minerals. The agricultural sector is still dominated by livestock breeding, but now includes significant amounts of cropping. In addition, a basic transportation network of railroads, roads, and aviation has been developed. Significant investment in the social sectors has resulted in near-universal adult literacy, a free health care system, and life expectancy approaching the spans in developed countries.

1.10 Industrialization, made possible by large investments by the Soviet Union, led to rapid growth during the 1960s and 1970s. Net material product grew nearly 8 percent annually during 1970-75, and by a further 4.3 percent annually in 1975-80. Gross industrial production rose by about 70 percent between 1960 and 1980, but agriculture lagged behind, with little change in the size of the livestock herd for the last 30 years. Industrial investments also permitted a growing volume of foreign trade as copper-producing capacity came on stream, but export growth could not keep pace with Mongolia's rising import dependence.

1.11 Until the early 1980s, Mongolia had fairly robust growth, despite the distortions and inefficiencies of the centrally planned economy. Since then, however, the economy has undergone increasing strains because of growing difficulties in the Council for Mutual Economic Assistance (CMEA) countries and the inadequacy of domestic resources to sustain efficient growth policies. This was reflected in the falling growth rate of real GDP,2/ from 7 percent in 1981-86 to 4.6 percent in 1987-89 (Table 2.1). The deteriorating external environment and the increasing fluidity of domestic economic policies and institutions led to a 2.1 percent decline in GDP in 1990 and a further 15 percent decline in 1991. Sharp increases in unemployment and inflation, both entirely new phenomena in Mongolia, have accompanied these output declines.

1.12 The convergence of three factors in 1990/91 created the present difficult situation. First, Mongolia's capital-intensive, import-dependent, centrally planned economy became incapable of generating self-sustained growth. Second, external capital flows from the Soviet Union, which had accounted for up to 30 percent of GDP, began to decline and ceased entirely in 1991. Third, the collapse of the CMEA system in 1991 resulted in severe dislocations in Mongolia's external trade, of which over 90 percent was with the USSR. Against this background, recent economic developments are reviewed in the following chapter.

2/ Mongolia's national accounts statistics are compiled according to the material balances approach to estimate Net Material Product (NMP), which is then converted to GDP according to the UN System of National Accounts (SNA). Particular caution is needed on the following points: (a) the extent, if any, of overestimation of growth that may have been engendered by the past regime's zeal to show Mongolia as a developed industrial country; (b) the adjustments required to move from NMP to GDP, especially the estimation of value-added in nonmaterial services and depreciation of capital stock; (c) the valuation problem due to "estimates at current prices" not always using prices actually paid by end-users and the lack of price indexes to arrive at the constant price estimates of GDP; and (d) conversion of GDP estimates in tugriks to dollars.

II. RECENT ECONOMIC DEVELOPMENTS AND THE EMERGING CRISIS

A. Background

2.1 This chapter analyzes recent economic developments in Mongolia and the government's response. In particular, it relates how the rapidly deteriorating external environment, especially the changed prospects for external trade and capital assistance, has created severe imbalances and generated serious production losses.

2.2 While Mongolia has experienced large external and domestic deficits for a long time, they did not generate monetary pressures because, until 1990, they were fully financed by concessional long-term assistance from the Soviet Union. In 1991, Soviet assistance was terminated. CMEA trade collapsed and markets for Mongolia's traditional exports went soft resulting in a deep loss of export earnings. Rapid and deep adjustment was needed. In the short term, the authorities have attempted to maintain consumption standards. This focus has resulted in substantial monetary growth and a consequent rise in inflation. The seriousness of the situation underlines the need for tight monetary and fiscal policies to effect the necessary reductions in both consumption and investment. This task is complicated by the simultaneous need to restructure macroeconomic policies and institutions for the transition to a market economy. This chapter deals mainly with the extent of the adjustment effort necessary to correct fiscal deficits, reduce monetary expansion, and restrain wages.

2.3 A note of caution is required when reviewing Mongolia's national accounts data and ratios of other macroeconomic variables to GDP. Despite continuing efforts by the government and several international agencies to adapt Mongolia's statistics to standardized international formats, much remains to be done before various data can be satisfactorily reconciliated. These difficulties are expected to be addressed in the next year or two with the help of technical assistance from the United Nations and other international agencies, including a component for the State Statistical Office in a Technical Assistance Project approved by the World Bank in December 1991.

B. Production, Expenditure, and Employment

Production

2.4 The industrial sector (including mining and electricity) until recently accounted for around 27 percent of GDP, but its poor performance in 1990 and 1991 contributed significantly to the decline in GDP (Table 2.1). Industrial NMP grew rapidly (9 percent per annum) during the first half of the 1980s, but slowed to 5 percent between 1985 and 1989 as a result of economic difficulties in the CMEA countries. Growing shortages of energy and imported spare parts led to stagnation in 1990, when industrial output grew by less than 1 percent, and to a substantial decline (12 percent) in industrial production in 1991. Lack of foreign exchange and the disruption of trade with the Soviet Union had a sharp contractionary impact on production in all the subsectors of industry, ranging from -8 percent in flour output to -50 percent in cement production.3/

Table 2.1: GROWTH OF NMP AND GDP AT CONSTANT (1986) PRICES, 1987-91
(percent)

	1987	1988	1989	1990	1991
Net material product	3.4	4.2	9.7	0.1	-23.6
Industry	2.8	3.7	11.4	0.7	-12.3
Agriculture	-6.4	2.4	13.8	-0.8	-6.9
Construction	19.1	11.8	9.6	-14.6	-28.9
Other	6.6	4.2	6.6	-16.0	-40.7
GDP	4.5	5.1	4.2	-2.1	-16.2

Source: Mongolian authorities.

2.5 Mining is of critical importance for Mongolia. Copper and coal exports are major sources of its foreign exchange earnings. Its copper-for-oil barter arrangement with the Soviet Union enabled Mongolia to survive the 1990/91 winter without major losses in production. Disruptions in the supply of spare parts, energy, and other inputs, however, limited copper output to around 320,000 tons in 1990 and 260,000 tons in 1991, compared to earlier levels of 360,000 tons. Coal production peaked at 8.6 million tons in 1988, declined to 8 million tons in 1989, and 7.2 million tons in 1990. This decline continued in 1991 when output was only 5 million tons, reflecting serious shortages of equipment and spare parts. Reduced coal production has curtailed electricity supply and heat generation and caused serious difficulties during the last two winters.

2.6 Agriculture, which contributes about 16 percent of GDP,4/ is particularly vulnerable to Mongolia's severe climate and its production fluctuates over 2-3 year cycles. Agricultural NMP, after declining by over 6 per-

---

3/ For instance, the output of flour, meat, milk and dairy products, and electricity declined between 8 percent and 15 percent; leather coats, carpets, knitwear, footwear, copper and molybdenum between 20 percent and 30 percent; sawn timber and cement, 50 percent.

4/ Considering that Mongolia is basically an agricultural country, agriculture accounts for a surprisingly small share of GDP. This is explained mainly by the following. First, some agricultural activities are recorded for definitional reasons under other sectors, e.g., processed agricultural products are included under industry. Second, in estimating GDP at market prices, almost all indirect taxes (e.g., price differentials) are attributed to the trade and distribution sector, which leads to overestimation of trade's share at the expense of the other sectors. Correcting for the latter distortion results in an increase in agriculture's share to 20 percent.

cent in 1987, enjoyed two successive years of growth before again falling in 1990 and 1991. The decline in 1990 was caused by a 10 percent fall in crop production because of cold weather, late rains during the harvest season, and shortages of diesel fuel and farm equipment. Although weather conditions in 1991 were favorable, shortages of inputs due to lack of foreign exchange and a delay in deregulating agricultural trade and prices continued to constrain crop production. Meat production remained virtually stagnant during the 1980s, mainly due to inefficient pricing policies and state procurement. However, the decline of about 150,000 tons (to 510,000 tons) in 1990 and an additional 50,000 tons in 1991 were probably caused by: herdsmen's desire to build up stocks following the easing of restrictions on the size of privately owned herds; lack of essential items in the domestic market that herdsmen need; and inadequate procurement prices and continued restrictions on private trading in livestock products.5/ In 1991, total meat production declined despite increased slaughtering by private herdsmen to trade for other consumer goods. This resulted in a decrease in the size of the national herd to 25.5 million from 25.9 million in 1990. Milk production also declined by 2.2 percent in 1990 and by a further 15 percent in 1991, although much of this probably reflects difficulties with the distribution system rather than production per se.

2.7 Industry has continued to be the leading growth sector, but its growth rate over the 1980s has declined as economic difficulties have mounted (Table 2.2). Interestingly, the distribution sector had the largest growth during 1986-90, reflecting higher unit costs and the growth in private consumption. By the same token, however, it was the largest contributor to the sharp decline in NMP in 1991.

Table 2.2: SOURCES OF NMP GROWTH, 1980-91
(percent shares of growth)

	1980-85	1986-90	1991
Agriculture	18.7	12.9	5.5
Industry	44.4	36.7	18.3
Distribution	22.1	37.2	59.1
Other	14.8	13.2	17.0

Source: Appendix Table 2.4.

5/ In January 1991, the government reduced state orders for meat by 15 percent, while raising mutton procurement prices by 60 percent; retail prices for mutton and goat were raised by 100 percent.

Expenditure

2.8 From Mongolia's national accounts data, patterns and changes in national expenditures cannot be studied in any detail.6/ Nevertheless, a rough picture of Mongolia's overall expenditure pattern is shown in Table 2.3.

Table 2.3: GROSS NATIONAL EXPENDITURE, 1986-90
(percent of GDP in current prices)

	1986	1987	1988	1989	1990
GDP at m.p.	100.0	100.0	100.0	100.0	100.0
Resource balance	36.2	29.1	28.0	33.1	26.8
Total resources/uses	136.2	129.1	128.0	133.1	126.8
Consumption	69.7	83.4	85.9	87.0	96.9
Public	24.3	24.5	24.0	23.2	22.0
Private	45.3	58.9	61.9	63.8	74.9
Investment	66.5	45.7	42.1	46.1	29.9
Gross fixed investment	51.2	46.9	44.1	44.8	32.1
Stock changes	15.3	-1.2	-2.0	1.3	-2.2

Source: Mongolian authorities and Bank staff calculations.

2.9 Mongolia has been able to maintain a very high negative resource balance because of large inflows of external resources (mainly from the Soviet Union), which averaged about 32 percent of GDP during 1986-89. Consumption over this period rose from about 70 percent to 87 percent of GDP, entirely reflecting the increase in private (or nongovernment) consumption to almost 64 percent of GDP in 1989. Investment, which originated mainly in the public sector, declined from a very high level of 66.5 percent of GDP in 1986 to about 45 percent in 1987 and continued at this level in 1988 and 1989. Thus, in the second half of the 1980s, public sector expenditure (both consumption and investment) was restrained in relation to GDP. The surge in private consumption (if not due to statistical error) is harder to explain, but seems to

---

6/ In addition to the weaknesses in GDP estimates, there are the following problems as well: (a) estimation of the resource balance in tugriks (i.e., net imports of goods and nonfactor services) is rendered difficult because of the exchange rate issue; (b) no breakdown of consumption expenditure between the public and private sectors is available; and (c) estimates of depreciation of fixed capital are suspect, and total gross investment cannot be broken down into public and private. Because of large differentials among various foreign exchange rates and categories of prices, these problems became so unmanageable in 1991, that State Statistical Office (SSO) could not estimate national expenditure. A World Bank/Economic and Social Commission for Asia and the Pacific (ESCAP) statistical mission, which visited Ulaanbaatar in July 1992, is expected to help SSO on this matter.

be the result of continued balance of payments support from the Soviet Union, even after major turnkey projects were completed in the mid-1980s.

2.10 Mongolia's extraordinarily high levels of investment reflect the highly capital-intensive nature of several major mining, power, and transportation projects that were carried out in the early 1980s to increase copper-producing and processing capacity. This is reflected in very high capital-output ratios for this period, on the order of 8-10. Once these projects were completed, investment receded to more normal but still high levels.

2.11 In 1990, Mongolia's rapidly changing economic relations with the CMEA and its new economic reform measures brought about significant changes in the pattern of national expenditure. First, external resources fell below 27 percent of GDP as a result of reduced Soviet aid; this drop would have been steeper but for the more than 50 percent devaluation. Second, faced with this revenue shortfall, the government started tightening and streamlining its current and investment expenditures. This led to a modest contraction in the public consumption ratio and a sharp drop in the investment rate. Third, the restraint in public sector expenditure, as a percentage of GDP, was greater than the reduction in external resources required. This would have created greater room for private investment had the incentives and means for it been in place. However, the reform program was still at an early stage and the increased resources available to the private sector were absorbed by higher private consumption.

2.12 A corollary of the rising consumption rate is the declining domestic savings rate (Table 2.4). Consequently, during the second half of the 1980s, a rapidly growing proportion of total investment, itself declining, was financed by external resources. This trend needs to be reversed if Mongolia is to embark on a path of self-sustaining development.

Table 2.4: FINANCING INVESTMENT, 1986-90
(percent of total)

	1986	1987	1988	1989	1990
Gross domestic investment	100.0	100.0	100.0	100.0	100.0
Gross domestic savings	45.6	36.3	33.5	28.2	10.4
Foreign savings	54.4	63.7	66.5	71.8	89.6
Memorandum item					
GDS/GDP (%)	30.3	16.6	14.1	13.0	3.1

Source: Table 2.3.

Employment and Wages

2.13 The production declines described above have already begun to show up in pressures on employment and wages. As a centrally planned command economy, Mongolia has not previously experienced open unemployment because the state found or created employment for every school leaver or graduate. Until recently, frictional unemployment was minimal (about 2 percent of the labor force) comprising workers temporarily out of work before being placed in another job.

2.14 Mongolia's population is growing rapidly, and 44 percent of the total is under 16 years of age (Table 2.5). Mongolia also has a relatively high labor force participation rate due to the state's historical commitment to provide jobs for everyone, the high level of educational development, and women's interest in employment. By contrast, the economy's capacity to absorb the growth in labor supply is limited because the leading sectors--mining, mineral-based industries, and livestock--are essentially capital- and land-intensive activities. On the other hand, labor-intensive activities, such as light industry and the retail sector, have been constrained by past development emphasis on capital-intensive material sectors. The policy of guaranteed employment has thus led to overmanning in state enterprises and the bureaucracy as well as a number of inefficient "make-work" projects.

Table 2.5: POPULATION AND EMPLOYMENT, 1988-90

	1988	1989 ('000)	1990	Structure 1988-90 (%)	Growth 1988-90 (% p.a.)
Total population /a	1,997.0	2,044.0/b	2,095.6	100.0	2.52
Under 16	n.a.	904.3	920.6	44.1	1.80/c
Active age	n.a.	995.1	1,028.2	48.9	3.33/c
Over active age	n.a.	144.6	146.8	7.0	1.52/c
Labor force resource	n.a.	928.0	n.a.	100.0/d	n.a.
Total employed	n.a.	764.0	n.a.	82.3/d	n.a.
Employment by sector /e	616.1	633.2	651.4	100.0	2.52
Material sphere	443.3	451.4	466.8	71.6	2.62
Industry	119.2	119.6	135.6	19.7	6.66
Agriculture	183.6	186.0	178.3	28.8	-1.45
Nonmaterial sphere	172.8	181.8	184.6	28.4	3.25

/a At the beginning of the year.
/b The census data of January 5, 1989.
/c For 1990 only.
/d For 1989 only.
/e Average annual figures.

Source: State Statistical Office.

2.15 The slowdown in the economy in 1989 and subsequent declines in production in 1990 and 1991 have affected employment adversely. Since 1990, new entrants to the labor force have not been guaranteed employment, and employees of some state enterprises have been laid off following enterprises streamlining or privatization. The government itself has released some 3,000 workers. As a result, the number of registered unemployed by mid-1991 increased to 36,000 (up 3.8 percent) from 20,000 a year earlier. Including nonregistered unemployed, the Ministry of Labor (MOL) estimates unemployment at about 45,000 (4.8 percent) in mid-1991. Rapid growth of private sector employment has taken up some of the slack, reaching 56,000 7/ or about 8.6 percent of total employment by mid-1991.

2.16 Although an overall unemployment rate of about 5 percent is not very high, the government is understandably concerned about this new phenomenon for two reasons. First, unemployment is concentrated mainly among the young urban population; 60 percent of the total live in the Ulaanbaatar area, where unemployment is almost 12 percent. Second, because of the sharp deterioration in the economy in 1991 and 1992 and an increase in redundancies as a result of privatization, the total number of unemployed has been rising rapidly, with an average of 6,000 people registering as unemployed every month in 1992, compared to 2,000 a year ago.

2.17 Wages had until recently been centrally controlled and remained virtually unchanged. Since retail prices had also been kept almost unchanged, real wages rose only as a result of promotions, productivity increases, and job reclassification. The wage structure also reflected the general pattern observed in other socialist economies in that wage scales were determined in great detail by industry and on an egalitarian basis. Monthly wages in the material sector rose only from Tug 526 in 1981 to Tug 568 in 1989, when average wages in industry were Tug 618, and in agriculture Tug 449. Bonuses came to be regarded as a wage supplement, distributed equally to almost everyone.

2.18 Starting in 1988, enterprise autonomy in determining wage and bonus payments was gradually increased. Nevertheless, average wages remained more or less unchanged in 1988-90 despite price increases, implying declines in real wages. In January 1991, most state enterprises and government institutions doubled all wages for workers to compensate for price adjustments. However, they did not offer any further wage increases in 1991, and continuing inflation, further eroded wages. The erosion continued in the first half of 1992 when civil servants and the employees of other budget units were given only 20-25 percent wage increases, while inflation was about 70 percent from the end of 1991. This was inevitable given the need to reduce aggregate consumption as part of the stabilization program. One exception to this general decline is private sector wages, which are about twice as high as public sector wages. This tight wage policy in the public sector is critical to the stabilization of public finance.

C. Need for Stabilization

Public Finance

2.19 A big part of the solution to Mongolia's crisis lies within the public sector, both in reducing the extremely high fiscal deficits and in

---

7/ This comprises 32,000 employed in 4,200 enterprises, 20,000 in about 3,000 cooperatives, and 4,000 self-employed.

restructuring the public finance system to one suited to a market economy. The consolidated state budget covers the central government, 3 cities, 18 aimags and 351 somons. Although the operations of state enterprises are not included in the state budget, they account for over two-fifths of budgetary revenue and receive loans and transfers from the budget to finance a substantial portion of their investment. Thus, the state budget accounts for a large part of overall economic activities. The state's importance is reflected in the high ratio of total government expenditure to GDP, which averaged about 64 percent in 1985-89. On the other hand, total revenue, although large by market economy standards, has lagged way behind expenditure, giving rise to a structural deficit of about 16 percent of GDP on average in the second half of the 1980s (Table 2.6).

Table 2.6: SUMMARY OF STATE BUDGET, 1980-91 /a

	1980	1987	1988	1989	1990	1991
			(million Tug)			
Total revenue	3,452.6	4,511.3	4,650.6	5,211.3	5,294.7	9,013.7
Tax	3,125.3	4,052.3	4,204.2	4,715.4	4,289.0	7,204.0
Nontax	327.3	459.0	446.4	495.9	1,005.7	1,809.7
Total expenditure	3,988.6	6,330.6	6,660.9	7,012.3	6,710.6	11,050.4
Current	3,337.0	5,038.0	5,146.1	5,382.8	5,434.5	9,918.3
Capital	651.6	1,292.6	1,514.8	1,629.5	1,276.1	1,132.1
Fixed capital	n.a.	446.3	416.8	441.8	412.5	n.a.
Capital transfers	n.a.	846.3	1,098.0	1,187.7	863.6	n.a.
Overall deficit	-536.0	-1,819.3	-2,010.3	-1,801.0	-1,415.9	-2,036.7
			(percent of GDP)			
Total revenue	51.1	46.5	45.1	48.6	50.6	55.9
Tax	46.3	41.8	40.8	44.0	41.0	44.7
Nontax	4.8	4.7	4.3	4.6	9.6	11.2
Total expenditures	59.0	65.2	64.7	65.3	64.1	68.5
Current	49.4	51.9	50.0	50.2	52.3	61.5
Capital	9.6	13.3	14.7	15.2	12.2	7.0
Fixed capital	n.a.	4.6	4.0	4.1	3.9	n.a.
Capital transfers	n.a.	8.7	10.7	11.1	8.3	n.a.
Overall deficit	-7.9	-18.8	-19.5	-16.8	-13.5	-12.6

/a Fiscal data in this and other text tables reflect some minor adjustments by IMF and Bank staff and may therefore differ from the original government data given in the Statistical Appendix.

Source: Ministry of Finance.

2.20 Until end-1988, budgetary deficits were fully financed by the Soviet Union through concessional loans, and in 1989 and 1990, Soviet aid still covered 90 percent and 80 percent, respectively, of total financing. However, with the cessation of Soviet aid in 1991, the slowdown of economic activity, and the introduction of fiscal reforms, public finances have undergone major and rapid changes. While new revenue instruments are emerging, the disappearance or weakening of traditional sources of revenue is causing significant revenue shortfalls. Expenditures are also proving difficult to cut and to restructure; hence, the deficit is growing and its financing is increasingly coming from monetary resources.

2.21 Revenues. Traditionally, the main sources of tax revenue have been turnover taxes and profit taxes on state enterprises and cooperatives. Together, they account for about 90 percent of total tax revenue and amount to 45 percent of GDP (Table 2.7). Turnover taxes have two components: the first

Table 2.7: STRUCTURE OF PUBLIC FINANCE, 1987-91
(percent)

	1987	1988	1989	1990	1991
Total Revenue	100.0	100.0	100.0	100.0	100.0
Current revenue	99.0	100.0	99.9	99.9	100.0
Tax revenue	89.8	90.4	90.4	89.9	79.9
Income taxes, of which:	39.8	43.4	44.8	44.2	28.9
Corporate taxes	37.7	41.4	42.9	42.7	27.7
Goods & services, of which:	51.0	51.1	48.5	36.8	27.9
Turnover & excise taxes	50.4	50.4	47.9	36.3	24.2
Other taxes	0.1	0.1	0.1	0.1	23.1
Nontax revenue, of which:	9.6	8.9	9.0	19.0	20.1
Social security & payroll taxes	5.6	5.8	5.8	4.0	9.6
Capital revenue	0.1	-	0.1	0.1	-
Total Expenditures	100.0	100.0	100.0	100.0	100.0
Current expenditures	79.6	77.3	76.8	81.0	89.8
Wages & salaries	13.1	13.2	12.9	13.5	16.9
Purchases of goods	24.6	24.0	22.7	25.7	24.0
Interest	0.5	1.5	2.5	3.4	-
Subsidies & transfers of which:	39.0	36.1	37.9	37.3	45.9
Social security payment	10.5	10.8	10.4	11.8	19.6
Other	-	-	-	1.1	3.0
Capital expenditures	20.4	22.7	23.2	19.0	10.2
Fixed capital	7.0	6.3	6.3	6.2	-
Capital transfers	13.4	16.5	16.9	12.8	-

Source: Mongolian Authorities.

is known as the import price differential, the difference between the import contract price and the (fixed) domestic wholesale price of the imported commodity. The share of revenue from import price differentials in the budget averaged about 36 percent in 1980-89 but has been declining since 1987 because of rising import prices. The second is the domestic turnover tax levied on some public utilities (e.g., electricity and water supply) and a few domestically produced goods (e.g., vodka, beer, and adult footwear), with vodka yielding by far the largest contribution (70 percent). The domestic turnover tax is included in the wholesale price of the taxed item. The combined share of import price differentials and domestic turnover taxes in total revenue is about 40 percent, equivalent to about 20 percent of GDP.

2.22 The share of income and profit taxes in the total revenue rose gradually from 28 percent (equivalent to 14 percent of GDP) in 1980 to about 45 percent (21 percent of GDP) in 1990. Profits are defined as the difference between gross sales revenue and production costs (including turnover taxes on inputs, depreciation and production taxes). Some loss-making enterprises are exempt from profit taxes and receive support from the budget. Until recently, profits of state enterprises and their taxes on them were planned by the authorities. The profits tax was in effect a mandatory transfer of funds to the budget.

2.23 Other sources of revenue accounted for less than 10 percent of budgetary revenues and represented 4.5 percent of GDP between 1980 and 1990. Taxes on individuals have not been an important revenue source. Nontax revenues comprise social security payments and fees obtained from cooperatives and state enterprises. Social security payments averaged around 4.5 percent of total revenues during 1980-90 and accounted for more than half of nontax revenue. Revenues from cooperatives and other sources make up 1 percent of overall revenues.

2.24 This revenue structure was based on the concepts of central planning. The move toward a market economy and ongoing tax reforms since January 1991 have implications for the level of revenues. These reforms, aimed at expanding the tax base and improving the elasticity of the tax system, include: the replacement of "planned" profit taxes on enterprises with corporate and individual income taxes; the introduction of a customs duty at a uniform rate of 15 percent to replace import price differentials; and preparations to convert domestic turnover taxes to a broader based sales tax, and the introduction of selective excise taxes in 1992.

2.25 While these tax reform measures are necessary, their immediate result, when coupled with the decline in production and trade, has been lower receipts from traditional sources of revenue. In addition, the revenue-generating potential of these new taxes has been, and will remain, limited in the short run until an effective tax administration can be organized and trained. For example, during 1991, realized revenue from import price differentials on consumer goods was only Tug 599 million, compared to actual receipts of Tug 1.17 billion in 1990. The newly introduced import duties, which will gradually replace import price differentials, yielded only Tug 295 million. This was not enough revenue to make up for the revenue loss from price differentials. Revenue from the profits tax on enterprises in 1991 was only slightly higher than a year ago, despite a 150 percent inflation in 1991. The main sources of revenue increase in 1991 were the turnover tax on petroleum, the excise duties, and the newly introduced windfall gains tax on enterprise inventories, which were mostly unrealized, hence financed by bank credit.

2.26 Expenditures. Mongolia's relatively large state budget has been absorbed mostly by current expenditures, whose share in total expenditures averaged about 78 percent (or 52 percent of GDP) during 1980-90. Within current expenditures, the largest category (44 percent) was social and cultural expenses, which included free food, health, social security payments, pensions, subsidies, and transfers to households and public establishments. As a result of changes introduced in late 1990 in the laws on pensions and social security and the cost-of-living adjustment following the doubling of prices, budgetary payments on this subcategory started rising sharply in 1991. National development expenditures, which include interest payments, purchases of goods and services and, until 1991, export subsidies, have been the second largest item (38 percent) in current expenditures. The share of wages and salaries in current expenditures has gradually declined from 20.4 percent in 1980 to 13.4 percent in 1990, but increased to about 17 percent in 1991 due to the doubling of wages and salaries at the beginning of the year.

2.27 A distinctive feature of the current budget has been the overwhelming importance of subsidies and transfers to households and nonprofit organizations, which accounted for 47-51 percent of the total during 1985-90 (subsidies alone made up about one-third of the total). The 1991 budget envisaged a sharp contraction (to 37 percent) in the share of this category; transfers exceeded subsidies for the first time because of newly legislated increases in social security payments. Social security payments in 1991 reached 19.6 percent, two-third larger than the 1990 share. Subsidies could not be reduced as much as budgeted, and the combined share of subsidies and transfers increased from about 37 percent in 1990 to about 46 percent in 1991. This remains the priority area for future action in rationalizing the budget.

2.28 Capital expenditures absorbed about 17 percent of total budgetary outlays (or about 10 percent of GDP) in 1975-86. Their share rose rapidly after 1986 because of the government's increased emphasis on housing, education, and health facilities, reaching a peak level of 23.3 percent of budgetary expenditure (15.5 percent of GDP) in 1989. However, with deepening economic crisis and declining public revenue, capital expenditures were cut back to 19 percent of the total (15.5 percent of GDP) in 1990 and 10 percent in 1991. In 1991, the government either slowed down or completely stopped the construction of several large projects because of resource and foreign exchange constraints. Investment cutbacks in 1990 and 1991, mostly in the material sector, reflected a policy decision to check the growth of the fiscal deficit as well as to reduce the government's role in the productive (material) sectors. Shortages of construction materials, both domestically manufactured and imported, also contributed to the decline in public investment.

2.29 Fiscal Decentralization. Local governments have started exercising a greater fiscal role, particularly on the expenditure side. Although the central government still holds all powers of taxation, local governments have been given increasing responsibility for collecting and using taxes. In the first half of the 1980s, local governments received about 30 percent of all budgetary revenues, but over the second half their share gradually increased to 53 percent. This increase is the result of the government's new policy permitting local governments to retain a greater portion of profits taxes generated by state enterprises within their districts.8/ The more significant aspect of fiscal decentralization, however, has been the increased spending at local level. As a result, the share of local governments in total

---

8/ Local governments are allocated certain segments of the tax base, including state enterprises, for the purpose of tax collection. This allocation is reviewed periodically. In addition, some taxes on individuals (e.g., private herd tax and individual income tax) and production taxes (salt and timber) are collected only by the local governments.

budgetary expenditures has increased, from an average of 35.5 percent in the first half of the 1980s to 50 percent in 1990. Most of this increased spending financed investments in schools, hospitals, and local infrastructure.

2.30 As already noted, the financing of Mongolia's budget deficits, which ranged from 13-14 percent of GDP in the first half of the 1980s to 15-20 percent in the second half, came almost entirely from foreign borrowing until 1990 (Table 2.8). In fact, on a net basis, the budget was accumulating bank deposits until 1989 i.e., exercising counter inflationary pressure. However, this concealed "indirect bank financing" by the central government, as a supplement to foreign resources, by advancing tax payments from and/or suspending subsidy payments to state enterprises, which in turn were resorting to bank financing. This practice helped to limit the size of the budget deficit to available foreign resources, while the growing bank loans to state enterprises were periodically capitalized.

Table 2.8: FINANCING THE BUDGET DEFICIT, 1980-91

	1980	1986	1987	1988	1989	1990	1991
			(Tug million)				
Total financing	536.0	1,645.9	1,819.3	2,010.3	1,801.0	1,415.9	2,036.7
Foreign, net	565.6	1,700.8	1,852.4	2,016.1	1,607.9	1,097.8	1,825.7
Disbursements	620.7	1,750.5	1,901.3	2,066.8	1,658.3	1,165.5	1,839.7
Amortizations	55.1	49.7	48.9	50.7	50.4	67.7	14.0
Domestic	-29.6	-54.9	-33.1	-5.8	193.1	318.1	211.0
Bank credit, net	n.a.	-420.2	-46.3	222.6	159.0	595.8	-212.6
Bonds	-	-	-	-	-	-	-
Other	n.a.	365.3	13.2	-228.4	34.1	-277.7	423.6
			(percent of GDP)				
Overall financing	8.0	17.7	18.8	19.5	16.8	13.5	12.6
Foreign financing	8.4	18.3	19.1	19.6	15.0	10.5	11.3
Domestic financing	-0.4	-0.6	-0.3	-0.1	1.8	3.0	1.3

Source: Ministry of Finance.

2.31 In 1989, the government decided to halt this practice. As a result and coupled with falling external resources, it incurred net bank borrowing equivalent to 1.8 percent of GDP in 1989 and 3 percent of GDP in 1990, despite a contraction in the budgetary deficit (Table 2.8). However, in 1991, the government revived its earlier practice of using indirect bank financing by taxing enterprises' unrealized "windfall profits" arising from revaluation of their stocks at the doubled prices, which raised Tug 2.1 billion, equivalent to about 23 percent of total revenue. This had the positive short-term effect of restricting the fiscal deficit to 12.6 percent, instead of 25 percent of GDP, and its monetary financing to 1.3 percent instead of 15 percent of GDP. However, it exposes the structural weakness of the revenue system, especially its inelasticity in the face of inflation, issues that will need to be addressed. Even so, the fiscal deficit has begun to have a significant impact on monetary developments.

Monetary Developments

2.32 Until late 1990, monetary policy in Mongolia, as in other centrally planned economies, passively accommodated the financing needs of the annual plan and the budget. The quantity of money was automatically adjusted to attain physical output targets given fixed prices and dependent on actual implementation of the plan. This policy was carried out by the State Bank, which until recently performed both central and commercial banking functions (i.e., a monobanking system with some 400 branches) under a national credit plan that set out credit and deposit targets for the entire economy, credit programs of the individual State Bank branches and direct lending to state enterprises, cooperatives, and individuals. The annual credit plan was determined by aggregating financing requirements of each State Bank branch, which in turn reflected the needs of state enterprises. As a result, interest rates were not a factor in the mobilization and allocation of capital or in managing aggregate demand.

2.33 Since late 1990, the Mongolian authorities have been establishing a new monetary management and financial system. The goal is to develop monetary policy instruments and institutions that can fulfill their conventional functions in a market economy and be an effective instrument for achieving internal and external balance.

2.34 Despite significant progress, monetary policy during 1991 remained completely passive and financed the budget deficit indirectly (para. 2.31) as well as the needs of state-owned enterprises, which was reflected in sharp monetary expansion. Also, a new contributing factor was the fourfold increase in private sector credit, mostly to the cooperatives. Currency in circulation, the main determinant of base money in Mongolia, grew an average of 12.8 percent annually in 1985-90, but increased by 128.3 percent in 1991. Money and broad money also rose rapidly in 1991: 70 percent and 56 percent, respectively. While some increase in money supply was necessary to accommodate the 1991 price adjustments, the rapid growth in credit to state enterprises and the private sector has contributed significantly to the continued rise in inflation (Table 2.9). Thus, monetary restraint will form a critical component of stabilization policies in the next two years.

Inflation

2.35 As in other socialist countries, Mongolia has until recently had an administered price system whose main objective was to maintain stable prices for consumer goods and production inputs. Retail prices remained almost unchanged in the 1980s (Table 2.10).9/ On the other hand, the wholesale price index, including both domestic and imported goods, increased by about 5 percent a year over the same period, while foreign contract prices for exports and imports rose, respectively, by about 3 percent and 6 percent per annum. Farmgate prices, which were set too low to support low prices for

---

9/ Nonetheless, retail unit prices of most goods in the official retail price index rose by between 4 percent and 125 percent during 1980-88, while prices of some goods declined by 25 percent on average. This suggests that the official data might have understated inflation.

Table 2.9: MONETARY SURVEY, 1986-91 /a

	End of Period /b					
	1986	1987	1988	1989	1990 /a	1991 /a
	(Tug million)					
Net international reserves	181.9	275.1	289.8	307.5	270.2	761.5/b
Other foreign assets, net /c	-529.9	-472.2	-250.9	-41.2	-364.1	802.8
Net domestic assets	4,557.9	4,571.6	4,735.3	4,821.2	6,460.7	9,994.6
Domestic credit	5,520.3	5,432.8	5,786.1	5,903.1	6,573.9	11,195.5
Government, net	-2,385.3	-2,431.6	-2,209.0	-2,050.0	-1,454.2	-1,666.8
State enterprises	7,608.5	7,558.7	7,606.2	7,562.4	7,549.7	10,454.4
Private sector, of which:	297.1	305.9	388.9	390.7	478.4	2,407.9
Cooperatives	(292.5)	(294.5)	(353.1)	(324.7)	(351.2)	n.a.
Other items, net	-962.4	-861.2	-1,050.8	-1,081.9	-113.2	-1,200.5
Broad money (M2)	4,199.9	4,374.5	4,774.2	5,087.5	6,366.8	9,953.6
Money	2,738.1	2,835.3	3,021.7	3,509.6	4,658.5	7,947.4
Currency issue	439.9	490.0	526.1	581.1	742.7	2,003.0
Less: Currency held in bank	-	-	-	-	-	307.5
Current accounts	2,298.2	2,345.3	2,495.6	2,928.5	4,013.1	5,571.0
Quasi-money	1,461.8	1,539.2	1,752.5	1,577.9	1,708.0	2,667.1
	(annual percentage change)					
Domestic credit	1.7	-1.6	6.5	2.0	11.4	-70.3
Government, net	-21.3	-1.9	9.1	7.1	29.1	-14.6
State enterprises	7.0	-0.7	0.6	-0.6	-0.2	38.5
Private, of which:	5.1	3.0	27.1	4.6	22.4	403.3
Cooperatives	(4.7)	(0.6)	(19.9)	(-8.0)	(8.2)	n.a.
Broad money (M2), of which:	-4.3	4.3	9.1	6.6	25.1	56.3/d
Currency in circulation	(7.8)	(11.5)	(7.4)	(10.5)	(27.8)	(128.3)/d

/a Data presented according to new classification system; to the extent possible, historical data have been revised accordingly.
/b Based on constant exchange rate of Tug 40 per $1.
/c Includes net balances held at International Bank for Economic Cooperation (IBEC), net borrowing from IBEC, and borrowing in rubles from the Foreign Trade Bank in Moscow, and capital subscriptions to IBRD and ADB.
/d Percentage change in the first six months of 1991.

Sources: Data provided by the Mongolbank and staff calculations.

agricultural raw materials and basic foodstuffs, remained virtually unchanged for three decades, until 1991.

2.36 Price reform is the most crucial component of the Mongolian government's economic reform program, which has been evolving since mid-1990. In this context, farmgate prices for agricultural products were increased by 30-70 percent from the beginning of 1991. All retail and wholesale prices except for 35 categories of key commodities 10/ were "freed" on January 20, 1991. Simultaneously, all retail prices, including controlled prices, were doubled, and wholesale and producer prices increased by an average of

10/ These items are estimated to account for about 40 percent of urban household expenditure and less than one third of rural household expenditure.

Table 2.10: PRICE INDICES, 1980-90
(1980 = 100.0)

	1981	1983	1985	1987	1988	1989	1990	1991	1992 (April)
Consumer prices	100.0	102.5	103.1	102.1	102.1	102.1	102.1	220.1/a	262.5/a
Wholesale prices	104.7	116.5	126.8	138.0	144.7	152.0	n.a.	n.a.	n.a.
Implicit NMP deflator	101.7	105.4	99.8	89.5	90.6	91.6	102.1	190.3	-

/a Taking the January 16, 1990 level (after the doubling of most consumer prices) as the base, this reflects the new consumer goods index introduced with IMF technical assistance and covering only 17 essential goods.

Source: Mongolian Authorities.

55 percent.11/ In June 1991, gasoline prices were raised fourfold. By October 1991, 18 of the remaining 35 categories of commodities with fixed prices were also "liberalized." In addition, producers were permitted to continue selling their output in excess of state orders at market-determined prices which, for both liberalized and controlled products, were two to three times higher than those in state and cooperative shops. Most recently (March 1992), further liberalization of consumer prices reduced the price-controlled goods and services to a few staples and basic services (i.e., flour, bread, rationed vodka, selected medicines, public housing rents, tariffs for public services and utilities).

2.37 In an attempt to develop appropriate price indexes, the government started about a year ago to sample 17 key prices in state shops, cooperatives and private free markets, and a larger sample survey is being developed. Sample data indicate that the cost of living (including fixed and liberalized prices) increased, in addition to the doubling of retail prices in January 1991, by a further 120 percent in 1991. There are indications that inflation accelerated during the first half of 1992 despite: the restraint that state enterprises can still exercise in raising prices, through "soft budget constraints"; the use of an overvalued exchange rate for most imports; the very small volume of transactions in the free market because of both continuing trade restrictions and shortages of goods; and the tightening of monetary policy.

Foreign Trade and Balance of Payments

2.38 Mongolia's economy is almost uniquely vulnerable to external economic shocks because of the relatively large size and particular composition of its foreign trade. Merchandise exports and imports accounted for about

---

11/ The apparent contradiction in this sentence between the freeing of prices of certain commodities and administratively raising the same prices represents the government's position on this issue.

22 percent and 50 percent of GDP, respectively, in 1988 and 1989.12/ Mongolia's foreign trade is characterized by a limited range of products and markets on the export side, and of sources on the import side, and by a large, chronic deficit. In 1988 and 1989, two categories of goods, namely, minerals (mainly copper and fluorite) and other nonfood raw materials (mainly cashmere, wool, camel hair, and hides) accounted for over 70 percent of total export earnings. Copper concentrate alone accounted for about 50 percent. As for market concentration, the Soviet Union purchased over 80 percent of Mongolia's exports and supplied a similar share of its imports. The Soviet Union also, until recently, financed Mongolia's large surplus of imports over exports, amounting to approximately $1.1 billion (31.6 percent of GDP) in 1988 and 1989 (Table 2.11). This foreign trade structure, however, came under great strain in 1990 and finally collapsed in 1991.

Table 2.11: SUMMARY OF BALANCE OF PAYMENTS, 1986-91
($ million)

	1986	1987	1988	1989	1990	1991
Trade balance	-587.3	-542.1	-628.7	-743.8	-314.5	-80.0
Exports fob	740.8	816.9	829.1	795.8	444.8	346.5
Imports fob	-1,328.1	-1,359.0	-1,457.8	-1,537.8	-759.3	-426.5
Turnkey projects /a	-510.7	-468.4	-391.9	-374.0	-264.3	74.7
Services balance	37.7	20.1	-12.2	-116.6	-72.6	0.2
Unrequited transfers	-0.1	-0.3	-0.3	3.9	7.4	43.6
Current account	-1,060.6	-990.7	-1,033.1	-1,230.6	-644.0	-110.8
Medium- & long-term capital	1,051.0	1,113.2	1,102.7	1,228.2	516.7	130.3
Disbursements	1,067.1	1,130.1	1,120.0	1,250.5	537.4	139.3
Repayments	-16.1	-16.9	-17.3	-22.3	-20.7	-9.0/b
Short-term capital /c	30.6	-20.0	-76.5	-33.3	66.8	-23.4
Capital account	1,060.4	1,024.9	1,037.9	1,236.6	583.5	106.9
Net errors and omissions	-21.2	-68.4	11.7	41.7	7.3	-43.9
Net change in reserves	0.1	-34.2	-4.8	-6.0	53.2	47.8
Memorandum items						
Exports of goods & services/GDP (%)	28.2	27.0	25.9	23.5	20.8	
Imports of goods $ services/GDP (%) /d	64.4	56.4	54.9	57.9	46.5	
Current account deficit/GDP (%)	36.3	29.6	27.2	34.6	28.3	
Net reserves in weeks of imported goods	2.7	4.5	4.8	3.7	3.5	2.2

/a Includes both goods and services; data are not available for disaggregation.
/b Excludes projected servicing of debt obligations to former members of CMEA.
/c Includes changes in the balances of nonconvertible currency deposits held by nonresidents, net borrowing from IBEC and other clearing accounts as reported by the State Bank.
/d Turnkey projects included in imports of goods and services.

Notes: Calculations based on official exchange rates. Data for 1989 and 1990 were reclassified to reflect standard international presentation.

Source: Mongolian authorities; IMF and World Bank staff estimates.

12/ Since trade performance in 1990 was affected by the impending transformation of CMEA arrangements and economic deterioration in both the Soviet Union and Mongolia, 1988 and 1989 data are used here to reflect the pre-reform trade structure.

2.39 In 1990, exports fell by 40 percent compared to the previous year, owing to changes in the CMEA trade and payments system, the breakdown in the Soviet economy, declining world prices of fibers and minerals, and the recession in the industrial countries. Other factors contributing to this dramatic decline included domestic production difficulties arising from power shortages, insufficient imported spare parts and equipment, and exceptionally warm weather during the last two winters, which softened Mongolia's traditional markets for cashmere, camel hair products, and leather goods.

2.40 Mongolia's most important mineral, copper, is produced by a joint Soviet-Mongolian enterprise, and its entire annual output (360,000 tons of ore) was, until recently, exported to the Soviet Union for processing. One third of export earnings from copper is left with the mining company to meet its requirements and the rest is shared with the Soviets. According to a new agreement with the Soviet Union (June 1991), Mongolia may now annually export 60,000 tons of copper ore to third countries, although this level was not reached in 1991. Unit prices for export of copper concentrate to the Soviet Union were about two thirds of the world market price during the first half of 1991 due to the lower copper content of Mongolian concentrate; and sales to third markets had to be made at about two thirds of the Soviet price, in part to offset additional transportation costs.

2.41 Exports of molybdenum (produced jointly with copper) and fluorite declined in 1990 because of unresolved payments problems with the Soviet Union. Coal exports earned about $17 million in the first half of 1990 but had to be suspended in the second half to meet domestic demand after a fire in the main coal mine. No exports were permitted in 1991 as priority was given to supplying the coal-based power plants. Exports of cashmere and cashmere products, which yielded $50 million (6 percent of total exports) in 1989, have suffered from the dislocation of trade with the Soviet Union, the recession in the industrial countries, warm winters in traditional markets, and the collapse of the international wool price.

2.42 Compared to a number of roughly similar market and socialist economies, Mongolia's import/GDP ratio is the highest by a significant margin.13/ This was largely the result of the Mongolian economy's integration, until recently, with that of the Soviet Union. About 1,000 enterprises and other installations built with Soviet assistance produced more than half of the national income, about 60 percent of industrial production, and 100 percent of the energy supply, all of which depended on equipment, spare parts and critical inputs imported from the Soviet Union. Inefficient industrialization and pricing polices also resulted in a high import dependence for such items as milk products (55 percent of consumption), vegetables and fruits (75 percent), eggs (50 percent), sugar (100 percent) and vegetable oil (100 percent), which could be partly satisfied domestically. Excluding turn-

---

13/ Mongolia's import/GDP ratio was 52 percent in 1988/89 compared to an average of 30 percent for Paraguay, Papua New Guinea, Romania, Bulgaria, and Viet Nam.

key projects,14/ almost 60 percent of remaining imports in 1988 and 1989 were in two categories of commodities: machinery, equipment, and vehicles; and fuel, minerals, and metals. Foodstuffs and other consumer foods made up another 25-30 percent.

2.43 In 1990, imports declined by about $755 million (49 percent) and exports by about $328 million (43.5 percent), reflecting the sharp reduction in Soviet aid and the limited cushion that Mongolia's meager reserves could provide. This sharp contraction in imports continued in 1991, with a further halving of the 1990 import level. Petroleum and food imports were the only categories in which the economy's normal requirements were met to any significant extent, owing mainly to barter arrangements with the Soviet Union (copper for petroleum) and food aid from the United States, Japan, and other countries.

2.44 Mongolia has also suffered from a deterioration in its terms of trade (Table 2.12). During 1972-85, contract prices for imports and exports among the CMEA countries were determined through a formula using a five-year moving average of world market reference prices. However, in 1986, CMEA traded-goods prices were fixed at the prevailing world prices and stayed there. As a result, Mongolia did not benefit from the decline in world petroleum prices or from the doubling of copper prices in 1986-89. Some improvement took place in 1989 when the price of petroleum from the Soviet Union was renegotiated downward to world market levels. Following the dissolution of the CMEA trade regime and the movement to dollar-denominated trade in 1990, relative export and import prices have substantially changed. In particular, the price of copper fell by 21 percent relative to the price of petroleum products. As a result of this and other price changes, Mongolia's terms of trade with the Soviet Union declined by 23 percent during the first half of 1991. This shrinkage represented a fall in the purchasing power of exports equivalent to 6.6 percent of GDP on an annual basis.

Table 2.12: TERMS OF TRADE, 1986-91
(transferable rubles)

	1986	1987	1988	1989	1990	1991 (1st 1/2)
Export price index (1980=1)	1.17	1.22	1.27	1.32	1.34	-
Import price index (1980=1)	1.54	1.59	1.62	1.64	1.67	-
Terms of trade index (1980=1)	0.76	0.77	0.78	0.81	0.80	0.75
Change in terms of trade (%)	-11.3	1.0	2.2	2.7	-0.2	-6.2

Sources: Mongolian authorities and IMF staff calculations.

14/ There are no disaggregated data for turnkey projects which, except for ongoing projects, came to a halt in 1991.

2.45 The direction of Mongolia's foreign trade has also begun to change as a result of the breakdown of trade, transportation, and payments relations with the Soviet Union. Within the CMEA, Mongolia conducted the bulk of its trade with the Soviet Union,15/ with a much greater market concentration than was the case for other CMEA countries.16/ In 1990 and 1991, Mongolia's trade with the Soviet Union and other former CMEA countries dwindled to a fraction of earlier levels but still accounted for a large proportion of total trade. Meanwhile, trade with the convertible currency area (CCA) increased rapidly during 1985-90, though from very low levels. In an attempt to boost its dwindling reserves of convertible foreign exchange, the government has encouraged exports to the CCA by introducing export subsidies. Thus, exports to and imports from the CCA, which balanced at about $18 million in 1986, increased to about $53 million in 1989. In 1990, exports for convertible currency declined to $43 million along with the general fall in exports due to production difficulties and unfavorable world market conditions. Imports from the CCA sharply increased, however, to $80 million because of the disruption of trade and financing relations with the CMEA. Mongolia's main trade partners in the CCA during the prereform era included Japan, the Netherlands, Switzerland, Germany, the United Kingdom, and Austria. With the opening up of the economy, trade relations are being developed with the United States, Australia, Republic of Korea and several other countries in the CCA. To this end, the government has negotiated Most Favored Nation (MFN) status with Japan, the United States, and the Republic of Korea, has applied to join General Agreements on Tariff and Trade (GATT), and has signed a cooperative agreement with the European Economic Community (EEC).

2.46 Capital flows to Mongolia were limited until recently to project loans (for turnkey projects and equipment associated with projects) and trade financing provided by the Soviet Union, and to a much lesser extent by other CMEA countries. These loans generally carried an interest rate of 1.5-2 percent per annum and a 15-year maturity, although the amortization payments were determined through bilateral negotiations for the five-year arrangements. Technical assistance loans--the Soviet term for turnkey projects and equipment loans--accounted for about two thirds of capital inflows on average during the last two decades, and the remainder has been trade loans. Capital inflow from other countries has so far been negligible, while there has been a capital outflow of $5-6 million per annum to China since 1986 for the repayment of debt contracted in the 1960s.

2.47 Until recently, almost all of Mongolia's external debt was owed to the Soviet Union. This debt was denominated in transferable rubles (TR) and, at the end of June 1991, amounted to about TR 10.5 billion. Repayments, how-

---

15/ Between 1930 and 1952, the Soviet Union was Mongolia's sole trading partner. While trade with other CMEA countries began in the early 1950s, it developed significantly only after Mongolia joined the COMECON in 1962.

16/ In 1989, the share of the Soviet Union in Mongolia's exports and imports was 81.1 percent and 89.3 percent, respectively; the corresponding ratios were 79 percent and 75 percent for Bulgaria and between 50-60 percent for Czechoslovakia, German Democratic Republic, Hungary, Poland, and Romania.

ever, have been suspended by mutual agreement since January 1, 1991. The government has been negotiating modalities for debt servicing and repayment with the Soviet Union and with the Russian Republic since the breakup of the Soviet Union in 1991, including the appropriate exchange rate for the transferable ruble. These negotiations are proceeding on the agreed principle that future debt service "should not impede Mongolia's economic development."

2.48 Faced with declining stocks of staple commodities and an abrupt decline in financial assistance from its traditional partners, in April 1991 Mongolia requested emergency food aid and quick-disbursing balance of payments support. Following meetings in Tokyo (September 1991) and Ulaanbaatar (October 1991) with the international development community, Mongolia received, by end-1991, aid commitments of about $245 million, comprising $124 million of medium- and long-term loans and $120 million of short-term credit. Of the $245 million, $125 million was for general balance of payments support; $26 million was contributions in-kind (mainly food and medicine); and $94 million consisted of technical assistance and a small amount ($20 million) of project aid. In addition, a May 1992 meeting of the Mongolia assistance group provided further aid indications of $320 million, which is expected to become available in 1992 and 1993. Mongolia's external indebtedness in convertible currency has thus been growing rapidly, and its projected debt-service ratio in 1992 already amounts to 14 percent of its exports of goods and services. The government has, therefore, established a Commission for Coordination of Foreign Assistance in the prime minister's office for coordinating and monitoring external borrowing by different government agencies.

2.49 International Reserves. Foreign exchange reserves increased significantly in the 1980s--in line with the policy to increase exports to the CCA--peaking in 1989 (Table 2.13). During this period, Mongolia's reserves were adequate in terms of months of imports from the CCA (42 months in 1989). With imports from the CCA increasing significantly in 1990, and with all external trade now being settled in convertible currency, significant drawdowns of foreign exchange have been made in the past two years. Net reserves turned negative by mid-1991, with gross foreign exchange reserves falling to about one month's imports.

Summary

2.50 In the past two years, Mongolia's economy has been hit by severe external shocks and is in the difficult process of adjusting to new realities. Its ability to consume and invest has been reduced rapidly and deeply, and tight monetary and fiscal policies will need to continue if serious inflation and payments problems are to be avoided. Given the authorities' objective of developing a market economy, the need for macroeconomic reforms is urgent. However, if the cost of adjustment is to be kept within tolerable limits, policies that begin to reverse the recent declines in production will be vital, while ensuring that social indicators do not show signs of reversal.

Table 2.13: INTERNATIONAL RESERVES, 1980-92
($ million, end-period)

	Net reserves	Gross Reserves			Liabilities
		Total	Foreign exchange	Gold	
1980	23.0	23.0	9.1	13.9	-
1981	21.8	21.8	8.6	13.2	-
1982	23.7	23.7	11.4	12.3	-
1983	19.3	19.3	7.3	12.0	-
1984	32.9	32.9	22.1	10.8	-
1985	57.5	57.5	40.7	16.8	-
1986	57.3	72.2	53.5	18.7	14.9
1987	91.7	148.5	128.4	20.1	56.8
1988	96.6	149.2	130.3	18.9	52.6
1989	102.5	278.9	260.1	18.8	176.4
1990	49.2	177.3	122.6	54.7	128.1
1991 June	-0.1	114.2	92.4	51.8	114.3
July	-2.9	112.9	61.0	51.8	115.8
1991	18.0	126.7	74.9	51.8	108.7
1992 March	7.7	102.4	50.6	51.8	94.7

Source: Mongolbank.

III. KEY REFORM AND POLICY ISSUES

A. Introduction

3.1 Mongolia's current economic difficulties, though mainly the legacy of its socialist past, have been greatly exacerbated by external shocks. Thus, the government is faced with the twin challenges of overcoming the immediate crisis and, at the same time, developing the new institutions required to manage a market-based economy. Its reform program attempts to address both challenges and includes policy measures to stabilize the economy and structural reforms to improve market signals, promote competition, and diversify its sources of foreign exchange. A brief chronology of the key reforms to date is shown in Box 3.1.

3.2 The government's response has been wide-ranging and ambitious and demonstrates its determination to restructure the economy radically and rapidly by replacing the old command-plan structure with market-based systems. The policy framework is largely the work of the coalition government formed in September 1990, and it continues to evolve. This chapter describes the main features of the reform program and seeks to identify the key issues still to be addressed. The reforms fall into three broad categories, discussed separately: reforms designed to strengthen the government's ability to manage the economy through indirect means; reforms required to enhance allocative efficiency and to increase export potential; and, reforms to weave a social safety net to protect the poor, the sick, and the elderly.

B. Macroeconomic Management

3.3 The authorities have moved with remarkable speed to dismantle the old central planning system and are now struggling hard to establish the new institutions needed to operate a market-oriented economy through indirect means of macroeconomic management. The latter is clearly the most critical area for continued reform efforts, considering the lessons of experience in Eastern Europe and China that difficulties arise when price and enterprise reforms take place without an appropriate macroeconomic framework.

3.4 A promising start has been made, but Mongolia's reforms need to continue focusing on three areas: financial sector reform, specifically the development of the central bank and of new commercially oriented financial institutions; fiscal reform, in particular the introduction of new taxes and the restructuring of budget expenditures; and planning reform, especially the creation of new systems of policy coordination appropriate to the needs of a market economy. These three areas are addressed below.

Financial Sector Reform

3.5 Initial Steps. Until 1991, Mongolia had a monobank system, and all central and commercial banking activities were carried out by one institution. The State Bank of Mongolia functioned like a cashier, directing credit according to the Planning Committee's instructions and handling foreign transactions in line with CMEA barter arrangements. Its four hundred branches around the

Box 3.1: KEY ECONOMIC AND STRUCTURAL REFORMS

1986

- Increase in domestic wholesale prices.
- Limited autonomy granted to public sector enterprises for investment.
- Introduction of long-term bank loans for investment.

1987

- Modification of investment planning system for setting overall targets.
- Expansion of investment autonomy of public sector enterprises.
- Rationalization of number of government ministries.

1988

- Reduction in five-year plan performance indices.
- Further decentralization of budgetary operations to local level.
- Limited liberalization of agricultural pricing and marketing in excess of state orders.
- Promotion of private sector cooperatives under new Law on Cooperatives.
- Introduction of more depreciated noncommercial tugrik/US dollar exchange rate.

1989

- Liberalization of intrapublic-sector enterprise pricing and expansion of operating autonomy.
- Modest easing of restrictions on private herd ownership.
- Elimination of monopoly of state trading corporations.
- Increase in selected administered retail prices.
- Easing of foreign exchange surrender requirements.
- Introduction of preferential domestic prices for exported goods.

1990

- Elimination of restrictions on private ownership of herds.
- Freeing of selected retail prices.
- Legalization of two-tiered banking system and establishment of two commercial banks.
- Rationalization of government ministries; elimination of State Planning Committee.
- Establishment of Customs Affairs Department and Tax Service Department.

1990 (cont'd)

- Promulgation of new Foreign Investment Law.
- Devaluation of tugrik vis-à-vis US dollar for commercial transactions.
- Introduction of foreign exchange auction system.
- Negotiation of most-favored-nation trade agreements with countries in the convertible currency area.

1991

- Increase in retail prices of most goods.
- Lengthened maturity structure of term deposits and increased interest rates.
- Substantial reduction of budgetary subsidy for imported goods and to loss-making enterprises.
- Devaluation of tugrik vis-à-vis US dollar to Tug 40 = $1.
- Adjustments to wages, pension benefits, and private savings deposits to soften impact of price increase.
- Privatization Law passed and program for small privatization initiated.
- Banking Law passed, and Bank of Mongolia established as the central bank. Separate commercial banks established.
- Direct export rights granted to selected manufacturers.
- Foreign trading rights issued on nondiscriminatory basis.
- Stock market regulation established.

1992

- Deregulated all prices (except for public services, utility tariffs, public housing rents, selected medicines, flour, bread, and rationed vodka).
- Eliminated mandatory state orders for exports.
- Passed Bankruptcy Law.
- Issue foreign trading licenses on a nondiscriminatory basis (except for copper scrap, cashmere, timber, and elk horns).
- Eliminated budgetary transfers to public enterprises.
- Introduced weekly monitoring of budgetary revenues and expenditures.
- Established a stock exchange.
- Raised central bank lending rate closer to inflation level.
- Simplified interbank clearing and payments arrangements.
- Assigned responsibility for transportation policy to a single coordinating authority, General Department of Transportation.

country accepted savings deposits and disbursed credit to enterprises and government agencies.

3.6 In May 1991, under a new Banking Law, the State Bank was divided into a central bank, called the Bank of Mongolia (BOM) or Mongolbank, and a foreign trade bank called the State Bank of Mongolia (International). The Bank of Mongolia's chairman is responsible to the legislature, thus making the central bank independent of the government. The commercial banking activities of the former State Bank have been transferred to seven new commercial banks, which have gradually taken over most of the former State Bank's branches. The Bank of Mongolia will eventually retain only 21 branches in 3 cities and 18 aimags. The Banking Law provides the framework for the development of a fully functioning central bank capable of managing money and credit using indirect instruments, leaving the allocation of resources to markets.

3.7 Since mid-1991, the new central bank has been tightening monetary and credit policies to contain inflation and impose financial discipline on the enterprise sector. Cash reserve requirements of 8.5 percent have been applied to the nonbank deposit liabilities of commercial banks and remaining central bank branches. These reserves were initially interest-earning, but interest payment on them has been stopped. In addition, the interest rate on the central bank's overdraft facility has been raised in two steps from 5 percent to 30 percent, the target being to achieve a positive real rate, once reliable price data are available. For the time being, it will be supported by quantitative ceilings on access to the facility. Since indirect instruments will take some time to become effective, the stabilization program recently agreed with the IMF includes quantitative targets for limiting quarterly and annual growth of credit. As reform progresses, further instruments of indirect management will be created.

3.8 The central bank has also begun to exercise its supervisory and regulatory functions. Banks established before the May 1991 Banking Law are to be relicensed, and those that do not meet the Law's capital adequacy requirements will be combined with other banks. The Bank of Mongolia is developing regulations and supplementary legislation to the Banking Law covering such matters as leasing, debt recovery and accounting standards.

3.9 Issues. Mongolia's macroeconomic performance in the short and medium run will depend on the central bank's effectiveness in three areas: imposing discipline on the rate of growth of money supply; developing its role as a central bank; and fostering the growth of the private sector, in finance and production.

3.10 The first priority is to maintain a tight monetary policy, considering that net domestic credit and currency grew by 70 percent and 128 percent, respectively, in 1991. This will require strict adherence to the agreed monetary program and firm resistance to the demands of state-owned enterprises for additional credit. Until most enterprises have been privatized, it will be important to avoid acquiring additional bad loans. For existing loans, an attempt must also be made to force the enterprises concerned to rationalize their operations because of the inflationary impact of granting further credit and the need to ensure access to credit for the nascent private sector.

3.11 A key prerequisite for reestablishing price stability will be to neutralize the high level of liquidity created since early 1991. Because the privatization program seems unlikely to achieve this, other routes must be explored. The government has recently commenced issuing bonds, with a first issue of Tug 300 million. With only an 8 percent interest rate, however, these bonds are unlikely to find willing takers, and forcing them on banks would be retrograde. Instead, the government should consider issuing price index-linked bonds, which could be an attractive savings instrument in present circumstances. Furthermore, housing stock still in public hands could be privatized over the medium term, thereby becoming a major source of revenue and of liquidity absorption.

3.12 To strengthen its central banking functions, the Bank of Mongolia has begun to train its staff in the new ways of doing business and is receiving significant technical assistance for this purpose. The present payments and clearing system will also have to be modernized because, in its present form, it inhibits efficiency in the banking sector and the availability of timely information for policymaking. The private banking sector may need the most attention.

3.13 In private banking, two issues deserve emphasis. First, following the transfer of former State Bank branches to the new commercial banks, every effort should now be made to operate these new banks as independent commercial banks. Since a major obstacle is doubtless these branches' bad debts with state-owned enterprises, the separation of such loans from the banks may be necessary to speed up the transfer. To avoid subsequent widespread failure, care will be needed to avoid monetizing such debts and generating inflation. Second, the central bank should play a major role in training the staff of the new commercial banks, especially in credit, risk, and project appraisal.

3.14 In terms of its impact on Mongolia's future development prospects, financial sector policy will need to ensure that the emerging private sector has adequate access to bank financing. This will require that, within any given macroeconomic target of permissible credit expansion, a growing proportion of total credit is redirected from the public sector (currently accounting for 95 percent of total credit) to the private sector. Privatization will contribute to this process. In addition, the improved finances (e.g., by increasing the share of "own" funds) of enterprises that remain state-owned would help reduce their claims on the banking sector as a proportion of total credit, thus allowing greater room for private sector credit.

Public Finance Reforms

3.15 Initial Steps. Mongolia's prereform fiscal system was geared in a classic way to the central planning system. The two major sources of revenue were: remitted profits from state-owned enterprises arising from the fixed price structure; and import price differentials, deriving from the wide disparity between import and domestic prices for consumer goods, many of which are imported. As reforms progress, both revenue sources will shrink. This means that the tax system will need restructuring to find new, more neutral levies appropriate to the needs of a market economy. The difficulty of this task, complicated enough, is compounded by the need for a drastic reduction in the fiscal deficit, which has been running at around 20 percent of GDP. The restoration of financial discipline is, therefore, the cornerstone of the short-term stabilization program, with the aim of reducing the overall deficit to 12 percent of GDP in 1992.

3.16 The first steps in this area were put in place with the January 1991 tax reforms. Intended to expand the tax base and improve the elasticity of the tax system, they include: replacing "planned" profit taxes on enterprises by corporate and individual income taxes based on market economy concepts; replacing import price differentials by customs duties at a uniform 15 percent rate; converting domestic turnover taxes to a more broadly based sales tax, and introducing selective excise taxes in 1992. Although these actions were all in the right direction, the authorities considered them insufficient to make up for losses from traditional revenue sources. Additional measures were introduced in September 1991, including: a 10 percent customs surcharge, raising the average rate to 25 percent; and, the doubling of excise rates on liquor, tobacco, and gold. Automatic payroll deduction of social security payments, which had been suspended, is also being reinstated.

3.17 On the expenditure side, about 80 percent of expenditures were current, about half of it in subsidies and transfers. In reform before 1990, the size of the bureaucracy had been reduced significantly, thus offering little prospect for further savings in the government's wage bill. Major savings in the short term have therefore been derived from a 30 percent cut in capital expenditures. Future capital expenditure will be linked to the availability of foreign project assistance.

3.18 A variety of other measures are being considered for the near term. These include administrative strengthening over both revenue collection and expenditures, a review of the structure of government to identify areas for further possible cuts, and the holding of wage and salary increases below the rate of inflation. Additional measures under consideration to strengthen both sides of the budget include the introduction of user fees and increased charges for public services, and for education and health services, cost recovery through a proposed national health program financed by contributions from employers and employees. However, all these measures remain to be worked out in detail.

3.19 Issues. The start that has been made in restructuring the budget will eventually provide Mongolia with the foundations of a market-oriented public finance system. However, in addition to all the vital measures under preparation, a variety of other issues need to be addressed in the medium term to improve the tax and expenditure structure and reduce the deficit.

3.20 In terms of budget structure, a major effort is underway to reclassify the budget along Western lines. In this regard, two issues seem to be relatively neglected at present. First, all enterprises should be moved off-budget as soon as possible, especially those that will remain in the public domain; otherwise, it may prove very difficult to harden their budget constraint. Second, a more rational system needs to be developed for allocating revenue and expenditure responsibilities between the central and local governments (aimags), not least so that local government expenditures can be regulated more tightly.

3.21 On the tax side, the big steps and main decisions have already been taken, but certain issues need to be reexamined. First, the elaboration of sales tax regulations should be undertaken with a view to their conversion in a few years' time to a value-added tax. This would imply the use of tax credits,17/ to avoid cascading taxation. Second, the present structure of income and company taxes seems to warrant more attention. Both income and company taxes are highly progressive, starting at very low rates.18/ With the scheduled completion of price reform in 1992, such wide ranges will be less necessary and hard to administer. Complex rules for personal income tax exemptions compound administrative difficulties. Moreover, the progressive nature of the company tax may encourage enterprises to break up into units of uneconomic size. Under the circumstances, early consideration should be given to simplifying tax rates and exemptions. This reform should be carefully designed because frequent changes in the tax structure are unadvisable.

3.22 Perhaps the most unusual feature of the company tax is the exclusion of wages and depreciation from costs for purposes of assessing tax liability. The government argues that allowing wages to be deductible would encourage wage hikes. However, the company tax is an inappropriate instrument for taxing wages because it discriminates against employment at a time of rising unemployment and encourages wages to be concealed in nonmonetary forms, such as food distribution. It also discriminates against the creation of new, labor-intensive enterprises in the private sector, and against self-employment. It is therefore recommended that tax rate revisions treat wages as costs and include a reasonable depreciation allowance to encourage investment. This does not mean that Mongolia might not need a tax-based wage policy but that different instruments should be used.

3.23 The final area that seems to offer scope for early results is a thorough review of subsidy policies. Subsidies account for a significant share of total expenditure (Table 3.1). With reforms in agricultural procurement and ownership, changes in the exchange rate, and the impending privatization of industry, most subsidies could be eliminated soon. While some price subsidies will have to be retained, they should be targeted in line with the social safety net. Controlling subsidies would also allow the government greater scope for incremental expenditures to protect the losers in the reform process, to retrain the workforce, and to provide vital economic infrastructure. The key to this is the speed of price and exchange rate reforms and privatization, discussed below.

Policy Coordination

3.24 Initial Steps. The heart of the old central planning system was the State Committee for Social and Economic Development, the Mongolian equivalent of the State Planning Commission found in all socialist economies. Signifying its determination to move away from the old system, Mongolia abolished the Committee in late 1990 and established instead a Ministry of National Develop-

---

17/ Crediting a producer in his tax bill for sales taxes paid on inputs used.

18/ Personal income tax rate schedule starts at 2.4 percent and rises to 50 percent. Company income tax rates range from 8 percent to 35 percent.

Table 3.1: STRUCTURE OF SUBSIDIES, 1989/90
(Tug million)

	1989	1990
Industry	340	447
Agriculture	502	528
Trade	478	347
Prices	170	96
Other	41	56
Total	1,531	1,474
Total current expenditure	5,383	5,469

Source: Appendix Table 5.4.

ment (MND) from the remnants of the old committees, plus the State Committee for Science, Technology and Higher Education. However, MND retains many of the functions and habits of a planning committee in state orders for agriculture and exports and in project preparation. Since August 1991, MND has also begun to perform the secretariat function for a newly established Economic Policy Committee, headed by the First Deputy Prime Minister.

3.25 Issues. The rejection of the old central planning system has been so strong in Mongolia that any suggestion that new forms of planning are needed is unwelcome. Especially during transition, however, an institutional framework and process are sorely needed to coordinate macroeconomic and development policies between ministries that no longer receive centralized direction. Through inexperience and policy disagreements, individual ministries and agencies have headed in different directions, and major policy initiatives have been taken without adequate interministerial discussion or consensus. Thus, the implementation of macroeconomic policy is fragmented--with agencies not sharing information, and dissipation of the full skills and experience of Mongolia's limited cadre of able decisionmakers.

3.26 In addition to its policy coordination function, the government needs to give attention to its other appropriate roles. These include the need for government intervention in cases of market failure, especially those related to the emergence of privately owned monopolies, and for improved methods for managing enterprises that remain public.

3.27 The other area where institutional development seems to be a priority is the improvement of the public sector investment program (PSIP) and the capacity of MND officials to carry out project appraisals suitable to the new structure of the economy. In mid-1991 review, a third of all PSIP projects was eliminated but, as the economy changes and the available pool of investment resources becomes apparent, PSIP will need to reassessed anew. Current methods focus on meeting output targets and on payback periods, with little attention to economic benefits and to cost minimization.

3.28 As the basis for the PSIP and a backdrop to the general formation of economic policies, MND, or some other central body, will need to develop a capability to formulate strategy. This goes beyond the short-term needs of the stabilization program or the reforms needed to establish a market economy. Examples of this sort of development planning abound in East Asian economies such as Japan, Republic of Korea, and Thailand. Four specific tasks seem to be important:

(a) long-term analysis of possible choices, options, and directions for the economy, taking an integrated look at resources, infrastructure, etc. For example, what would be the implications of faster mining exploitation? Of continuing population growth at current rates?

(b) convening interministerial groups, with outside experts, to assess important projects from various perspectives (such as a large mining project with important implications for transportation and energy). Such activities might be directed toward producing special reports to the legislature.

(c) general reviews of the developmental implications of government programs.

(d) evaluations of the effectiveness of various government programs, with a view to providing feedback on their cost-benefit ratios. These would provide an independent view of the programs supported by various ministries and could bring problems to the surface quicker than would otherwise occur.

C. Improving Incentives

3.29 In the move from the command plan to a market economy, the role of incentives is paramount. Perhaps the hardest economic management lesson of reform in socialist countries is that the key to creating successful markets lies in removing obstacles, rather than in taking direct action. This boils down to removing barriers to competition and refraining from sheltering public enterprises from the impact of competition.

3.30 In this regard, reforms are necessary in three main areas, all fully recognized in Mongolia: prices and markets; the external sector; and enterprises. Major actions, described below, have been taken on all three fronts. The order in which these are discussed is deliberate, because the government's present intentions with respect to sequencing raise some questions. Experience in Mongolia and in other reforming socialist countries suggests that perhaps excessive reliance is being placed on the role of privatization relative to other reforms. This discussion is not intended to discourage privatization in Mongolia or its present timetable, but rather to urge the authorities' continued attention to the related reforms on which the ultimate success of privatization depends.

Price and Market Reforms

3.31 Initial Steps. Until the end of 1990, Mongolia's official price structure was similar to those in other socialist countries that followed the Soviet model: low energy prices, subsidized food and housing, free social services, cheap capital goods, and very expensive consumer goods. These price differentials were made possible through a rigid system of price controls and distribution through state channels, designed to contain final consumption and thus to generate heavy funding for capital-intensive industry. In Mongolia, the price differentials on imported consumer goods--which account for about half of total supplies--were equivalent to an estimated tariff of 250 percent. Housing rents in Mongolia average about Tug 300 per month, including heating, which represents about 20 percent of the average wage of Tug 1,500.

3.32 Official price data are unreliable and, historically, reflect only official price changes. Nevertheless, data for 1980-89 reveal that wholesale prices, which enjoyed some degree of flexibility in the 1980s, rose much more rapidly than retail prices, considerably eroding the yield from the "taxation" of retail margins.

3.33 Major price adjustments were made in January 1991. Some realignment of relative prices also was done, especially for intermediate and primary goods, to reduce the need for budgetary subsidies. Retail prices fixed by the government were doubled, to raise them above wholesale prices, while the increases in wholesale prices were usually less than 100 percent. Farmgate prices were raised sharply (30-70 percent), as were tariffs for public services, and the tugrik was devalued from Tug 5.63 = $1 to Tug 7.1 = $1. Budgetary subsidy funds were cut sharply, from Tug 1,474 million in 1990 to Tug 700 million for 1991, and their scope was greatly narrowed. Most wages were adjusted to compensate fully for the price changes.

3.34 In addition, the January 1991 measures were a step toward price liberalization. They reduced the number of centrally determined public sector tariffs and limited controlled prices to:

(a) 35 categories of retail prices (down from 220 before);

(b) 10 categories of imported goods;

(c) wholesale prices of certain goods still subject to state orders; and

(d) certain other wholesale prices of basic goods.

Some goods were subject only to maximum prices, some were subject to two-tier pricing, with above-quota sales allowed at liberalized prices,19/ while the prices of other goods were freed.

3.35 In another important development in January 1991, rationing coupons for ten items were introduced. Rations are issued to families according to

---

19/ For example, 15 percent of meat was intended to be sold on free markets and the percentage was to rise in later years.

their size, with no allowance for their age composition. The rationed quantities vary a little by city/aimag, depending on the availability of specific commodities. Table 3.2 shows the rations for a family of six in Ulaanbaatar in June 1991.

Table 3.2: MONTHLY FOOD RATIONS, JUNE 1991

Meat	16.2 kg
Flour, grade 1	10.2 kg
grade 2	10.0 kg
Rice	1.8 kg
Sugar	3.5 kg
Butter	2.4 kg
Vegetable oil	1 bottle
Tea	1 block
Soap	2 blocks plus detergent
Vodka	3 bottles

Note: For family of 6 in Ulaanbaatar.

Source: Government of Mongolia.

3.36 In September 1991, the prices of half of the remaining 35 controlled commodities were liberalized, reducing the value of controlled sales to the equivalent of 40 percent of urban household expenditure and 20 percent of rural household expenditure.20/ Further liberalization took place in March 1992, leaving only public utilities, transportation, housing rents, selected medicines, flour, bread, and rationed vodka subject to price controls. While state orders for agricultural products will continue to dominate distribution through the 1992/93 winter, market distribution is expected to dominate in the rural sector from mid-1993.

3.37 Issues. It is generally recognized that the private sector's response to the government's price reform efforts has been disappointing. However, private traders' access to either domestic or imported goods is highly restricted because state order system and distribution system still predominate. Rationing and price controls on many consumer goods has effectively excluded private traders from this system and, in any event, the controlled margins are too small to be attractive. As long as the state order system is rigidly maintained, price reform will not lead to market development.

20/ The items remaining controlled after this round include: rationed goods; petroleum products; selected consumer goods such as tent covers; medicine; and rents and public utilities.

3.38 The government has said it would remove these barriers before the end of 1992, and the list of commodities that will remain subject to control is similar to those in many market economies. It is very important that the government stick strictly to its timetable and accompany the price moves by simultaneous and matching liberalization of the state marketing system. This implies the replacement of rationing with a targeted social safety net. This reform would promote the success of the trade and privatization reforms discussed later in this chapter.

3.39 These changes, to allow privatization to work, dwarf any related issues in this area. However, the ongoing role of the state in this area deserves attention. Continued state determination of the prices of energy, housing, and much transportation seems reasonable. However, these prices must be adjusted to reflect long-run marginal costs. They were held low until 1991, have not been increased by the same margin as most other prices, and already account for a substantial proportion of subsidies. An urgent priority therefore is for analysis to determine appropriate adjustments for such prices even though inflation and exchange rate movements will pose problems.

3.40 The government should be ready to correct for market failures of which two types. First, some markets may be very slow to develop, causing problems for producers. Agriculture is the most potentially serious case, especially meat and grains. The government should be ready to offer <u>minimum</u> support prices, below expected market prices but above variable costs. The second area relates to possible market failure because of monopolies. Many industries in Mongolia have only one enterprise and, after price liberalization and privatization, such enterprises may seek to exploit their monopoly power by charging unreasonable prices. In Mongolia--as in other socialist countries--the sophisticated administrative skills needed to deal with this through direct intervention are unlikely to be present or easily developed. Rather, the solution will be to proceed on a parallel track with trade reforms, allowing imports to provide the necessary competition. This liberalization should be phased in gradually, to avoid wiping out large sections of industry overnight. In any event, it will be constrained as long as acute foreign exchange shortages persist.

3.41 <u>Factor Prices</u>. The successful liberalization of product prices would require producers to respond to commodity price signals by adjusting the level and composition of their production in the short run and the size and structure of their capital assets in the medium to long run. For this, enterprises need flexibility in their use of labor and capital. The immediate liberalization of factor markets in Mongolia is more problematic than for product markets. The proper operation of factor markets requires further reforms, notably in defining ownership and governance of enterprises and strengthening the financial system. Private owners (or independent managers in state-owned enterprises) might be in the best position to provide countervailing force against wage pressures. For liberalized credit markets to work well, solvent banks, market-based lending practices, and appropriate regulation are needed. Until such institutions become fully operational, factor markets may have to be regulated.

3.42 During the transition period, when stabilization has a very high priority, wage increases must be modulated to prevent a wage-price spiral.

Such restraint can be effected through: freezing or limiting increases in the wage fund or average wages and employment in state enterprises; moral suasion, backed by tight credit and fiscal measures, to check wage increases in the private sector; and limiting the increase in minimum wages. Mongolia has come a considerable distance in removing restrictions on labor mobility and wage determination by enterprises, with a view to improving incentives to reward gains in productivity. The government is also keeping wage increases in the public sector below the inflation rate. Nonetheless, private enterprises have been offering much higher wage increases than the inflation rate. Government would be advised to monitor this situation carefully, using its credit control to ensure moderation during this critical period.

External Sector Reforms

3.43 Initial Steps. Under the old, monopolistic trade system, 95 percent of Mongolia's trade was with the CMEA countries, handled by the large state-owned enterprises and by five foreign trade corporations (FTCs).21/ The government recognizes the need both to diversify its sources of foreign exchange, and to reform the trade regime into one that reflects and supports the move to markets. Similarly, the old foreign exchange regime involved full surrender of foreign exchange earnings and administrative allocation of foreign exchange under an annual plan. Foreign investment has been high in Mongolia, but solely from the CMEA countries before 1990 and concentrated in mining and related processing activities. With the collapse of the CMEA system, the government has recognized the need to move rapidly in this area and has already initiated reforms in the foreign exchange system, foreign investment, and the trade regime.

3.44 In the foreign exchange regime, two major changes have occurred. First, a series of devaluations has taken the exchange rate from Tug 3 = $1 in June 1990, first to Tug 5.6, then Tug 7.1 in May 1991. In June 1991, a three-market structure was set up: the commercial rate of Tug 40 = $1; Tug 7.1 = $1 for barter trade; and a free market rate in a thin market, where rates ranged between Tug 100 and Tug 150 = $1 in 1991. In May 1992, the barter and commercial rates were unified at Tug 40 = $1, while the rate of the free market was around Tug 250 = $1. The free market has emerged because of the new foreign exchange retention scheme, under which full surrender is required only for state orders. Foreign exchange earned above orders and earned by private exporters can be retained in full. Enterprises and cooperatives not subject to state orders may retain 50 percent and 90 percent, respectively, of their earnings. These retained earnings may be held in foreign exchange accounts or sold. This is the source of foreign exchange for the third market, but a small one at present.

3.45 Mongolia has high hopes for foreign direct investment. It passed a generous foreign investment law in 1990, which includes provisions for unre-

---

21/ Mongolimpex handled CCA country trade. Four others handled CMEA trade: Teknikimport handled imports of machinery and equipment; Rasnoimport handled imports of consumer goods; Autoneftimport handled imports of vehicles and petroleum products; and Mongolexport handled all exports.

stricted repatriation of capital and remittance of profits and dividends. The Ministry of Trade and Industry takes responsibility in this area.

3.46 In the area of trade, decentralization has begun by the issuing of trade licenses to private and public enterprises. Some 340 such licenses had been issued by late 1991. The government has said it would eliminate licensing requirements, except for statistical information purposes, and to phase out the state order system. Nevertheless, in 1991, the government issued $385 million of export orders, of which 81 percent was for barter trade with the Soviet Union, compared with total projected exports of $432 million. Thus, the state order system still dominates trade, and almost all trade contracts in 1991 were signed by the state FTCs. Preparations for further diversification of trade have been launched by MFN treaties with Japan, the United States, the Republic of Korea and by a cooperative agreement with the European Communities. Mongolia has also applied for GATT membership.

3.47 The major additional reform being proposed is to move from the rigid import plan via state orders to an "indicative import plan," with categories of imports identified with sources of foreign exchange. Except for barter trade and "emergency imports," centralized distribution of imports is to be phased out over time.

Foreign Trade

3.48 The private sector's apparent lack of response to these trade and exchange reforms is easy to explain by: its lack of experience in such matters, the persistence of the state order system, the shortage of supply in the domestic market, and the poor world market situation for wool and cashmere. In addition, the continuation of barter arrangements with the former Soviet Union republics means that reforms in this area must be designed carefully. Moreover, the FTCs' expertise in trade matters, must be recognized because such skills are scarce.

3.49 Nevertheless, significant progress in trade is hard to foresee as long as the mandatory state order system is in place. This system should be dismantled as soon as possible and replaced by voluntary contracts at freely negotiated prices.22/ Mineral exports to the Soviet Union are a special case and will have to continue as a separate arrangement.

3.50 Eliminating the state order system and the rigid foreign exchange allocation system with respect to imports is very important. While special arrangements may remain necessary for barter imports from the Soviet Union, and perhaps, in the short term, for some targeted "critical" imports funded by official aid, all other imports must be urgently liberalized to provide competition to domestic monopolies and to facilitate and stimulate exports.

3.51 With the disappearance of the state order system, FTCs will no longer be needed as state instruments, and they can become trading houses,

---

22/ Although the government announced in March 1992 the dismantling of the mandatory state orders system for exports, this decision had not taken effect by mid-1992.

specialized in foreign trade. Their earnings would come from on margins between procurement and export prices, or between import and domestic prices. The state will, however, continue to perform residual functions, including export promotion (trade fairs etc.) and advisory service to exporters. The nucleus of these activities should be developed out of the FTCs.

Foreign Exchange Policy

3.52 The new foreign exchange policy is a big improvement over the old one in two respects: it shows that the authorities recognize the need to move toward a unified exchange rate; and the new rate structure comes closer to a realistic, market-based rate, at least vis-à-vis cash transactions. Despite this progress, the present policy still has two major shortcomings: Mongolia still has sharply differentiated, multiple exchange rates; and depreciated rates are not fully passed on to the end users. Mongolia holds the present commercial rate as a nominal anchor against inflation since, in such a heavily import-dependent economy, a price-exchange rate spiral could easily develop.

3.53 Regarding multiple exchange rates, until recently the most serious shortcoming was the very appreciated rate for barter transactions, 80 percent of total foreign trade in 1990. This conflicted with the objective of encouraging exports and their diversification as well as efficient import substitution. The government could only justify and sustain this high barter exchange rate if it kept the state order system, soft budget constraints for state enterprises, price controls, and restrictions on the movement of capital and labor, all scheduled for phasing out. What causes concern now, however, is that the effective implementation of exchange rate unification and further depreciation of the rate as may be needed might be hampered by delays in reforms in the above areas.

3.54 The foreign exchange retention scheme, while contributing to the existence of multiple exchange rates, encourages exports to CCA countries by enabling exporters to raise their "average" rates of exchange and by giving them access to free foreign currency. Nonetheless, it is a second-best option and should be eliminated with the state order system and compulsory surrender of foreign exchange. It operates through and makes possible the parallel foreign exchange market, which has been officially tolerated since mid-1990 and became de facto a part of the official exchange rate system. Because the parallel market is still thin, that exchange rate (about Tug 150 = $1 in October 1991) cannot be taken as a representative, market-determined rate. It serves as a useful index of changes in foreign exchange supply during transition, but it can be eliminated as soon as the related reforms in the foreign exchange system have been implemented.

3.55 The major remaining shortcoming of current foreign exchange policy is that the depreciated official rate of Tug 40 = $1 is rarely passed on to the end users of imports. This is mainly because the resultant domestic prices are not considered "affordable." For instance, shortly after the June 1991 devaluation, Mongolian International Air Transport (MIAT) raised its fares to cover the increased tugrik cost of its foreign exchange liabilities. A sharp decline in the number of passengers soon forced it to rescind the decision and instead resort to central bank financing. The sharp devaluation should have generated a large shift in relative prices, with increases in the prices of imports, close import-substitutes, and exportables relative to those of domestic (nontraded) goods. Such a shift has not taken place because of import and exchange controls, the rationing of some import commodities (e.g., rice), and the predominance of administrative pricing. Thus, instead of being exposed to large relative price changes in line with the rising price of foreign exchange (official and shadow), Mongolia's producers and consumers have been subjected to progressive tightening of supply and growing shortages. This practice is severely reducing the impact of the devaluation and should be stopped, by lifting administrative interventions.

3.56 In summary, the two key steps that appear to be necessary are to further unify the multiple rates as soon as possible, and to eliminate obstacles to the impact of the exchange rate on the domestic economy. Only then will a more reasonable judgment be possible about the appropriateness of the exchange rate.

Foreign Direct Investment (FDI)

3.57 The opening up of Mongolia and the enactment of a foreign investment law have already generated 32 joint venture agreements with new partners, 22 of them signed in the first half of 1991. They mostly involve commodities such as cashmere, camel wool, horse hair, meat, and minerals, but some are in trading and tourism. All these ventures utilize Mongolian inputs, and none is an assembly-processing venture so popular in other Asian countries, especially Southern China. To encourage further projects, the government is considering establishing development zones or even a processing zone.

3.58 Mongolia would do well to designate one location just for export enterprises, where transport arrangements can be coordinated and supplies of power, heat, and water guaranteed. However, the government will have to be realistic about the types of foreign enterprise likely to come to Mongolia and their potential impact. Most of them will probably follow the recent pattern, seeking to add value to Mongolia's natural resources, especially in animal by-products. Transport costs will probably make processing of imported materials uneconomic, and Mongolian labor is not cheap to compensate. Significant investment in raw material processing, if it comes, will depend on improvements in export transport. Therefore, expectations of short-term benefits from FDI should be modest.

3.59 The two areas where immediate action seems to be most warranted are in strengthening FDI administration and in selective promotion. Mongolia is very distant and must therefore make the foreign investment process as simple as possible, preferably via a "one-stop" agency where foreign investors can obtain all necessary permissions as well as information about potential local partners. In addition, such an agency should selectively promote foreign investment, by forging institutional links with overseas agencies that can target potential foreign investors in Mongolia's export industries. This is an appropriate use for technical assistance.

Enterprise Reform and Privatization

3.60 Initial Steps. The development of the private sector is a key element of the government's economic strategy. It involves both the promotion of new activities, by providing an enabling legislative framework, and privatizing a third (by asset value) of existing public enterprises (Table 3.3). The authorities hope for rapid progress in this area, as the key to cementing the new market economy. Privatization and new private sector activities are designed to replace the previous system of state-owned enterprises operating under mandatory planning and distribution.

Table 3.3: NUMBER AND VALUE OF STATE ENTERPRISES TO BE PRIVATIZED (April 1991)

Privatization category	Number of enterprises				Value (million Tug) of enterprises			
	Ulaanbaatar	Darhan & Erdenet	Aimags	Total	Ulaanbaatar	Darhan & Erdenet	Aimags	Total
Large privatization (blue coupons)	90	28	226	344	3,881	1,570	5,304	10,755
Small privatization (green coupons)	498	48	1,055	1,601	3,035	428	2,185	5,648
Agricultural coop.	1	0	277	278	7	0	3,732	3,739
Partly state-owned	101	25	238	364	9,873	4,437	2,801	17,111
Total	690	101	1,796	2,587	16,796	6,435	14,022	37,253

Source: The State Privatization Commission.

3.61 Despite the attention lavished on privatization, promotion of new private sector activities has not been neglected. It began in 1988 with the promotion of private sector cooperatives and has spread since 1991 with the promulgation of the company law, bankruptcy law, consumer protection law, and antimonopoly law. The number of private cooperatives has grown from 180 in 1988, employing 3,500 persons, to nearly 3,000 in 1991, employing well over 20,000 (excluding the livestock cooperatives). Other private firms have appeared since the reforms began, and in October 1991 numbered some 4,200, with 32,000 employees. Most of these firms provide services and produce light consumer goods for the domestic market. Including an additional 4,000 self-employed, some 56,000 people work in new private sector activities, about 8.6 percent of total employment of almost 650,000.

3.62 The privatization program has completed about a year of its critical implementation phase through a voucher system (Box 3.2) similar to those current in the Czech and Slovak Federal Republic, Poland, and Romania. In addition, a stock exchange was created in February 1992 to permit share trading after privatization and to facilitate the large firms' privatization process. The voucher scheme is to cover most of the 1,600 small enterprises and the 340 large enterprises slated for complete privatization and the 364 firms to be partially privatized. The privatization of small firms and shops is well under way, with more than 1,000 firms already privatized. In addition to privatization by voucher, some small enterprises and shops are being leased and sold. The "large" privatization, originally, scheduled for a year beginning in October 1991, has been extended to 1994. The only enterprises to remain in state ownership are in mining, energy, rail and air transportation, communications, and water supply. These are large in terms of asset value but small in number.

Box 3.2: MECHANICS OF PRIVATIZATION BY VOUCHERS

1. Mongolia's privatization program is being implemented through free distribution of vouchers that will be used in bidding for publicly owned assets. It has two distinct components: (a) small privatization, which includes some 1,600 small businesses, all agricultural assets, livestock, and others with a total book value 1/ of Tug 9.4 billion; and (b) the privatization of 340 large, state-owned enterprises with a book value of Tug 10.8 billion and partial privatization of further 364 firms with a book value of Tug 17 billion.2/ Each citizen is given two vouchers. Green vouchers have three tickets and are for the purchase of small assets. Blue vouchers have one ticket, for purchase of big assets. The face value of each citizen's vouchers is about Tug 10,000, so that the total national voucher value amounts to about Tug 20 billion and corresponds approximately to the book value of assets to be privatized. This represents about one-and-one-half years' GDP at mid-1991 prices and far exceeds the financial savings of households, which are only about Tug 1 billion.

2. Small properties have been sold mostly at auctions, arranged by local authorities under guidelines prepared by the Privatization Commission, with no reserve prices. The public has been informed by listing the assets to be auctioned in newspapers across the country. Any individual can bid for assets by simply taking part in the auction with their vouchers; no cash is used in auctions. The highest bid wins the asset, and the Privatization Commission issues the ownership certificate to the winner. Individuals can trade, buy, and sell the green vouchers for cash, but cannot use them for bank credit. Banks may provide brokerage services for coupon holders, but local markets are not regulated in any way.

3. Large firms are also sold by auction through brokers and the stock market. Since the opening of Mongolia's first stock exchange in February 1992, 21 large firms have been privatized and 16 more are on the waiting list. The mechanics of large privatization is as follows. First, the Privatization Commission decides which enterprises are to be privatized each week. These enterprises are converted to joint stock companies, and 10 percent of their shares are granted to the present employees, who are then allowed to participate in the auction on an equal basis with others. The remaining shares are sold in batches with successive blocks of shares sold sequentially. Once the auction is announced, individuals bid with their blue vouchers for a number of shares through brokers located across the country. After collecting the bids, the brokers phone in a bid for a batch of shares, in terms of vouchers, to the stock market. The share batches are sold each hour, and the broker with the highest bid for the batch wins the shares and distributes the shares to his or her clients. The batches are sold in this way until all the shares are placed. Blue vouchers can be transferred up to three times but cannot be freely traded or sold to foreigners. They must be used to buy shares in the large firms which may then be traded on the stock market and sold to foreign investors in accord with the general provisions governing foreign investment. The voucher scheme is to charge a fee of Tug 200 per person for the vouchers (except for some 75,000 poor citizens). A revenue of Tug 300 million will accrue to the privatization fund to cover such items as brokers' commissions; two months' severance pay for an estimated 20,000 workers in the firms being liquidated; training for enterprise directors, brokers, bank officers, and accountants; public awareness programs; and communications and other office expenses.

1/ Book value is the depreciated value of investments at historical cost, not revalued for inflation. The book value of all assets is therefore substantially below replacement cost because of depreciation and the high rates of inflation in 1990 and 1991.

2/ As of April 1991, the total book value of state assets in Mongolia, including assets in the nonmaterial sectors, was estimated at Tug 51 billion. Of these, the material sectors' assets, which would be subject to privatization, had a total value of Tug 37 billion, including Tug 13 billion for shares to remain in the hands of the government.

3.63 The company law was an important milestone, as it defined ownership, and specifically the state ownership of existing enterprises, all of which have had to reregister. This has enabled the government to be in a position to define both its privatization program and its remaining ownership responsibilities with some certainty.

3.64 Livestock herds and most state farms are also to be privatized; some 60 percent of the herd has already been spontaneously privatized. Pastureland will remain public, the privatizing of farmland awaits passage of the Land Law. In the meantime, some leasing arrangements have been introduced.

Privatization

3.65 The privatization program will transform the face of the Mongolian economy permanently. The initial, breathtaking timetable for completing the process in 1992, however, seemed overhasty and might have led to widespread enterprise failure and to some backlash against reform. The new timetable for completion by 1994, while still ambitious, is welcome and much more realistic. To avoid "drift" in existing enterprises, however, a final, realistic timetable must set as soon as possible and adhered to.

3.66 The key issue with respect to the timetable for privatization is the sequencing of related reforms. Price and domestic trade reforms will dramatically affect the valuation of existing enterprises and the prospects for creating new private enterprises. This suggests that privatization phases should be synchronized with price and marketing reforms. Thus, enterprises in sectors already freed of price controls and state orders should be privatized first; others should await the completion of price reforms. This is another reason for avoiding delays in price and market reforms. Piecemeal privatization over a long period of time could have negative consequences because of its effects on individual decisions. Significant delay could yield to the takeover of enterprises by their workers and the decapitalization that has been observed in other countries. Thus, the publication of a timetable for each enterprise would be most appropriate.

3.67 The debt of firms to be privatized is a particularly difficult issue, particularly with the largest enterprises. Canceling outstanding debt of Tug 10 billion and the enterprises' deposits of Tug 4.5 billion has been suggested. Treatment of this issue also affects the development of the banking system and has implications for the market. Cancellation seems inappropriate and potentially inflationary. However, an exchange of some of this debt for long-term bonds seems a reasonable possibility, perhaps to be held by the new development bank or fiscalized through creation of a special fund within the budget framework. This issue needs to be addressed with considerable care.

3.68 The possible macroeconomic effects of privatization also merit the authorities' early attention. First, many firms are likely to run into difficulties once they are removed from state support. Because their need for temporary assistance in restructuring may be difficult and inappropriate to ignore, and the government should recognize this possibility in its fiscal planning. Similarly, individual share selling to finance consumption may have monetary repercussions. Thus, the privatization program would seem to depend on a careful fiscal and monetary policy stance.

3.69 While good progress has been made in defining an overall legal framework for privatization and a new private sector, less attention has been paid to one key regulatory aspect. Mongolia's accounting and auditing standards are still inadequate and few professionals are trained in these skills. A major effort is needed in this area if a market system is to be developed, based on share capital. Shareholders need information based on consistent accounting and audit systems to make sound decisions.

Private Sector Development

3.70 The attractiveness and priority of the privatization program should not distract attention from the needs of the new private sector and its necessary policy framework. Good progress has already been made in the legislative area, but more is needed. The private sector will need credit, for example, and that specific provision should be made for it in the credit plan. Similarly, the completion of the reform of the state order system is a critical next step; this will not only stimulate the creation of private trading companies, but also provide new enterprises with access to raw materials and energy, currently a severe constraint.

3.71 As the private sector develops, the government will have to consider technical assistance needs of new enterprises (bookkeeping, technology acquisition, health, and safety) and the appropriate institutional set-up for it. Here, international experience abounds. Ancillary services of this type are likely to sprout most rapidly in rural areas, because rural dwellers will probably see the most rapid gains in income from the reforms, after price corrections. This would put heavy demands on transport and on local government, but could quickly bring new jobs to the countryside.

Public Enterprise Management

3.72 Although over 2,000 enterprises are to be privatized with assets valued at over Tug 20 billion, a much higher level of assets will remain in public ownership in mining, energy, transport, and telecommunications. Little thought appears to have been given to the issue of corporate governance for the remaining enterprises. It will, however, be vital from a fiscal standpoint and for its supply implications because these enterprises provide the private sector with many essential inputs. This, an entire topic in itself, will need serious attention, with regard to: adjustment of tariffs and user-charges for full cost recovery; appropriate systems of preventing administrative interference in the day-to-day operations of enterprises; efficient ways for government to exercise its ownership functions such as through boards of directors or holding companies; and ways to permit the poor to continue to have access to public services.

D. The Social Safety Net

3.73 Even without the transition to a market economy, Mongolia would have faced severe short-term difficulties from external shocks to its economy. However, the break-up of the state-owned enterprises will remove the safety net for many citizens and the government recognizes its obligations in this regard. The rural nature of the economy offers some cushion because many affected persons still have close ties to rural areas and food sources. Some migration from cities to the rural areas occurred in 1990/91, but a segment of the urban population without rural ties will bear the brunt of the adjustment.

3.74 Several preparatory steps have already been taken. A severance pay system for redundant workers was instituted and local governments were given resources in the 1991 budget to distribute either as welfare funds or for job creation. Further, the fees raised from issuing privatization vouchers are to be used for retraining or job creation. While cost-recovery principles are to be introduced in health and education, provisions are being made to ensure continued care for people who cannot pay. The base pension, now below the poverty line, will be reviewed in light of price developments in 1991 and 1992.

3.75 Appropriate cost-recovery systems are one good direction for change, but the health and education system will have to be tended with care against break down. In several reforming socialist economies, the break-up of state-owned enterprises--which provide many such services directly or indirectly--has led to a rapid deterioration in standards and coverage, with potentially serious long-term effects. Therefore, sufficient budgetary resources will have to be provided to maintain a social safety net during the transition, especially in primary health care and primary education, particularly in rural areas.

3.76 The biggest question, however, derives from price reform and the abolition of the ration system scheduled for 1993. In preparation, the State Statistical Office is developing an index of minimum living standards to establish an objective measure of poverty. The government recognizes the need to protect the most vulnerable through targeted assistance, which is the most appropriate use of fiscal savings derived from a reduction in generalized subsidies. The key point here, however, will be to make protection of the poor consistent with the new market economy. Therefore, to the extent possible, such protection should be offered through income supplements, not through price controls or subsidies.

IV. DEVELOPMENT PROSPECTS

A. Background

4.1 Mongolia has been hit by severe external shocks at the same time as it is seeking to bring about a radical transformation of its economy. Under any circumstances, this would make the assessment of development prospects hazardous. In addition, the external shocks have not yet worked themselves through Mongolia's economic system. Indeed, the probability that Mongolia will be affected by a continuation of external problems seems quite high. In particular, the economic difficulties of the former Soviet Republics raise particularly difficult problems for Mongolia's export prospects and its associated essential imports. If essential imports continue to be unreliable or unavailable, the impact on Mongolia would be serious indeed, requiring an even sharper adjustment than the one already envisaged. The scenario described below was drawn up by the government in August 1991 on the assumption that the Soviet Union would be able to fulfill the barter trade agreement of July 1991, and that the necessary reforms would be completed on schedule.

4.2 The seriousness of Mongolia's economic situation and the extent of the adjustment required make the case for shifting to a market economy as quickly as possible. Stabilization would be necessary with or without structural reform, because the source of the shocks is external. In the judgment of the authorities, and the mission's, that a market system will be much better equipped than a centrally planned system to provide the necessary flexibility to absorb these external shocks and return the economy to a path of sustainable growth. The scenario described below assumes that stabilization would take about two years to achieve and growth would resume in 1994. However, current uncertainties suggest that a period of negative or no growth could be extended further, either because of insufficient policy reforms or because of a continued deterioration in Mongolia's external situation, or both.

B. The Government's Program and Scenario

4.3 The government has prepared and begun to implement an impressive program of economic reforms and stabilization policies.23/ They are directed at arresting the current economic decline while setting the stage for sustained recovery, containing inflation, and making progress toward balance of payments viability. However, the program's realization may require firmer and bolder implementation of reforms by the government (Chapter III), with a commensurate private sector response. It also assumes that barter trade with the former Soviet Republics will continue as agreed by the Soviet Union and Mongolia.

23/ The government program is summarized in an official document entitled "Memorandum on Economic Reform and Medium-term Policies" (September 1991). It has a quantitative framework for 1991-94 with special emphasis on the first two years (Table 4.1).

4.4 After a two-year decline (1990 and 1991), the strength of the recovery of GDP will depend on how far and how fast the economy's current bottlenecks can be eased and on producers' response to economic reforms. Economic recovery will be facilitated by improved availability of foreign exchange from exports and external aid and by the timely development of new market-oriented institutions. While this will help create an environment conducive to growth, producers' response will depend on the strength of incentives (i.e., prices and other factors affecting profitability), overall price stability, and confidence in government policies. These in turn will hinge on the success of the government's price and trade reforms, privatization program, and macroeconomic management. This is discussed below with reference to three critical macroeconomic indicators: production, the saving-investment balance, and the external balance and foreign-borrowing requirements.

Production

4.5 Economic recovery is expected to be led initially by the agricultural sector. While agricultural performance is subject to year-to-year fluctuations depending on weather conditions, growth over the medium term is expected to return gradually to its prereform rate of 4-5 percent as the shortage of critical imports is eased and producer prices, distribution, and ownership of productive factors are liberalized. Both the government and the donor community recognize the urgency of agriculture's recovery and are directing significant resources to its critical needs. Agricultural producer prices were freed with effect from the beginning of 1992. Their full effect, however, will only be felt when the recent decision to abolish the mandatory state order system for agricultural products is effectively implemented, with full participation of the private sector in agricultural marketing. The supply response to the liberalization of farmgate prices will be enhanced as herd ownership and crop farming are privatized. The government plans to eliminate all barriers to private marketing of agricultural products by end-1992 and to start by mid-1993 phasing out the centralized procurement of agricultural commodities by the state. All these reforms will be meaningful only if the transportation of agricultural products is also privatized and/or deregulated, and government subsidization of retail prices of farm products do not undermine private trading.

4.6 Industrial output, comprising manufacturing, mining and energy production, is expected to remain below capacity in the short run because of shortages of spare parts, raw materials and energy. While this situation is expected to ease with the improved flow of aid and export earnings over the medium term, recovery of production is likely to be restrained by the closure or restructuring of uneconomic units. Efforts to encourage direct foreign investment through the new company and foreign investment laws, the establishment of small- and medium-sized enterprises through special programs and decentralization of industrial conglomerates, and the upgrading of technology in those enterprises which are viable in new market conditions will set off a gradual process of structural adjustment in the sector in line with more rational economic prices and incentives, and thus serve as medium-term sources of growth in industry, especially in agroprocessing.

4.7 The energy sector is of critical importance to Mongolia's recovery, particularly the coal-based power plants. In the short run, energy supply is expected to be improved by relieving current shortages of spare parts for coal mines and coal-based power plants and by importing new equipment needed for the transport of coal. The barter agreement with the former Soviet Union (copper for petroleum), if fully implemented, would largely meet Mongolia's need for petroleum products. Mining value-added can be increased in the medium term through the fuller use of existing capacity if new export markets can be secured. A good start has been made with limited exports of copper concentrate to Japan in 1991. Small-scale mining, particularly in construction-related minerals and precious or semiprecious metals and stones, will probably be developed by domestic capital alone or jointly with foreign capital, once prices and trade are deregulated.

4.8 The easing of transportation bottlenecks will be critical to achieving new, viable sources of export earnings. In this regard, three aspects are crucial: the recently signed agreement with China on the use of Tianjin port; the need to improve the transshipment of goods by rail at the Mongolian-Chinese border; and upgrading airport facilities at Ulaanbaatar. These improvements will facilitate transport flows as trade is increasingly routed through China rather than Russia in search of diversified export markets.

4.9 The government envisages that the above policies will be adequate to limit the decline in GDP to 5 percent in 1992 and, after a year of zero growth in 1993, to resume average growth of 3 percent annually thereafter.

Saving and Investment

4.10 For the next few years, Mongolia will need to manage its scarce savings and foreign exchange very prudently. Investment will therefore have to be limited to the essential minimum until savings begin to recover after the adjustment program is complete. However, the efficiency gains stimulated by the reform program can be expected to generate growth with only low levels of investment. The magnitude of such investment is shown in Table 4.1. Budgetary investment will focus on socioeconomic infrastructure, and a "core" investment program will be prepared before the end of 1992.

4.11 Resources for such an investment program are expected to come mostly from external sources. While tax reforms and expenditure cuts should bolster budgetary savings, the latter may continue for some time to be drained by income and capital transfers (consumer and producer subsidies, respectively), leaving a negative balance. With the progress of privatization, price reform, better targeting of subsidies, and fiscal reform, budgetary savings could start financing government investment in the final years of the period. Nonetheless, the overall fiscal balance would remain negative over the entire period.

4.12 Overall, private savings, starting from a low base indeed, are expected to recover slowly after adjusting to lower income levels and then to rise gradually in line with further banking reforms and with the growth of the private sector.

4.13 The rapid acceleration in inflation in 1991 will need to be checked implying that the overall fiscal deficit should not be monetized and that the private sector's access to credit would steadily increase as it acquires for-

Table 4.1: KEY MACROECONOMIC INDICATORS, 1990-94

	1990	1991	1992	1993	1994
	(percent change)				
Output					
Real GDP	-2.1	-16.2	-5.0	0.0	3.0
Nominal GDP	-2.0	54.1	37.7	25.0	18.5
Prices					
GDP deflator	-0.4	84.0	45.0	25.0	15.0
Consumer prices	0.0	120.0	50.0	30.0	20.0
	(percent of GDP)				
Total investment /a	32.1	14.1	14.0	14.0	14.0
Gross national savings /a	3.4	4.0	3.0	5.2	7.5
Current account deficit /a	28.7	10.1	11.0	8.8	6.5
Budget and Money					
Revenue	50.7	55.9	48.5	48.5	48.5
Expenditure	64.1	68.5	60.4	58.5	57.0
Overall deficit	-13.4	-12.6	-11.9	-10.0	-8.5
Broad money	60.5	61.7	54.9	53.8	53.5
Currency in circulation	7.1	10.5	9.7	8.1	7.2

/a The program does not provide data on these items beyond 1991.

Source: Government of Mongolia, "Memorandum on Economic Reform and Medium-Term Policies," September 10, 1991.

mer state enterprises. The program therefore envisages a tight monetary policy, supported by newly introduced cash reserve requirements as well as direct credit controls. This demand-management policy, coupled with the positive supply response expected to result from price and trade liberalization, is expected to lower inflation from 120 percent in 1991 to 50 percent in 1992 and falling gradually thereafter.

Trade Prospects and External Resource Requirements

4.14 The sudden collapse in Mongolia's major export markets, especially for leather, cashmere and meat products, was reviewed in Chapter II. The external situation will continue to hamper the recovery of exports from their depressed level of $350 million in 1991, but this constraint may ease after 1992 if workable barter trade arrangements can be made with the former Soviet Republics. On the other hand, prospects for diversifying markets for traditional exports are limited in the short term because of anticipated excess supply in the world copper market, continuing weak demand for cashmere, and the relatively low quality of Mongolian meat products. Moreover, to diversify its exports, both in terms of geography and commodity, Mongolia will need to overcome serious transportation problems and to break into competitive world markets. Because all this takes time, export recovery will be modest over the period under consideration.

4.15 Mongolia's dependence on imports in the prereform era was unusually high because of turnkey projects financed by the CMEA countries, and the abundant import financing from the Soviet Union. Despite the response of other financing agencies, the present depressed level of imports will improve only slightly over the next two to three years, partly because of an expected further deterioration in Mongolia's terms of trade and partly because of the need to build up its international reserves. The limiting of imports will be achieved through both a realistic exchange-rate policy, coupled with newly introduced customs duties, and the continued use of the foreign exchange allocation mechanism.

4.16 However, even if the authorities can pursue the minimum investment/minimum imports scenario described above, Mongolia would still need a substantial inflow of external resources to maintain its production, consumption, and investment at basic levels. The most crucial period is the next 18 months (1992/93) when bottleneck relief would help bolster the reform program and lay the foundation for future recovery. Donor meetings in Tokyo (September 1991 and May 1992) and Ulaanbaatar (October 1991) suggest that external financing requirements for this initial phase of the transition period, may be available on appropriate terms and would take Mongolia through end-1993. It would amount to over $550 million (para. 2.48). Indeed, considerable levels of external assistançe will need to be mobilized if a reasonable level of imports 24/ is to be maintained (Table 4.2). Since Mongolia cannot be considered creditworthy for much commercial borrowing (paras. 4.22 and 4.23), most of this assistance should be on concessional terms.

C. Risks and Other Possible Outcomes

4.17 The scenario outlined above was based on two critical assumptions: that the external environment will not deteriorate further; and that the government's reform program and policies will be effectively implemented on schedule. The greatest risk comes from the possibility of a further collapse in trade with the former Soviet Republics. Already, internal difficulties in the republics have prevented the delivery of many items under the July 1991 barter agreement. Petroleum supplies at times are running 50 percent below schedule and there are severe shortages of critical items like explosives for the coal mines. While the government's program emphasizes policies to develop trade with nontraditional partners, the Russian Republic is projected to continue to account for about 80 percent of Mongolia's total trade, and to provide the major market for its most important export, copper concentrate, as well as being the source for all essential imports of petroleum.

4.18 If the present difficulties in trade between Mongolia and the former Soviet Republics persists, the present stabilization and reform program would

---

24/ The import levels in Table 4.2 already reflect some scaling down of the import figures of the government's September 1991 program as a result of further deterioration in Mongolia's foreign trade during 1991.

Table 4.2: EXTERNAL FINANCING REQUIREMENTS, 1991-94
($ million)

	1991	1992	1993	1994
Requirements				
Imports /a	501.2	555.0	485.0	550.0
Services	-0.2	15.9	23.0	25.0
Receipts	26.5	38.1	40.0	45.0
Payments	26.3	54.0	63.0	70.0
Increase in reserves (net)	-31.2	27.8	20.0	30.0
Debt amortization	9.0	16.1	24.3	40.0
Others /b	50.6	11.6	18.3	20.0
Total requirements	529.4	626.4	570.6	665.0
Financing				
Exports	346.5	357.0	398.0	450.0
Grants	43.6	26.6	9.0	10.0
Concessional loans	108.5	122.2	65.0	/c
Direct investment	0.0	5.0	5.0	10.0
Commercial loans	30.8	40.0	0.0	/c
Total financing	529.4	550.8	477.0	470.0
Gap	0.0	75.6	93.6	195.0
Memorandum item				
Debt service ratio (%) /d	5.7	13.9	15.1	16.0

/a Includes "turnkey" projects.
/b Includes errors and omissions.
/c Included in "gap."
/d In percent of exports of goods and services.

Source: "Mongolia: Recent Economic Trends," May 6, 1992, prepared for the May 1992 aid group meeting in Tokyo.

have to be redesigned, with a much more severe adjustment and reduction in living standards. Considering the major uncertainties involved, no attempt has been made to quantify such a scenario. However, trade would shrink even further below foreseen levels, resulting in a continued sharp decline in output, and an extension of the period before recovery could be expected. Although the international community would probably respond to such a situation, imports as a share of GDP would fall sharply and this would require even larger devaluations, with consequent inflationary pressures. Investment could be expected to fall below the depressed levels projected.

4.19 Such a situation would affect the industrial sector most heavily and, consequently, internal distribution. Import-dependent areas of industry, energy but also processing industries such as leather tanning, would be particularly hard hit. The greatest concern, about the coal and power sectors, given Mongolia's harsh winter climate, would call for particular external efforts. While such outcomes are not projected at this stage, it is important to be aware of their potentially devastating impact in Mongolia's import-dependent economy. Finally, one key feature of Mongolia's economy provides a degree of resilience and comfort: the rural sector, and especially the livestock sector, offers a base that is relatively immune to import fluctuations. Some migration to rural areas where basic living standards can be maintained has already been observed. In extreme circumstances, one outcome in the near term could be a process of partial deindustrialization and a temporary return to a predominantly rural economy.

4.20 Even if the above dramatic outcome does not materialize, a considerable risk remains that the government's own targets may not be achieved because of policy failures, either of design or implementation. Several issues alluded to in Chapter III of this report bear highlighting here:

(a) Significant progress has been made in price reform and the relaxation of some restrictions on domestic and foreign trading by private business. Nevertheless, price controls and trade restrictions remain in force in key areas such as agricultural products and basic consumer goods where a quick supply response is feasible and where the private sector would have the best chance to succeed.

(b) The privatization program is proceeding more slowly than originally envisaged. It may therefore result in a prolonged period of uncertainty for both private and state enterprises and an excessively large number of business failures and closures, with adverse effects on output and employment.

(c) Exchange-rate policy until recently applied a highly overvalued rate to more than 80 percent of foreign trade. It continues to fall short of what would be needed to provide an adequate incentive to exports and import substitution.

(d) At interest rates less than a quarter of the inflation rate, banks cannot attract deposits or discourage loan requests for unproductive uses.

(e) The fiscal program could be made much stronger by measures such as introducing a value-added tax, an effective global personal income tax, and by reducing subsidies.

4.21 Continued close attention to these reform areas will be needed if the overall targets are to be achieved, even in the absence of further external deterioration. Taken together with the external uncertainties, the present scenario must now be considered optimistic. Since the program was designed in August 1991, the balance of probability has shifted toward a more conservative outcome in the next two years.

D. Creditworthiness

4.22 Mongolia's medium-term development assets include its well-educated labor force, abundant agricultural and natural resources, and the basic resilience of the rural economy. Although the authorities are fully committed to the reform program, Mongolia's near-term balance of payments prospects are subject to considerable risks because of the economic conditions in its main trading partner. However, these risks are likely to become smaller over time as Mongolia receives foreign aid and direct foreign investment from new sources, helping to diversify its foreign trade away from traditional markets.

4.23 Almost all of Mongolia's external debt was owed until recently to the Soviet Union in transferable rubles. However, the amount owed to countries in the convertible currency area have started to grow rapidly since mid-1992 under the umbrella of the Mongolia Assistance Group. In the absence of a track record and given the prevailing uncertainty, Mongolia is not regarded as able to borrow from commercial sources on market terms, nor can its reasonable capital needs be sustainably met without concessional assistance. For the foreseeable future, it must therefore rely on official sources for most of its external capital requirements. Recently contracted debt as well as expected inflows of concessional aid in the coming years are projected to give rise to a debt-service ratio of 15-20 percent over the medium term. Given the country's rich mineral and natural resources and its export prospects once its transformation to a market-based economy is completed, these projected debt-service ratios should not unduly strain the balance of payments. However, this assumes that the servicing of Mongolia's debt to the former Soviet Union, which is large relative to the size of its economy, remains manageable. This assumption is itself based on the understanding between the former Soviet Union and Mongolia that the repayment of this debt should not hamper the latter's economic development.

Main Sectors and Selected Issues

Table of Contents

Main Sectors and Selected Issues

This annex consists of a preliminary review of the main sectors of Mongolia's economy and of selected issues. It draws upon the still very limited literature available on Mongolia outside the former Council for Mutual Economic Assistance (CMEA) countries, on the work undertaken--and some still underway--by several bilateral and multilateral agencies during the past year (notably by the Asian Development Bank, the United Nations Development Programme, and the United Nations Specialized Agencies), and on data and information gathered by the first World Bank economic mission. Under the circumstances, it does not purport to present a comprehensive view or detailed analysis at this stage, but rather a set of sectoral notes as background to the overall report.

Agriculture

Overview

1. Prior to the 1921 revolution, Mongolia was a simple agrarian economy with the majority of its population living as seminomadic herdsmen. Despite the industrialization policies pursued since the 1940s, agriculture, especially extensive livestock-grazing, still plays an important role in the economy, much greater than its 20 percent share in GDP implies. It is a key element in the social fabric of Mongolia, employing about 90 percent of the population in rural areas and 30 percent of the total labor force. It accounts for about 44 percent of total exports, mostly livestock products. Agriculture has important linkages with the rest of the economy and provides more than 75 percent of the raw materials and other inputs for leather and shoe factories, wool processing mills, milk, and bakery plants. The major agricultural activities are animal husbandry and crop farming. About 70 percent of agricultural value added comes from animal husbandry, which accounts for 94 percent of land use. Agricultural GDP in Mongolia shows significant year-to-year fluctuations because of severe variations in weather conditions. However, a rising trend is discernible and annual growth averaged 2.7 percent during 1986-90. But the sectoral NMP fell by 7 percent in 1991 as a result of the transitional difficulties experienced by the economy.

2. The main production units in agriculture continue to be state farms and agricultural cooperatives. At the end of 1989, the 52 state farms and 255 agricultural cooperatives cultivated only a small proportion of Mongolia's arable land, to 827,000 ha. The state farms, working about 75 percent of the cultivated land, account for 70 percent of main crop output. In contrast the agricultural cooperatives, which are based on production associations, control about 25 percent of the cultivated land but account for about 90 percent of meat output and 70 percent of milk produced.

Structure of Agriculture

3. The Mongolian agricultural sector is characterized by a dual structure of extensive and intensive production systems. The intensive system, which is applied by the state farms engaging mostly in crop production, has

absorbed the available capital and is the focus of agricultural development. The extensive livestock farming has become a raw material base for the intensive system. Exports from the extensive subsector have been used to finance imported inputs for the intensive subsector. The limited growth of production in the intensive subsector is achieved at a high input cost. This is the result of a development strategy biased toward industrial development, which was pursued by all former socialist countries.

4. Until recently, most of agricultural output originated in the state and cooperative sector. Private ownership was limited to a small proportion of animals which cooperative members were allowed to own privately. In 1990, cooperatives accounted for 44.5 percent of total gross output of agriculture, state farms and enterprises 33.3 percent, and households 22.2 percent. Agriculture was centrally planned and the state took full responsibility for production, supply of inputs, and distribution and sales of produce. The state owned all land, most livestock and virtually all farm equipment, and production was organized by 325 state farms and large cooperatives. Each year every farm was required to submit a list of machinery, chemicals and other inputs that was aggregated to determine the sector's input needs. State orders were set for deliveries of meat, milk, wool and wheat by individual state farms and cooperatives at government-determined prices. The rigidities imposed by central planning did not permit the realization of agricultural potential and gave it little chance to respond to the diversifying preferences and needs of the population. The inadequacies of this system have only recently emerged because Mongolia's partners in CMEA used to make up for shortfalls in domestic output and provided ready markets for its exports.

5. Livestock husbandry has traditionally been the main agricultural activity in Mongolia. Since 1959, most livestock has been state-owned. However, in 1990 limits on private ownership were abolished, some state-owned cattle were sold at low price or given on long-term lease to smallholders, and the share of privately held animal stock rose to 40 percent. As a result, the total herd increased to 26 million in 1990, from about 22 million in 1987. The main animals bred are sheep, goats, cattle, horses, and camels for their wool, hair, skin, meat, hides, and tallow and smaller amounts of milk and butter.

6. Animal husbandry has remained largely pastoral, and it is heavily dependent on environmental and climatic conditions. Improvements have been limited to the supply of winter housing for stock, and water supply. There are no sophisticated methods to control endemic or parasitic diseases, although veterinary boards and laboratories have been set up in all aimag and somons. Most medicines are imported. Yearly losses are often as much as 1 million newborn stock and almost as many adult stock; due to severe shortages of medicines, the number of deaths increased by at least 100,000 in 1991. In line with this pastoral system and owing to lack of incentives and poor pricing as a result of state order system, productivity has been low and the potential of the livestock subsector has not been realized. For instance, average wool output is less than 2 kg per head. At mechanized dairy farms the average milk yield is about 2,600 liters per year per cow and 1,200 liters per year per cow in simple dairy farms. Meat production remained virtually stagnant during the 1980s and barely reached 498,500 tonnes in 1990, resulting in

shortages. Milk production declined by 15 percent in 1991 which, among other things, reflected lack of sufficient fodder.

7. Expanding crop production and bringing additional lands under cultivation has been a major goal of agricultural policy. Following the 1959 virgin lands policy, there have been substantial production increases in wheat and other cereals, potatoes, vegetables, hay, and fodder. However, these increases mask low yields owing to the soil's low natural fertility and insufficient rainfall. Of the 1.3 million ha under cultivation, 35,500 ha are irrigated in 140 systems. The average yield for cereals is only some 1.1 tonnes/ha. In normal years, Mongolia produces enough wheat and potatoes to meet domestic needs, but only a third of its vegetable, fruit, and fodder needs. About 75 percent of crop output is produced on state farms. Poor pricing policies and state orders have hindered crop development and diversification. The annual average output in the late 1980s was some 800,000 tonnes of grains, 150,000 tonnes of potatoes, 45,000 tonnes of vegetables, and 500,000 tonnes of fodder.

8. The existing stock of agricultural equipment, all from the former CMEA countries and mostly the Soviet Union, includes 2,600 crawler tractors, 500 heavy tractors, 8,000 light tractors, 2,500 combine harvesters, and 2,000 reapers. The collapse of the CMEA trade arrangements have created severe shortages of tires, spare parts, transmission belts, and batteries. As a result, 40-50 percent of the existing stock of equipment is out of service and to the detriment of production. Because of reduced harvesting capability, crop output was lower by 14 percent in 1990 compared to 1989. Conditions deteriorated further in 1991; an estimated 25 percent of the year's crop was not harvested. This situation also threatens the 1992 harvest. In addition, stocks of fertilizers (ammonium sulfate, triple superphosphate, and potassium chloride) and other agricultural chemicals (herbicides and pesticides) are virtually exhausted and there were no imports at all in 1991. It is doubtful that the former Soviet Republics, the traditional supplier, will be able to deliver Mongolia's usual 72,000 tonnes a year.

9. While overall investment in agriculture rose by Tug 2,530 million (54 percent) in the 1980s, the share of capital investment in agriculture declined from almost 20 percent in 1980 to 13.7 percent in 1989. Of the total investment in the "productive sector" (industry, agriculture, transport, trade, etc.), 20 percent went into agriculture in 1989. Capital investment in agriculture was inefficient as it was concentrated in the establishment of large and overcentralized complexes, which were poorly suited to the economic conditions of Mongolia.

10. Main agricultural exports are primary products, including meat, leather goods, camel wool, and cashmere. In 1990, agricultural exports accounted for 43 percent of Mongolia's total export. However, exports, until recently, were restricted to the Soviet Union and Eastern Europe. Countries with a broader range of choice are unlikely to accept Mongolian products, unless their quality is improved substantially. In the past, annual imports of major agricultural inputs, such as machinery, spare parts, seed, fertilizers, fuel and chemicals, were as high as Tug 290 million to Tug 310 million. In 1989, these goods accounted for 36 percent of total imports.

Reforms 1/

11. Privatization. Most state farm assets have been privatized through dividing them into smaller units and farming agricultural companies. Ownership transfer has principally been through "coupons," although the state remains the largest shareholder. Agricultural cooperatives are being transformed into companies, with the existing members taking up issued shares, and their activities are limited to the provision of extension, transport, and veterinary services for a fee. About 70 percent of the national livestock herd had been privatized by June 1992. Land has not been privatized.

12. Price Policy and Reform. Government-determined prices for agricultural products have nominally been discontinued and replaced with floor prices or guideline prices. These prices are paid for government procurement under state orders and serve also as minimum prices for commodities sold through other channels. Most output prices, particularly for livestock, result in an implicit producer tax as they are substantially below border prices, even though they were raised several-fold (e.g., six- to sevenfold in the case of free-market prices for some crops) over the past two years. In the case of input prices, most inputs for crop production are imported and not subsidized, with the result that prices for these items increased about tenfold between 1990 and 1992. On the other hand, many inputs for the livestock subsector, particularly pharmaceuticals (imported and domestic) continue to be heavily subsidized. Only nominal charges are levied for veterinary services, and the cost of transporting fodder is absorbed by the government budget.

13. Market Policy and Reforms. Market reform has progressed more slowly than price reform. State orders are still the main marketing mechanism. In recent years, however, state order procurement of livestock/livestock products has declined, and now almost two thirds of livestock marketing occurs outside of state orders. Nevertheless, state orders represent the largest remaining economic distortion in the agricultural sector as they impede the development of efficient prices and alternative market channels as well as supply and export responses. As a transitional step from a centrally planned state marketing orders system to a market economy, the government established in June 1991 a joint-stock company for spot and futures trading in livestock products. Crop commodities will be added to trading at the commodity exchange after the 1992 harvest.

14. Land Reform. A draft land law is under discussion in Parliament. It would allow Mongolian citizens to own land up to 0.3 ha, essentially residential property. For agricultural use, both Mongolian and foreign citizens can lease unlimited amounts of land up to 60 years, but subleasing is prohibited. Leasing fees, based on land productivity indicators, are to be reviewed periodically. Rangeland will not be leased. To avoid adverse effects on grazing land or access to it from excessive leasing of land for crop farming, bringing any new land into cultivation will have to be approved by an environmental committee.

1/ This section draws on a working paper drafted by A. Nyberg in July 1992 in preparation for the Bank's first Structural Adjustment Credit operation in Mongolia.

Issues

15. Despite reforms, Mongolian economy is still characterized by over-centralized supply of inputs, and distribution and marketing of output. Privatization of livestock has made significant progress, expanding ownership of herds and, hence, decentralization. On the other hand, progress in privatizing agricultural land and crop production, apart from some lease arrangements, has been slow. State farms are being split up into smaller companies to facilitate privatization. However, the criteria to be used for dividing assets are not clear. This issue needs serious attention from government.

16. Government ownership of the Agricultural Supply Service (ASS), traditionally the sole importer, supplier, and distributor of inputs, continues. ASS has been unable to fulfill its role since the collapse of the CMEA trade arrangements, its distribution network is not functioning, and within the Ministry of Agriculture there is no agreement on the future role and prospects of ASS. Hence, the provision and distribution of agricultural inputs is a major problem as the old structure based on the concepts of central planning is proving unsuitable for the present task. A newly established agency, the Import Supply Corporation of Agricultural Machinery, will assume some ASS functions, but the details of this arrangement are not clear yet.

17. The dependence of agriculture on climatic conditions and its seasonality have major implications for processing and storage facilities. In general, milk production is high in summer but low in winter while the opposite is true for meat production. Crop production is also low in the winter. Hence, Mongolia must develop processing and storage capability to ensure that foodstuffs are available all year. For example, 312 million liters of milk are produced each year but, for lack of storage, large amounts have to be turned into butter, and there are milk shortages. Meat processing and storage facilities are also insufficient. The centralized system of slaughterhouses, comprising three big abattoirs and two meat processing factories in the three main cities, make it difficult to process herds since animals have to walk 200-1,000 km from rural areas which takes months. With the capacity of these facilities limited to only 63,000 tonnes of meat a year, animals are often processed at weights well below their summer maximum, leading to output losses. Cold storage capacity is also low, 19,500 tonnes of meat.

18. The Ministry of Trade and Industry (MTI) has been responsible for marketing all commodities. The MTI's Wholesale Supply Board (WSB) ensures the supply of food grains to the population through its local wholesale and retail branches. Despite the government's declared policy of relying on market mechanisms, state orders for major agricultural products have not been totally eliminated, and the central distribution and marketing system under the control of MTI is still in operation. While it may not be possible to eliminate the existing distribution system quickly or completely, the government should start considering alternatives and allow private firms to go into the food distribution business. State orders are a related issue. Although most agricultural prices have been largely deregulated, up to 70 percent of agricultural output remained under the state orders system in 1991.

19. The government should consider and start developing strategies for action on a number of other issues. With total pastoral land remaining

unchanged and a growing herd, overgrazing is becoming an environmental problem. The government declared that pastoral lands would not be privatized, but user fees or taxes to reduce overgrazing have not been introduced. Veterinary services are inadequate and are of poor quality, leading to endemic parasitic animal diseases that lower the livestock productivity. Intensive crop farming has reduced the quality of soil and increased farm area subject to erosion. Privatization will impel legal reforms to avoid common property problems. A framework to develop land tenure arrangements, leasing, taxation, rules on livestock movements, and procedures for negotiation and arbitration need to be established.

Industry

Overview

20. The industrial sector accounts for a third of national income, employs a fourth of the labor force, and is the largest contributor to GDP. Industry's share in GDP rose from 29 percent in 1980 to 34 percent in 1990, reflecting increased investments in electricity generation, mining (copper in particular), forestry products, construction materials, metallurgy, and machinery. Heavy industry's share in gross industrial output rose from 48 percent in 1980 to 52 percent in 1990. Light industries, including leather, textiles, shoes, detergents, and printing products, account for 25 percent of gross industrial output; food industries, including meat, flour, bakery, and milk products, account for 20 percent. The present industrial structure with predominant energy and raw materials subsectors is a result of a development strategy focus on expanding heavy industry through government direct intervention in resource allocation for the past three decades.

21. The growth of gross industrial output in the first half of the 1980s averaged 9 percent annually. Despite a slow down in 1985-89, it was still high, averaging 5 percent annually. However, it stagnated in 1990 and declined by 12 percent in 1991. Lack of foreign exchange resulting in shortages of imported raw materials and spare parts caused a sharp contraction in all subsectors, ranging from 10 percent in electricity production to 26 percent in copper production. Almost all factories operate well below capacity and, in some, production has stopped. The restoration of economic growth will in the first instance require the fuller utilization of existing productive capacity which depends, to a large extent, upon the availability of foreign exchange.

Structure of Industry

22. Industrial development took the form of investing in state enterprises according to annual plan targets and priorities. Investment in industry grew from one third of the total in early 1970s to around 40 percent in early 1980s. About 70 percent of the industrial investment were externally financed, mainly by the CMEA countries and particularly the Soviet Union. In 1986, the share of industrial investment rose to 39.3 percent before it sharply dropped to 27.5 percent in 1989. This may be attributed to the reduction of direct government investment as part of its reform program after 1988.

Another factor is recent emphasis on investment in transport and communications. Within the industrial sector, priority has been given to investment in electricity and fuel subsectors. In terms of resource allocation, heavy industries have held a predominant position. Investment in light industry has focused mostly on food, woodworking, wool, and leather subsectors.

23. As a result of past government policies the industrial and processing facilities in Mongolia remain heavily concentrated in a few areas and in a small number of state enterprises, reflecting the predominant position of the public sector in a centrally planned economy. At the end of 1990, most of the more than 400 large public enterprises, were operating at a loss. More recently, the private sector has started to develop in retail trade, small manufacturing, and handicrafts but it remains small. The structure of production is expected to change rapidly over the next three years, if the privatization of large SOEs is carried out as planned.

24. Mongolia's industrial exports consist mainly of raw materials, semi-processed goods and some finished goods such as leather and wool products. All of capital goods and most finished goods are imported. In 1990, 91 percent of all exports went to CMEA countries, and 88 percent of all imports came from this group. This excessive dependence on the former CMEA economies for export markets, technology, and inputs, has seriously hurt Mongolia's terms of trade. After the demise of the regime, the government decided to turn to a new development strategy for diversifying its export markets with the help of joint ventures with foreign firms to import technology and gain access to international markets. To this end, the government has already adopted a liberal foreign investment law.

Reforms

25. In 1988, the Law on State Enterprises was enacted to give enterprises greater autonomy in production, investment, and marketing as well as flexibility in wage and profit allocation. To further the reform in this area, the law was replaced by the Company Law of 1991. The Privatization Law went into effect on July 1, 1991. Small-scale privatization is 80 percent complete. With the opening of the Mongolian Stock Exchange (MSE) in February 1992, large-scale privatization has also begun. As of mid-1992, 21 of the largest 400 enterprises were privatized. The Privatization Commission plans to privatize a hundred companies by year-end.

26. To withdraw from direct intervention in labor management, the government has started to draft the Industrial Disputes Settlement Law. Tripartite arbitration and special labor courts are under consideration. Employee benefits are governed by the Labor Law, and the new Pension and Benefits laws covering minimum wages and other compensation.

27. In March 1990, the Foreign Investment Act was enacted to provide a legal basis and some incentives for foreign investment. Amendments to the law to improve the incentive structure for foreign investment are under consideration.

Issues

28. Several structural problems hamper the development of Mongolia's industrial sector to tap its natural resource base. The organization and production structure is a key issue. Concentrating industries in a few locations has advantages and disadvantages. Economies of scale, reducing transport volumes, and facilitating central administration are among the advantages that probably led to the current structure. However, these advantages are limited in industries processing items widely available throughout Mongolia and whose output is mainly for domestic markets. Sometimes, transport volumes are unnecessarily increased, while the scope for economies of scale may be very small. Such is the case for construction materials and livestock products. Establishing processing plants in the countryside seems to be desirable and requires the encouragement of private sector involvement. Although large size plants located near to the workforce may be able to continue to operate, new policies should foster the relocation of industries and reduction in their size. Several industries need substantial upgrading, which may be less for some than starting over with new installations and processing methods. Small new processing industries serving, domestic or local markets initially, could offer the highest growth potential. For export products, transport costs will be an important consideration in selecting the plant location and the extent of processing.

29. Mongolia's industrial sector is inefficient, characterized by capital-intensive industries with outdated and inefficient technology and heavy dependence on imported inputs. The capital-output ratio steadily increased between 1940 and 1990, indicating the growing capital-intensive nature of investments. This policy might once have been desirable for importing technology, but today the number of uncompetitive state enterprises and their low productivity suggest that past investment has not been efficient. The capital-output ratio rose from 4.6 in the first half of 1980s to 5.5 in the second half. Since the productivity of key industries influence the efficiency of the whole economy, this is a source of concern. To compete internationally, Mongolian industries will need to improve their efficiency and cost effectiveness. Another efficiency issue relates to the protection of domestic industry from foreign trade. The geographical location of Mongolia, its current exchange rate policy, and the present tariff regime are enough protection for industry to exploit ample import-substitution possibilities.

30. The government's technology modernization program identifies as priority areas the following industries: export products based on domestic raw materials; mining; construction materials; chemical industries (e.g., phosphatic fertilizers) using domestic resources; copper products; and other metal products. However, the program raises important questions and appears inconsistent with the overall strategy of economic liberalization and privatization. For example, it calls for modernizing state-owned enterprises that are to be privatized. On the other hand, it states that the public sector should minimize its investments in industry. In addition, investment in some of those enterprises may not be economically viable. Moreover, the source of financing for technology upgrades is not clear. More important, if state-owned enterprises are to be privatized, government should allow their new owners to restructure enterprises as they see fit.

31. Uncertainties about the management of enterprises that will not soon be privatized are sources of concern. The privatization program, apart from

reducing the role of the government in the economy, aims at restructuring the industrial sector to increase efficiency and competition. While large-scale privatization has started and seems to be moving, the process is expected to last at least three years. This means that many enterprises will stay in the public sector for quite a while. How they will be managed in the meantime is unclear, particularly the loss-making ones. So far, their losses and their credit needs have been covered by borrowing from banks, a main cause of monetary expansion. While not adding to the budget deficit directly, this contributes to public sector borrowing and risks crowding out the private sector. For the enterprises remaining in the public sector, hard budget constraints must be imposed and their access to unrestricted bank credit curtailed. Banks are lending to them, not on the basis of commercial viability, but because they are state enterprises. These enterprises should be subject to the Bankruptcy Law to ensure that they operate on a commercial basis.

32. The government also has a small and medium enterprise program (SME), which seems to be very desirable given the size of domestic markets and the need for private sector development. The Ministry of National Development has formulated the initial policy which attempts to address such questions as the appropriate technology for SMEs and how technological renovation would be undertaken. Responsibility for the program lies with the Ministry of Labor, reflecting the government's interest in its employment creation potential. However, the multiministry management of the program should be streamlined to facilitate coherent and efficient implementation. The government contemplates special financing and incentives for the program, including reduced tax rates; budget increases for investment; and credit lines for foreign exchange.

33. Decentralization and small and medium enterprise development should reduce production costs, if transport restraints can be alleviated. Eventually, the process would also lead to lower consumer prices. Unemployment in the larger cities should encourage some urban dwellers to accept employment in rural industries. The realization of these benefits, however, will require successful coordination of the SME program with other reforms, such as the accelerated liberalization of prices, exchange rates, and interest rates. An important issue that needs to be addressed is the efficient allocation of credit. The role of the banking system in SME development should be promoted, and the appraisal skills of the newly emerging commercial banks should be developed.

34. Unemployment and need for retraining of management and labor are emerging as important issues as the restructuring of the economy gets under way. Weakened external and domestic demand at a time of accelerated privatization program could worsen unemployment (para. 2.16). For the transition to a market economy, Mongolia does not have enough managers who are knowledgeable and experienced in market functioning. Mongolia's labor force is well educated, but its educational system and curricula in technical and business-related higher education require reorientation. Simultaneously, an economy-wide intensive retraining of workers and managers in new technologies and company management under competitive market conditions is needed. This will require innovative practices to blend diverse technologies, since the new and old ones will have to coexist during the transition.

Energy

Overview

35. Electricity, generated with domestically mined coal and imported diesel fuel, is the principal source of energy in Mongolia. It is also one of the major industrial subsectors, accounting for about 11 percent of the total industrial value added (equivalent to 2.5 percent of GDP in 1990) and employing about 16,000 people. As a result of the government's industrialization policy, investment in electric power has been high, about 30 percent of the total industrial investment in 1980-89. Consequently, electricity supply doubled between 1980 and 1988, expanding at an average annual rate of 9 percent. Average per capita consumption was some 1,375 kWh in 1990, comparable to middle-income countries, although about one fourth of the population, mainly in the rural areas, remains without electricity. In 1990, industry accounted for about 90 percent of total electricity consumption and residential and office use for the rest. As a result of the economic crisis, electricity production fell by about a quarter during the last two years (1990/91)

36. The Ministry of Energy and Fuel, established in the 1950s, is responsible for the government's energy policies and the management of power generation and coal mining. It also runs the central heating system. There are, in addition, a number of agencies indirectly involved with energy issues. They are: (a) the Energy Scientific Institute, which is responsible for research, experimental work, and the design of heating and electricity facilities; (b) the Mining Industry Institute, charged with research into fuel processing and nonpolluting fuels; and (c) the Coal and Chemistry Design Center responsible for research on chemical applications to energy.

Structure of Energy Sector

37. Mongolia's total installed generating capacity is 845 MW but dependable capacity is around 800 MW. Electricity is produced by two distinct systems. The Central Electricity System (CES) consists of five coal-fired thermal plants with a capacity of 690 MW (three in Ulaanbaatar, one in Darhan, and one in Erdenet). It accounts for about 80 percent of the country's installed capacity and generates 87 percent of electricity (3,000 GWh in 1990). Of this, over 90 percent was generated by two large plants in Ulaanbaatar. The CES is connected to the Soviet grid by a 220 kV line to Irkutsk. The CES covers 30 percent of Mongolia's territory and supplies electricity to main cities and to six central aimags where 50 percent of the population live. The five main stations are Soviet designed, use obsolete technology, and are highly polluting and inefficient. Their estimated gross efficiency is less than 60 percent, with high own-use (almost 20 percent) and high transmission and distribution losses (almost 13 percent). Losses in the heating distribution system are also high, because above-ground pipelines are extensive and poorly insulated. The CES is profitable despite its inefficiencies, and tariffs covered costs amply in 1990. Increases in 1991, the first time since 1960, brought tariffs to Tug 0.35/kWh for industrial and public use and Tug 0.50/kWh for residential use.

38. The other system, the decentralized electricity production and distribution system, is comprised of diesel-powered generators in 11 aimags with an installed capacity of 119 MW, and of a 36 MW coal-fired plant at Dornod. In 1990 this system generated about 400 GWh or 12 percent of domestic production. All the equipment is of Soviet and Czech origin. The costs of the decentralized system are higher, but residential and public users pay the same as the central system users. While industrial users pay more (Tug 0.93/kWh), the tariff is still too low to cover costs. The resulting subsidy is the largest in the 1991 budget, accounting for more than 50 percent of total subsidies.

39. Despite rapid growth in its electricity generation, Mongolia imported electricity from the Soviet Union (about 28 percent of total consumption between 1980 and 1985 and 8 percent between 1986 and 1990) as the coal-based generation system was unable to adjust to fast load variations. During excess supply periods, Mongolia used to export electricity to the Soviet Union, but the amount was no more than 2 percent of domestic generation. In 1990, net imports were 152 GWh. Mongolia had to stop electricity imports in 1991 because of a hard currency shortage. For the past two decades, all requirements for oil products were met by imports from the Soviet Union. In 1990, such imports absorbed about 40 percent of Mongolia's total foreign exchange earnings. The dislocation of the traditional trade arrangement with the Soviet Union since late 1990 has affected the flow of oil products particularly. In 1991, oil product imports from the Soviet Union accounted for about 70 percent of the contracted amount under the Soviet Union-Mongolia barter trade agreement (Mongolian copper concentrate for Russian oil products). It is doubtful that the country can get a similar amount in 1992, as Russian oil production is expected to fall below domestic needs. This means that, unless oil from other sources is substituted for Russian oil, the decentralized electricity system that uses fuel oil will not produce sufficient electricity.

Issues

40. The collapse of the CMEA trade arrangements and the economic crisis have seriously affected the supply of petroleum and critical spare parts required for power plans and for coal production. This had led to a growing energy shortage since January 1990. Forced outages in 1991 resulted in direct losses of 372 million kWh, or $18 million valued at the Soviet electricity import price, and forced lower capacity utilization in industry, from 61 percent in 1990 to 59 percent in 1991. Gross power generation declined by 15 percent in 1990 and 10 percent in 1991. The decentralized system is also operating at only 50 percent capacity because of shortages of fuel oil and spare parts. Unless critical spare and replacement parts and diesel generators are available, electricity supply will continue to decline further in the coming winter months with serious consequences for industrial production and for the population. To ensure fuller utilization of the existing capacity in order to forestall electricity shortages is the most critical short-term issue in Mongolia.

41. The most important longer term need is to expand the electricity generation capacity. By the end of 1993, the present capacity and imports from Russia, assuming they can be resumed, will probably be insufficient. The

Ministry of Energy estimates that electricity demand will more than double by the year 2000. In the circumstances, the development of a 600 MW minehead power station at Baga-nuur to feed the central grid should be a priority in investment plans. The 80 MW plant presently under construction at Ulaanbaatar should also be completed. The provision of sufficient energy is critical to sustain economic growth.

42. While coal is the lowest cost energy source and its use is appropriate for electricity generation, the government should use the opportunity provided by the need to expand capacity to diversify Mongolia's power generation sources. The potential for hydropower, for example, should be part of the energy policy. Hydropower is also likely to reduce pollution from burning coal. While a proposal has been made to build a hydropower plant in the northwest and to connect the Mongolian and Chinese grids, its feasibility has not yet been determined.

43. Overhaul and upgrading of the existing power plants and distribution network will be needed to reduce inefficiency and pollution and to improve conservation. However, the availability of coal in determining such improvements must be taken into account. For instance, the third power plant in Ulaanbaatar uses coal from a nearby mine with high extraction costs and of a different type from coal from other mines. Therefore, the rehabilitation of the plant may be less cost effective than installing new capacity elsewhere. Coal or hydropower-based plants in some western aimags which now use diesel-based generators, if justified by load densities, might reduce costs and increase efficiency. With demand approaching the established capacity and given the lead time to construct new plants, energy conservation should be high on the government's agenda. The need to improve energy efficiency in the industrial sector is particularly acute.

44. The greatest contribution to efficient energy use and conservation will come from sound pricing. Energy pricing policies need to be reviewed and adjusted to reflect full costs so as to encourage conservation. Current tariff rates cover costs only because the price of domestic coal is lower than international prices. Electricity pricing is not based on long run marginal costs (LRMC) and does not reflect the true resource cost of electricity to users. The authorities should estimate LRMC and price electricity accordingly and, to promote conservation, introduce peak load and progressive tariffs. The government might also wish to review tariffs for the diesel-powered systems in the highly subsidized aimags.

Mining 2/

Overview

45. The mining and minerals sector plays a crucial role in the Mongolian economy. The production and export of minerals accounted for 20 percent of GDP and over 50 percent of exports in 1991. The sector employed some 20,000 people in 1991. Mongolia is well endowed with over 600 deposits of more than 80 kinds of minerals, including copper, coal, fluorspar, molybdenum, silver, gold, uranium, oil, iron, tin, tungsten, zinc lead, phosphates, wolfram, fluorspar. There are also around 170 largely undeveloped deposits of construction materials such as granite and marble. At present, 35 deposits are being exploited and 90 or so are in the process of development. One uranium mine is under exploitation at present in Dornod aimag.

46. A number of institutions have policymaking responsibilities in the mining sector. The State Mining Bureau (SMB) has responsibility for all mineral development with the exception of oil, gas, coal, and construction materials. The Mongolbank has the authority on matters regarding precious metals. The Ministry of Energy (MOE) is in charge of coal mines and supervises *Mongol Nuurs* (the Mongolian Coal Corporation), which runs the mines and implements the policies of the MOE. The Ministry of Trade and Industry (MTI) is responsible for the marketing of other mineral resources, including copper. A number of government agencies also provide support in the formulation of mining policies. They are: (i) the Center of Mongolian Coal and Chemical Technology which reports both to the MOE and the Academy of Sciences; (ii) the geological center, responsible with overseeing exploration and exploitation; (iii) the State Committee on Environmental Control, which is responsible for mine reclamation issues.

Structure of the Sector

47. Copper Subsector. The mining sector in Mongolia is dominated by the Erdenet copper/molybdenum mine and process plant, located 350 km to the northwest of Ulaanbaatar. Erdenet can be considered a significant producer by world standards (110,000 tonnes contained copper per year). More than 80 percent of sector revenues are derived from the processing of copper/molybdenum ore. The production of molybdenum concentrates represents a relatively minor by-product, consisting of less than 5 percent of the copper value, at current prices. It was formed in 1971 as a joint venture between Mongolia and the Soviet Union (51 percent Mongolia). Following the break-up of the Soviet Union, it is not clear who now represents the former Soviet Union's share--presumably the Russian Republic. The mine has progressively grown in scale to its present annual output of 20 million tonnes ore, containing 0.8 percent copper (Cu) and 0.012 percent molybdenum (Mo). The processing plant has been producing regularly since 1974, approximately 350,000 tonnes copper concen-

---

2/ This section has essentially been extracted from the draft "Mining and Minerals Sector Brief" (April 16, 1992) prepared by the World Bank's Asia Technical Department (Energy Division) for the Mongolia Technical Assistance Project (Credit 2321-MOG).

trates (35 percent Cu) and 1,500-2,000 tonnes molybdenum (47 percent Mo). Following ongoing exploration at and around Erdenet, the copper reserve's life has been extended to 60 years. However, bearing in mind that copper grades are forecast to deteriorate to 0.5 percent, ore production will need to be expanded to maintain concentrate production levels. A review of cut-off grades in the process plant is needed to optimize the value of exports in relation to mine life.

48. Copper ore is mined at the Erdenet open-pit with traditional technology. All the equipment is of Russian origin and is close to international standards. In recent years, Erdenet has experienced difficulty in obtaining equipment, spares, and consumables (fuels, lubricants, and explosives) from the former Soviet Union. As a result, in 1991, production of copper concentrates fell by 25 percent to 260,000 tonnes. This directly affected the barter trade in petroleum products. Since the situation cannot be expected to improve in the short term, the Erdenet joint venture needs urgently to find alternative supply sources for fuels and other consumables, as well as spare parts and equipment to protect against shortages of such imports from the former Soviet Union.

49. Under the original joint venture agreement, all copper concentrates were to be exported to the Irkutsk smelter in Soviet Siberia. The former Soviet Union has relaxed this requirement, and Mongolia was permitted to export a portion of the concentrates to other countries to generate hard currency. The export markets outside Russia include Japan, China, and Western Europe. In 1991, a new agreement was reached whereby one third of the copper concentrates were to be delivered to Irkutsk; one third, Mongolia would be free to export; and the remaining third would be destined to Irkutsk or elsewhere to maximize foreign exchange earnings for the joint venture's own use. This agreement is currently in force. The former Soviet Union might be willing to permit Mongolia to export all concentrates internationally to earn hard currency.

50. In the absence of Western-style accounting statements (income statement, balance sheet, etc.) a full assessment of the financial and economic viability of the Erdenet operation is difficult to make. However, the operation seems to be internationally competitive. Indeed, during the early years of mining of fluorspar by Mongolsovtsvetmet, Erdenet cash flow was utilized to cover negative cash flows from the fluorspar mining, suggesting a financial viability at Erdenet. Net income from operations at Erdenet is reported to be Tug 110-120 million per year. However, care needs to be exercised in interpreting "net income" which may well not have the same definition as western accounting.

51. Coal. Coal is the main primary energy source for electricity production and the most intensely mined natural resource in Mongolia. Coal mining is also a major industrial activity, accounting for about 4 percent of total industrial value added and providing employment for 4,400 people. CES power stations and the power station at Dornod are the largest consumers, accounting for 61 percent of total coal output in 1990; industry and construction accounted for 13 percent; communal and public services 10 percent; and, exports to the Soviet Union 7 percent (1990). Coal production increased steadily during the 1980s; it peaked at 8.6 million tonnes in 1988, but

declined to 8 million tonnes in 1989 and 7.2 million tonnes in 1990. The declining trend continued during 1991 when output reached only 6.5 million tonnes, well below historical consumption levels.

52. Mongolia's total coal reserves are estimated at 100 billion tonnes, among the world's largest. Most deposits are poor quality (2,400-5,100 kc/kg calorific value), ranging from high-moisture brown coal/lignites to high-ash bituminous coals. The exception is the Tavan Tolgoi mine; though small (100,000 tonnes annually), it produces a huge (1 billion tonnes) of coking coal at the site, from a deposit that has a 20 mtpy production potential (10 million tonnes of coking coal and 10 million tonnes of thermal coal). All coal in Mongolia is low in sulfur, less than 1 percent.

53. There are 16 coal mines, excluding a new mine (Shive Ovoo) currently under construction, which is scheduled to start production in 1992. All mines are owned and operated by the Mongolian Coal Corporation (MCC) or Mongol Nuurs under the Ministry of Energy. The 14 open-pit mines account for 95 percent of total supply, with the two largest mines at Baga-Nuur (4 million tonnes annually) and Sharyn Gol (1.6 million tonnes annually) accounting for over 70 percent. None of the remaining 14 mines (only two of which are underground) produces more than 0.5 million tonnes annually, and the annual output of 10 local (aimag) mines averages only 10,000 tonnes. The two main mines supplying the thermal power plants are fully mechanized and the technology is relatively modern. Equipment, all Soviet-made, is comparable to that in western open-pit mines. However, productivity of capital stock and labor is low, owing to shortages of spare parts, auxiliary equipment, and bulldozers as well as explosives and other consumables. In some mines, productivity has declined owing to increasing stripping ratios, most visibly at the Sharyn Gol mine, which reached around 5 m^3 overburden per ton.

54. The breakdown of CMEA trade has seriously affected the coal subsector. Since late 1989, procurement and delivery of replacement equipment, spare parts, explosives, fuels, lubricants, and batteries have become increasingly problematic, disrupting coal production and resulting in significant output losses. The situation worsened in 1991 and, because of increasing shortages of key imports, the availability and utilization of existing equipment have been declining. Particularly affected is specialized mine transport equipment (dump trucks and bulldozers), whose availability declined by as much as 60 percent. In addition, in mid-1991, 13 of 40 (40 ton) and 6 of 25 (27-ton) dump trucks were old and inoperative. This is reflected in declining overburden removal, which was 26 percent lower at Sharyn Gol and 42 percent lower at Baga-Nuur than planned. The equipment bottleneck was relieved in the first half of 1992 when financing because available from the donor community for necessary imports of specialized machinery.

55. Production costs in the open pit mines range from Tug 25-75 per ton, extremely low by international standards, reflecting low labor costs and the degree of mechanization and capitalization. Following the June 1991 devaluation, imported material and labor costs increased, though not pro-rata, and are still low by international standards. Coal prices range from Tug 110-204 per ton (as of late 1991), depending upon the calorific value, which is well below international levels, and the opportunity cost of imported coal. However, this price range covers production costs, and all open-pit mines are

financially viable, except for Sharyn Gol which is marginal at present prices. The Nailakh underground mine with production costs in excess of Tug 300 per ton is not viable but, because its reserves are nearing exhaustion, will continue to be subsidized in order to minimize the socioeconomic consequences of closure.

56. Given the importance of coal to Mongolia's economy, a balanced strategy will have to be developed. Equipment and operations at existing mines need rehabilitation for continued economic exploitation. Exploitation of new mines may need rail links and, if so, those costs will have to be included in their economic analysis.

57. Fluorspar. Mongolia is the third largest producer of fluorspar after the People's Republic of China and Mexico. Total revenue from fluorspar mining and processing is modest, amounting to $33 million per year, 14 percent of sector earnings. The seven main fluorspar mining areas are concentrated in an area some 350 km southeast of Ulaanbaatar. Six of the mine areas are operated by a Mongolian/Soviet JV--Mongolsovtsvetmet, the seventh by the Mongolian/Czech JV--Mongol-Chekhoslovakmetal. The JV arrangements are the same as at Erdenet. All mines except one are open-pit operations utilizing close to state-of-the-art mobile (shovel-truck) mining equipment.

58. The mine areas produce various grades of fluorspar ranging from 35 percent run-of-mine (ROM) ore to 95 percent metallurgical grade. Some ROM ore is fed to a processing plant at Bor Undur to produce high grade (92-95 percent) fluorspar, referenced as "acid grade" (normally 97 percent+) by Russian republic consumers. All fluorspar production from the JV operations is sold to industrial (steel and chemical) demand centers in the former Soviet republics and CMEA countries. The transport distances to East European markets are very substantial and must make the economics of the operations close to marginal at best. Nevertheless, the former Soviet Republics seem to find the captive Mongolian JV operations financially acceptable. Mongolia fluorspar CIF prices are likely to be competitive with fluorspar from the People's Republic of China (the main fluorspar producer, capturing an ever-increasing market share), given the transport distances involved from China. Most of Mongolia's trade in fluorspar since 1991 has been in hard currency, except for lower grade ores which are still traded on barter.

59. Gold. Gold mining in Mongolia is small scale and restricted to simple alluvial operations that have to be suspended in winter. It provides less than 1 ton of gold per year, contributing 3 percent of sector revenues. Production fell in 1991 to 0.67 tonnes. Three alluvial operations are at Tolgoit/Ikh Alt (a joint venture with the former Soviet Union), Sharyn Gol (until recently a joint venture with Bulgaria, but now fully Mongolian-owned), and Duvunt (Mongolian). Two new alluvial operations at Haylast and Tsagaan Chuluut are under construction, the former by a Mongolian/Soviet Union JV and the latter by Mongolian interests; both are planned to be operated as Mongolian ventures. Gold output is in the form of impure ore, assaying only 80-90 percent gold. Detailed production costs of the alluvial operations are kept confidential by the government but, at best, they probably yield profits of $1-2 million per year. Exploration in the Tolgoit/Sharyn Gol area has identified additional alluvial gold reserves as well as reserves amenable to underground mining.

60. Other Minerals. The only other mineral production/exports of economic significance are tin and tungsten, which together contribute only 0.2 percent ($1 million) of sector revenues per year. Tin has been mined at Modot, some 200 km east of Ulaanbaatar, by a Mongolian/Czech JV but was taken over by Mongolian interests in 1991, following voluntary withdrawal by the Czech partner at the time of extremely depressed international tin markets. A 49 percent share in this operation is currently being privatized through the voucher system. The mine produced 100-120 tonnes tin concentrates in the mid-1970s but production in the 1980s was not recorded, implying that it was insignificant. Tin grades are reported as 1.15 kg/tonne tin. Concentrate sales to "free world" smelters are currently being made at about $2,000 per tonne. Cash operating costs are reported to be on the order of $1,200 per tonne concentrate, which makes the operation profitable. A number of private Mongolian operators produce, collectively, only 7-10 tonnes tin concentrates per year. A new tin mine is under construction at Janchivalan by Mongolian interests, whose production potential is understood to be limited.

61. A Mongolian/Hungarian JV operated until recently the Tsagaan-Davaa tungsten mine, 100 km northwest of Ulaanbaatar, but because of depressed tungsten markets, the Hungarian partner withdrew in 1991. Production of tungsten concentrates (60 percent WO_3) reached 125 tonnes in the late 1970s but declined to 45 tonnes in 1990. Mongolia is also constructing a new tungsten mine at Ulaan-Uul. But bearing in mind the extremely difficult geographical and infrastructure conditions in the area (the far west of Mongolia) as well as the depressed state of the market, the new mine is of questionable economic potential.

62. Finally, the only other mineral operation in Mongolia of any size is the uranium mine at Erdes in northeastern Mongolia. This mine area, which borders on the former Soviet Union, is operated by the Russians who lease the land from Mongolia. Little, if any, access to, or information about the deposit seems to be available to third parties. Conflicting reports suggest that the mine may be close to exhaustion.

Reforms

63. The government's mining policy is in transition and, following the reforms in other sectors, the government has been reviewing its mineral sector development policy. The SMB is preparing a new mining law to formalize licensing, royalties, and profit repatriation issues. The government's mining policy, which had historically relied on Soviet bloc assistance, began a new phase with the passage of the Foreign Investment Law with effect from May 1, 1990. This law provides for foreign participants to "invest in any branch of the national economy unless the MPR legislation stipulates otherwise" (Article 3.1). Guarantees of management in joint ventures, exemption from nationalization, repatriation of profits and international arbitration of disputes (if this is agreed in the investment contract) are among the features of the law. Further guarantees will soon be provided by the Multilateral Investment Guarantee Agency (MIGA) which Mongolia will join in the near future. The law also provides for a maximum corporate tax rate of 40 percent and a guaranteed rate for foreign investors that will not exceed the local investors' rate. A tax holiday of up to three years is also given, starting with the first profit-making year.

Issues

64. Legal. Mining law is the priority issue in the sector. Although the SMB has been preparing one, its completion has been delayed, and this is already having a negative effect on potential foreign investment. Several foreign investors have made attempts to participate in the development of Mongolian mineral resources, in particular, gold. But Mongolian policy limits participation by foreign investors to 49 percent in hardrock gold operations and it prohibits alluvial gold operations. This policy is consistent with the Foreign Investment Law's phrase "unless MPR legislation stipulates otherwise" (Article 3.1). Foreign investment in the mineral sector is likely to be slow in coming while these restrictions remain. The government must clarify its mining investment policies. Furthermore, as these policies will be reflected in the new Mining Act, policy clarification is urgent.

65. Regulatory. All current mining operations apparently operate without formal mining leases. This is understandable, if not legally sound, for enterprises where the government is the majority shareholder. Private operators, however, apparently have no security of title. As the preparation of an act progresses, the draft should embody internationally accepted principles of a mining code that satisfies the expectations of private investors and the needs of the government to provide effective supervision of the sector. Especially important are that:

(a) Mineral rights granted should be exclusive for a determined area.

(b) Exploration and mining rights granted should be as comprehensive as possible, i.e., granted for all minerals. They will normally exclude only hydrocarbons and, possibly, building materials such as sand, gravel, etc.

(c) The Mining Code should respect the principle of minimal government intervention in mineral exploration and development, while reserving the right to assess the overall economics of the project prior to granting leases or concessions.

(d) The Mining Code should guarantee that, if a mineral discovery leads to a viable ore body, the right to mine, process and market minerals will not be unreasonably withheld.

The Mining Law is only a first step. The major tasks of drafting implementation regulations and designing administrative procedures will remain. Training needs will be substantial.

66. Institutional Deficiencies. The functions of the above agencies are not well defined. The government's role as shareholder and as administrator-regulator should be separated. This step is critical to give government institutions the necessary transparency in the eyes of potential foreign investors. To interact efficiently with foreign companies, SMB's small staff needs to be considerably expanded with personnel who are conversant with the financial and economic evaluation of potential mineral prospects.

67. Government Policy. The government desire to maintain the minimum 51 percent equity participation in future mineral development presents a seri-

ous risk that foreign interests may not develop in the manner and with the speed desired. The rationale for the government position lies in its desire to receive the major share of profits from the exploitation of minerals, which are seen as national assets. In addition, after so many years of relying on the former Soviet Union, some government officials view the maintenance of major government equity in mineral development as a guarantee against any possible future domination by China.

68. Promotional Plan. The government is committed to promotion of further mineral development and has recognized the need for foreign initiatives, but government entities are ill-equipped to organize this task effectively. Mongolia has a substantial, well-documented geological data base but, government agencies have hesitated to make it available for foreign commercial exploitation. The only apparent promotion has been the government's receptivity to potential investors visiting Mongolia. The first opportunity to meet with the international mining fraternity (Denver, Colorado, February 1992) was largely unsuccessful due to the uncertain enabling environment and government interest in maintaining major equity participation.

69. Infrastructure. Future mineral development in Mongolia will face substantial infrastructural difficulties. There is almost no transport infrastructure, except the rail line traversing the country from the former Soviet Union to China and small branch lines from that artery to existing mines. This is a major constraint for bulk commodities, including copper and coal. In addition, outside the CES grid, power supply is undeveloped. In the Gobi desert, where potential coal and copper operations have been identified, the development of railroad, power, and water supply would be a prerequisite for mineral operations.

70. Trade Routes. As a land-locked country, Mongolia has limited options for exporting its minerals. The traditional trade route goes north into Russia and then westward, via the Trans-Siberian rail line to the former Soviet republics and CMEA countries. As Mongolia strives to diversify its markets, new trade routes need to be developed. One option is the old route north and then east to the port at Vladivostok. However, this haul, over 4,000 km, would seriously damage the economics of most Mongolian mineral development opportunities. In addition, this port is closed six months a year due to freezing temperatures and icing. The alternative is south and east through China. Indeed, major developments in the Gobi desert would open up the opportunity to develop a new Chinese-gauge rail line south to connect to the World Bank-financed Inner Mongolia line being constructed to provide a coal route east. To this date, however, no meaningful discussions on this route have been held between China and Mongolia.

Transport

71. Despite rapid industrial development, Mongolia's transport infrastructure remains seriously inadequate. This hinders the flow of factors of production and distribution, the availability of commodities, and the development of internal markets. It is also likely to hamper domestic and foreign private investment, once the country recovers from its present crisis. Given the size of the country and its widely spread resources (including popula-

tion), the development of transport and communications will be a challenging and difficult task. The transport sector grew relatively rapidly during the 1980s, averaging about 5 percent annually. In 1990, it accounted for over 11 percent of GDP and employed about 48,000 people.

72. Ulaanbaatar, the capital, is the main generator of traffic; the corridor north to the Russian border is the most intensively used. Darhan, the second largest city, is about half way along this corridor, at the junction with a branch to the west that serves the third largest city, Erdenet. These three cities account for about 35 percent of the population and most industrial activity. Population densities in the rest of the country are very low, averaging less than one person per km^2. Outside this main corridor and its extension to the southern border with China, the transport network is rudimentary, comprising low standard roads, some navigable rivers, one rail line to Russia in the northeast, and a number of low standard airports.

73. Personal mobility by modern means is low. Many individuals in the countryside ride horses. Motorized road transport is also used, but no good records are available. Total inter-city travel is under 1,000 km per person annually; this compares to 550 km in China and 6,000 km in Japan. Freight intensity is high in the areas served by the main rail line, and low elsewhere. Some 75 percent of Mongolia's freight moves by rail. Almost half is domestic coal, most of it for the main power plants in Ulaanbaatar. Foreign trade accounts for most of the balance of rail traffic, both imports of consumer and industrial goods and fuel and exports of copper concentrate and manufactured or semiprocessed animal products. Roads carry the remaining 25 percent of freight, more than half of it construction materials. Average freight in Mongolia is about 3,400 ton/km per person annually, compared to 1,000 in China, 3,700 in Japan, and over 15,000 in the former Soviet Union.

74. Freight transport flows are likely to change as trade is increasingly routed through China, rather than Russia. Industrial decentralization will result in smaller plants sitings throughout the country to serve nearby populations, thereby reducing transport intensity. Improving power plant efficiency could greatly reduce the need for coal transport--perhaps by one-third; and, increasing the concentration of copper ore at extraction points could also reduce freight volumes. Overall, however, transport intensity is likely to increase with economic growth, and selective modernization is needed throughout the system.

<u>Structure of the Sector</u>

75. <u>Railways</u>. Mongolia has some 1,800 km of rail line and an additional 200 km of shunt-lines and side tracks. The gauge is the same as in Russia, but wider than in China. Gradients up to 2 percent and many bends limit train weight and speed. Wooden sleepers are used and, because they are not chemically treated, they have to be replaced every 6-7 years. Signaling and telecommunications systems are insufficient. The rolling stock comprises Soviet-made locomotives and wagons. Repairs used to be made in Soviet facilities but are now carried out in two ill-equipped depots in Mongolia; spare parts and fuels, imported from the former Soviet Union, are in short supply. In 1990, the railways transported 14.5 million tonnes of freight and 2.5 million passengers, which is below capacity. Domestic traffic accounts for 8 million

tonnes, of which 80 percent is coal, mainly for the power stations. Trade with the former Soviet Union accounted for 6 million tonnes of freight, ex ports for 2.5 million tonnes, and imports for 3.5 million tonnes. Transit traffic was about 1 million tonnes, one third of the level in the mid-1980s, and was expected to be only about 100,000 tonnes in 1991. The railway is a Mongolia-Soviet Union joint venture with equal ownership. It was built by Soviet construction organizations and financed with Soviet loans. It has regularly shown an operating profit; however, most profits were distributed to the 16,000 employees providing an average 25 percent wage supplement in the form of housing, schooling and medical allowances.

76. The Trans-Siberian route through Russia has recently encountered problems and its costs are high. As a result of internal problems in the former Soviet Union, shipments take three months or more between Mongolia and Europe, and sometimes get lost altogether. In 1991, freight cost $1,800 per TEU to Eastern Europe. The route north and east to Vladivostok or Nakhodka, over 2,000 km away, also takes some three months. The route south across China is much shorter, some 1,000 km from the border to the port of Tianjin, but was little used until recently. Transit is hampered by the gauge differential and inadequate transshipment facilities. Wheels under passenger wagons are changed relatively quickly, but freight is reloaded manually. The lack of equipment for handling is particularly cumbersome for bulk cargos and containers and results in unpredictable waiting times. Freight costs $680 per TEU to Tianjin.

77. Road Transport. Despite its large territory, Mongolia has only 42,000 km of main roads--an average 27 m per km^2--of which only 1,300 km are paved and most in poor condition. State roads, connecting the aimag centers, account for about 10,000 km. In the past, 50-60 km were added to the main network annually, absorbing half the road budget; the other half was used for road maintenance. Standards are low due to a shortage of resources and of mechanized methods, and poor initial construction. Roads are the responsibility of the State Roads Corporation and its agencies in each aimag and their funding comes partly from a tax on the sale of fuel products. Traffic volumes are light, increasing near the main cities. It is estimated that 70 percent of freight tonnage is carried by road, although only 25 percent in terms of ton-km. The motorized vehicle fleet comprises 40,000 units, of which 27,000 are trucks, 2,500 buses, 6,000 cars, and 4,000 agricultural vehicles, mainly tractors. There are also more than 10,000 trailers. Some 70 percent of the fleet is more than six years old; about half the trucks have run more than 500,000 km. Most trucks are 5-ton vehicles and fuel inefficient. Vehicle shortages have recently been aggravated by lack of spare parts, tires, and batteries, and about 30 percent of the bus and truck fleet is currently inoperative.

78. Five agencies are responsible for interurban passenger and freight transport. The seasonality and directional imbalance of traffic--70 percent of freight is distributed from Ulaanbaatar and the rest goes to Ulaanbaatar--increases transport costs, especially for long distances. Each aimag has its own transport company for shorter distances and their privatization is planned in the near future. At present, tariffs are officially set; the intracity tariff covers only 80 percent of costs.

79. <u>Air Transport</u>. With a vast territory and low population densities that cannot justify high standard surface networks, long-distance passenger transport within Mongolia is mainly by air. The number of passengers has grown at about 5-6 percent per year over the last 15 years. In 1990, about 774,000 passengers were carried an average distance of 700 km. Air cargo has decreased in the last three years, along with declining trade volumes (both foreign and domestic), and was less than 11,000 tonnes in 1990, almost half of it luggage and mail.

80. Mongolia's extensive domestic air transport network links the 21 major population centers and 160 smaller centers throughout the country. There are five asphalt-concrete surfaced runways. Ground equipment is up to 30 years old. The Civil Aviation Authority oversees the aviation subsector, but the airline company (MIAT) is responsible for airport management.

81. MIAT (Mongolia International Air Transport) is the sole domestic carrier. It has about 70 aircraft (45 12-seater and 16 50-seater) but fewer than 50 are normally operational and most are more than 15 years old. MIAT's facilities are minimal, and has no hangar for repairs and maintenance. Staff has been increasing and is now about 1,500. International air transport is less developed: in 1990, only 50,000 passengers were carried. This, however, represents a significant growth compared to 20,000 in 1987 and only 12,500 in 1980. There are direct links only with Irkutsk, Moscow, and Beijing, served by AEROFLOT and MIAT (with an aircraft leased from Aeroflot). China's CAAC introduced flights between Beijing and Ulaanbaatar in August 1991. Other international carriers are reportedly considering establishing air links with Mongolia, although Ulaanbaatar's airport ground facilities are below international standards. MIAT showed an overall operating profit of Tug 34 million in 1990. It joined ICAO in 1989 and sets international tariffs as well as ground fees in accordance with IATA's procedures. Domestic tariffs, however, do not cover aircraft replacement cost.

<u>Reforms</u>

82. Long-distance transport companies will probably remain under government ownership for the foreseeable future, but aimags' transport enterprises have already been divided into smaller units to facilitate their privatization. There are about 80 companies with 200-500 vehicles each and many smaller companies, each having 50-200 vehicles. In all, 70 percent of vehicles are to be privatized through the coupon system or outright sales. The taxi service in Ulaanbaatar has already been privatized. Many trucking companies have their own repair shops.

83. The government intends to keep civil aviation under public ownership. Its immediate concern is that MIAT is currently hampered by shortages of imported spares, and many aircraft are grounded. Beyond immediate repair needs, MIAT needs to modernize its fleet and improve ground facilities. It is evaluating the use of Fokker-100s and other aircraft for domestic routes, and the building of a hangar for repairs and maintenance. It has ordered two Boeing-757s, although a leasing arrangement, a joint venture, or permitting other airlines to increase their service may be more appropriate in the short term. Tariff increases will also be needed.

Issues

84. The most urgent issue in the sector is the lack of imported spare parts, tires, batteries for all kinds of vehicles, basic road construction materials and equipment, spare parts for the locomotives and the rolling stock. Based on recent import volumes, the transport sector's total import requirements are estimated at $80-100 million per year. The Bank and some donors provided financing for critical imports in 1992, but a substantial financing gap remains to fully satisfy the import needs of the sector.

85. Improved transshipment is essential to facilitate Mongolian exports and imports through China, the shortest land route to the sea and to Asian markets. One proposal is to build a reloading facility in Mongolia with an annual capacity of up to 1 million tonnes at Zameen-Uud, close to the Chinese border but in the harsh Gobi desert; another proposal envisages extending the Chinese gauge into more hospitable terrain in Mongolia; a third consists of improving the existing facility in China, through a joint venture. The latter may be the more economical solution, but will require Mongolian investment in China.

86. The railways need a wide range of modernization projects to reduce operating costs. Examples of such projects include the following: to renovate the wagon fleet, thus lowering traction costs; to introduce automatic telephone and cargo control systems (UNCTAD has proposed instituting the ACIS wagon tracking module); to provide staff training in modern technologies and practices, and to establish cooperative ties with other railways in nearby countries; and, to establish, probably in the private sector, small-scale facilities for repairs and supplies, e.g., concrete sleepers, crushing stone, renewal and planing of wheels.

87. International documentation, insurance and claims, chartering, and other practices are all new to Mongolia and will have to be learned. As a first step, the government established a national freight forwarding company, TUUSHIN, in 1990 with help from UNCTAD/ESCAP. The company deals with container shipments; so far it handles imports only, some 20 TEUs per month, but expects to begin handling exports and to build up a multimodal service. It is building four container stations near rail lines and will need to invest in equipment and in staff training.

88. Transport tariffs were not doubled when other prices doubled in January 1991; this has worsened the financial performance of transport entities. Tariffs will have to be liberalized if privatization is to be successful and if excessive subsidies are to be avoided for nonprivatized enterprises.

89. Vehicle replacement is a very high priority. This would achieve fuel savings of at least 25 percent which is extremely important because a large proportion of export earnings goes for imported fuel. Vehicle imports are no longer restricted except by lack of foreign exchange, and Mongolia should start importing more efficient types. Vehicle choice and investment should be largely in the hands of the private sector, except for long-distance passenger transport companies. Improvement of vehicle repair shops is also important; many lack adequate equipment.

90. Low population densities and related low traffic volumes cannot generate adequate returns for most road upgrading; nevertheless, paving some road sections may be economically justified. The Transport Department has prepared an overambitious network development plan that includes the building of 1,200 km of paved roads before 1995 and a further 2,000 km between 1995 and 2000. A road master plan is being prepared with ADB assistance to identify priorities, as well as feasibility studies for four links: Erdenet to Darhan, 180 km; Ulaanbaatar to Baga-Nuur, 90 km; Urhangay to Kar Khorum, 80 km; and Kar Khorum to Tsetserig, 130 km. The studies are to be completed by end-1992.

91. Construction capacity should not constrain road development. The law allowing foreign companies or joint ventures to operate in Mongolia will facilitate the transfer of modern technologies and provide training for local construction workers. The road agency has little experience with bidding and will need to develop procedures for it. Improving road maintenance should also be economically justified. Obsolete equipment and technology need replacing, and staff need training in modern techniques. A road-user charge study should be done to see whether road users contribute enough to cover marginal costs.

92. Ulaanbaatar's airport will need to be upgraded to handle the expected increase in international traffic. However, an UNCTAD report indicates that the runway is not well situated and that geography limits the types of aircraft that can use it. The government is therefore considering converting a military airport at Nalaikh, some 50 km from Ulaanbaatar, to commercial use. Nalaikh would need new terminal facilities. Two other military airports could also be converted to civilian use.

Telecommunications

Overview

93. Since the 1920s, Soviet aid has enabled Mongolia to establish a national postal and telecommunications network as well as a limited international communications network. The development of telecommunications reflects the characteristics of the spatial distribution of Mongolia's population and the vastness of the country. The telegraph and telephone networks cover only a small fraction of the country; services are concentrated in the reasonably accessible urban areas. The urban areas have the basic infrastructure, but its quality severely inadequate. Direct long-distance calling, telex, and facsimile, and data transmission services are not yet available. This situation hinders the flow of information and creates bottlenecks in the development of both external and internal markets.

94. Telecommunications are under the jurisdiction of Mongolian Telecommunications Authority (MTA), which was a ministry until recently. MTA has full authority on postal services and on technical services related to radio and TV transmissions. With respect to telephone services, MTA controls only the Ulaanbaatar exchanges and the domestic trunk network while the aimags have operational authority at the local exchange level.

Structure of the Sector

95. Telephone Services. In spite of the difficulties posed by geography and a small population thinly scattered over 18 aimags, a large proportion of Mongolia's population has access to telephone services. There were 4 lines per 100 people in 1990 (up from 2.5 in 1980) for the country as a whole, which compares favorably with China (0.5) and Thailand (1.7) but not with Malaysia (7.3). The density is higher in cities: for instance, 6 lines per 100 persons in Ulaanbaatar (33,500 lines), which accounts for one fourth of the population. In smaller towns, where half of the population live, 2 telephones are shared by every 100 persons, and some districts have no telephone exchange. Between 1980 and 1990 the exchange capacity increased from 42,630 lines to 76,600, reflecting an average annual growth of 5.5 percent. Smaller exchanges with varying capacities of 300-2,000 lines are located in aimag centers and somons. Combined domestic and long-distance traffic in 1989 was 19.2 million minutes, compared to 10.9 million minutes in 1980.

96. The telephone services are generally low in quality. Exchange lines are fully utilized, circuits congested, and equipment outdated. The waiting list for new lines is almost as long as the list of current customers (53,000 registered applications and probably more unregistered demand, mostly in Ulaanbaatar, versus 76,600 lines in use). Local charges for official and residential telephones at the end of 1990 were Tug 68 ($1.70) and Tug 20 ($0.50) per month, respectively. Installation and transfer charges ranged between Tug 250 and Tug 120. Local calls are not metered and there is no record of the volume of local traffic. Long-distance calls are charged according to distance and duration, businesses paying almost twice as much as residences. The charge per 3-minute varies between Tug 3.60 ($0.09) and Tug 15 ($0.037). These charges have given MTA an operating surplus. Telefax services are not yet available. International connections remain poor. International telephone services are available to the former Soviet Union via Intersputnik, to China via an open-wire system, and since August 1990 to Hong Kong via Asiasat-1. They are handled semiautomatically, and the quality of service suffers from noise, echo, and long waiting times.

97. Telegram and Telex. Telegraph services are provided through teleprinters in post and telecommunications offices. Available statistics point to a different trend in telegraph traffic than telephone traffic. During 1980-87, telegraph traffic grew 2.7 percent per annum but declined in 1988 and 1989. However, this is probably due to the expansion of telephone services, and further falls in telegraph traffic can be expected. Telex services are not developed in Mongolia. There are only 80 subscribers, all in Ulaanbaatar and mostly government agencies and trading companies.

98. Postal. Mongolia has a motorized intercity mail delivery and a reasonably well-developed postal system. However, our knowledge of it is limited.

99. TV and Radio. There are 16 radio transmitters operating in VHF, short, medium and long wave ranges, some with FM; a monthly fee is charged to radio owners, Tug 10 for households and Tug 20 for businesses. Almost every family has a radio, an estimated 20 radios per 100 person, 450,000 in all. There are two TV programs, one Mongolian and one from the former Soviet Union.

The monthly fee for using a TV is Tug 20. On average, there are seven TV sets for every 100 persons, and it is estimated that 65 percent of the population can watch the two available programs; but the distribution is uneven. Almost every family in the larger cities has a set, compared to one for every 270 families in the rural areas. Only 100 of the 350 somons have access to direct TV transmissions. The total number of TV sets is estimated at 150,000.

Reforms

100. Since 1990, the Mongolian government has taken steps to improve the telecommunications network and to satisfy the demand for telephone services. A French company (ALCATEL) recently installed an additional exchange with a 27,000 line capacity (combined for local, national transit, and international calls) in Ulaanbaatar. A number of projects are also under consideration: (i) an Intelsat earth station, with a grant from the Japan International Cooperation Agency (JICA), to improve international communications by a 1,000 line national transit exchange combined with a 100-line international exchange. It will cost $7 million and is scheduled to begin operation in 1993; (ii) one earth station and the installation of 100 domestic satellite stations using Asiasat to improve domestic communications, telecommunications and broadcasting (a $4 million contract for this project has been signed); (iii) Negotiations are under way with Daewoo, a South Korean firm, to install digital exchanges with 20,000 lines at an estimated cost of $8.7 million. An export credit is being sought from South Korean sources.

Issues

101. Alleviating congestion and improving the quality of both domestic and international service through increased capacity, the replacement of obsolete equipment and new technology are among the major issues facing the sector. While the government has been trying to improve the situation, its efforts have been on rather piecemeal, without sufficient consideration of longer term objectives. A May 1991 mission from the International Telecommunication Union (ITU) and a subsequent ADB mission have noted the technical problems and incompatibilities of the French and Japanese proposals. Both the ITU and ADB have also recommended the formulation of a master plan for development of telecommunications in Mongolia. Such a plan could identify sectoral priorities and assess the feasibility of various proposals under consideration by MTA.

102. The organizational and financial restructuring of MTA is needed to make the government responsible for policy formulation as well as an autonomous company for operating telecommunications services. MTA was created in 1990 to achieve this objective but in reality functions as a government department in all respects. Policy formulation and regulatory issues do not seem to be separated. MTA is in charge of the postal system, telecommunications, as well as the broadcasting services; operational authority at the local exchange level rests with the aimag governments. This structure is fragmented and is not conducive to the development of an efficient telecommunications sector. Therefore, there is a need for institutional changes. Both ITU and ADB have recommended that: (a) the postal and broadcasting services should be separated; (b) MTA should be truly autonomous and its services be centralized--i.e., the aimag governments should not be involved in the tele-

communications sector; and (c) an independent regulatory body should be created. Government has, in principle, agreed with these recommendations but has not yet taken any action.

103. On the financial side, the issue is MTA's relationship with the government budget. At present, the government controls MTA's budget and receives all its revenues and allocates investment funds from the central budget. The arrangements are convoluted and need to be straightened out. If MTA is made an autonomous, commercially oriented company, this problem could easily be solved. A related issue is the personnel system of MTA. Its current system resembles a civil service, and the authority is overstaffed. The ratio of staff to 100 telephone lines is about 7, whereas it is under 1 in most industrial countries. The staff, however, is well qualified. All were recruited from the School of Information Technology: 10 percent engineers, 30 percent technicians, and 15 percent operators. However, they will need additional training when new technology is introduced.

104. The level and structure of domestic services need to be reviewed and appropriate adjustments be made to reflect costs. The present tariffs are too low, particularly when equipment procurement and replacement costs in foreign exchange are taken into account. Part of the excess demand for telephone services is due to inappropriate pricing policies.

Education

Overview

105. Like other former socialist economies, Mongolia has put special emphasis on education and human resource development and as a result, it has an elaborate educational system. Expenditures on education have been traditionally high, 20 percent of the state budget in 1981; 25 percent (14 percent of GDP) by the end of 1990. Much of the pre-1990 system has developed along the Soviet lines, particularly tertiary education, with the number of places and the content of the courses determined to a high degree of detail by quantitative manpower planning, and educational establishments largely separated from research institutions. However, in line with other changes in the economy, the educational system is also changing. Reform plans for the sector have been prepared and a new education law has been passed, although much remains to be done in practice. Employment in the sector, including principals, teachers, support, and maintenance staff, increased from 50,987 in 1985 to 64,935 in 1990, 10 percent of total employment in the economy.

Basic Educational Indicators

106. As a result of an extensive and well-developed infrastructure, access to basic education has been satisfactory. The gross primary enrollment ratio is effectively 100 percent. The literacy rate is 97 percent--defined as the percentage of persons of 10 or more years of age having completed at least three years of school, and 89 percent of children complete the eighth grade and 50 percent graduate from the tenth. Within the under-34-year-old age group, only 2 percent failed to complete secondary school; 16 percent of the

total workforce has some higher education. Currently, 440,000 students are enrolled in the elementary and secondary schools, 30,000 in specialized schools, 20,000 in vocational schools, and 18,000 in higher level institutions. About 510,000 persons, 25 percent of the population, attend some form of school during the year.

107. The achievements education have been generated by appropriately designed government policies. School attendance is required until about the age of 17. Kindergarten, primary, and secondary education are free of charge; 80 percent of postsecondary students receive scholarships. Students pay for their textbooks at a subsidized price of Tug 15-20 per book. Educational standards, within the context of the existing system, seem reasonable. A highly selective entrance exam is given for continuing higher level studies. For example, of 400 applicants to a technical school, only the best 20 are accepted. The competition process to enter specialized schools allows widespread participation from students in rural areas.

Structure of the Sector

108. Kindergartens provide education for children aged 3-7 years. Their number increased from 680 (62,740 students) in 1985 to 909 (97,210 students) in 1990. The percentage of children in the kindergarten age group rose from about 20 to 30 percent over this period. In 1990, about 85 percent of all kindergartens were financed from the state budget, the remainder by state enterprises. The student-to-teacher ratio was a reasonable 21.4.

109. Primary education consists of grades 1-6, covering students aged 7-12. Secondary education comprises grades 7-10. At present there are two types of primary/secondary schools. The first one is "complete" secondary schools, providing 10 years of schooling, including the 6-year primary school cycle. Currently, there are 260 complete primary/secondary schools. The other type provides eight years of schooling, i.e., 6 years of primary and 2 years of secondary. The number of primary and secondary schools increased from 590 (25 percent of which in 10-year schools) in 1985 to 634 (43 percent in 10-year schools) in 1990. Enrollment in the primary/secondary school system increased at an annual rate of 1.2 percent over the same period. In the primary/secondary school system, the student to teacher ratio was a respectable 20.8 in 1990.

110. Educational facilities in the system are well utilized. To limit costs, school buildings are used from 8 a.m. to 10 p.m. The younger children attend the morning shift and the older adults the evening courses. In 1990, there were 289,800 places for the 440,900 children, yielding a utilization ratio of 1.52. Ten percent of all primary/secondary students attend schools rated as in poor condition. To facilitate access to education, the system provides dormitories in aimag and somon centers for the children of herdsmen. In 1990 64,632 students lived in dormitories but only 55,234 beds were available.

111. Mongolia has five universities: the Mongolian State University, Pedagogical University (which includes institutes for foreign language, teacher training, kindergarten training, and teacher retraining), a Medical University, an Agricultural University, and a Technical University. In addi-

tion, there are two teacher-training colleges for primary schools and kindergartens. Enrollment declined from 26,000 in 1983 to around 17,000 in 1990, and the number of university graduates also declined, from 4,971 to 3,150. In the past, Mongolian students also received higher education abroad, mostly in the Soviet Union and East European countries, but this outflow has slowed to a trickle.

112. In 1990, there were 31 technical schools with 18,476 students, 44 vocational schools with 29,067 students, and 26 vocational secondary schools with 20,285 students. Between 1985 and 1990, three new technical schools opened but enrollment declined from 22,978 to 18,476. Enrollment in vocational schools also fluctuated between 27,700 and 34,150 during the same period, while that of vocational secondary schools has increased steadily, reaching 20,285 students in 1990.

Reforms

113. Since 1991, the Mongolian government has been implementing an ambitious and far-reaching reform program to improve the education sector's efficiency and relevance to a market-based economy. As a first step, it adopted an Education Law on June 27, 1991, designating education as a social policy priority area. In July 1991 a national committee for universities was established. Under the law the state will provide free general education but will charge tuition for professional degrees. It allows the establishment of private schools which need to register with the Ministry of Education and have their curricula, teachers, facilities, etc. approved. The ministry is establishing a review, control, and auditing unit. The response of the private sector has been good, and five private colleges were opened in 1990/91.

114. The Ministry of Education has established three basic institutions to teach the economics of free market systems: one within the Mongolian State University for macroeconomic management; and two colleges, the Business College and the College of Market Economy, to train and prepare brokers, dealers, and other financial intermediaries. Western curricula have been adopted, as well as the Western system of BA, MA, and PhD degrees instead of the Soviet diploma system. However, professors and teaching materials are not yet available. Efforts are concentrating on retraining teachers for the new colleges, and staff in government agencies. A private school of economics has also been established.

115. Higher level education is being decentralized and will be subject to a fee. University branches and technical schools are to be established in aimag centers. So far, three branches for agriculture and medicine have been established. Under the reform program, local governments will be in charge of managing and financing local schools. Students of higher level, vocational and technical schools would start to pay a fee but would also be able to obtain a government loan for this purpose. A better integration of education and production would be pursued through apprentice plans, which could reduce costs at vocational schools, and by training centers attached to enterprises or business firms.

116. The school system will have additional "paths" to enable earlier specialization. Primary school will still be compulsory for eight years, but

children can take a break or shift after the sixth grade if they choose to attend specialized evening classes or vocational courses; gifted children can pursue paths in arts and sciences in special schools after the sixth grade, instead of the eighth. For a foreign language, students can choose Russian or English from the fifth grade. New curricula are being developed along these lines. Parliament has voted to switch from the Cyrillic to Mongolian script by 1994. Courses in Mongolian script for children and adults have started, and a daily one-hour TV program teaches the script.

Issues

117. Although an education law has been enacted and the government is eager to establish an education system to meet Mongolia's needs under the new conditions, the specifics and sequencing of reforms are not yet determined. A comprehensive sector study is needed to identify priorities, available resources, and the capabilities of the Ministry of Education. There is a general consensus that the quality of education should be raised and the system made more flexible to reflect the needs of a market-based economy. This is the major reform objective and will require the changes summarized below. As noted above, the government has already acted on many of these issues.

118. Reforming the education curricula, particularly in the vocational, technical, and tertiary education areas. The content of courses must be revised substantially; new courses, foreign languages, modern textbooks and laboratories, need to be introduced; and existing facilities need to be modernized. Efforts in those areas, however, will be complicated with the planned conversion of all teaching from the Cyrillic to the traditional Ourgen script. Indications are that the quality of education cannot be improved without improving the quality of teachers. Most teachers are qualified at the institute level and their education is not thought to be up to date. They must be retrained and their skills increased to introduce new curricula and courses to prepare students for life in a market economy.

119. Increasing the capabilities of the Ministry of Education to implement and monitor reforms. The ministry has 33 staff at its headquarters. This is not sufficient to develop and implement a major reform program, with new curricula and textbooks. Mongolia can benefit greatly from the experiences of other countries, and the scope appears ample for both multilateral and bilateral assistance to Mongolia in modernizing and reforming education. Steps are already being taken to address some of these issues, and an internationally supported Higher Education Policy Center has been proposed.

120. Reducing the cost of running the system without compromising on standards. This will require cost-effective methods of teaching and increases in the efficiency of resource use. Low population density results in high education costs, but some savings may be possible, for example, by consolidating facilities or classes, especially in higher education. Introducing a limited user fee is likely to be useful. Exploring distance-teaching alternatives to boarding school for children of the nomadic population should be considered seriously. Increasing local autonomy in determining the content of courses and greater use of apprenticeship programs is likely to reduce costs also. The proposal to establish university branches at the aimag level may have to be reviewed. The Bank is likely to be instrumental in this respect by

undertaking a study analyzing the macroeconomic and sectoral aspects of the reform program.

Health

Overview

121. Mongolia has a relatively well-developed medical infrastructure. However, since it is a large and sparsely populated country, achievements have naturally come at a high cost: expenditures on health absorbed about 8 percent of GDP during 1980-88 and 5 percent in 1989-90. Medicine is a major employer: as of end-1990, there were 6,180 doctors, of which 70 percent were women, about 11,300 nurses, and some 8,000 technicians and lower level workers. The medical system, which increasingly has so far provided services free of charge, has recently been coming under pressure as revenues of the central government (as percent of GDP) keep declining. The Mongolian authorities realize that radical reforms are needed, and the reform process is already under way, although the specifics have not yet been formulated.

122. The Ministry of Health is responsible for policymaking and coordination. Of its staff of 60, 40 are professionals. However, the capabilities of the ministry in terms of implementing a major reform are not known, and it is likely that it will need extensive technical assistance.

Basic Health Indicators

123. Mongolia compares favorably with other Asian nations in terms of coverage of and access to health services. The number of doctors and middle level personnel per 10,000 population increased steadily from 5.2 and 40.5, respectively, in 1960 to 22.9 and 88.8 in 1990. The number of hospital beds per 10,000 population increased from 19.7 to 119.5 over the same period. Immunization coverage of one-year-olds was over 85 percent for the main diseases. Life expectancy is high at 60 years for males and 62.5 percent for females. The population growth rate has been high, between 2.7 and 3 percent in 1970-90, owing to earlier government policy of encouraging large families. As a result, the population is very young--over a half of the population is under 18. Due to the expansion of medical coverage, the death rate declined from 12.2 per 1,000 to 7.9 during 1970-90. Death rates are higher in rural areas where communications and transport facilities are poor and medical assistance is delayed. Viral diseases are the leading cause of death among adults. At the end of 1988, Mongolia had reported no cases of AIDS. In 1987 an AIDS research center was opened at the Institute of Hygiene and Virology and its specialists were trained in laboratory techniques by the World Health Organization (WHO).

124. Infant mortality is still high. After rising from 1965 to a peak in 1985 (76.8 per 1,000 live births), it declined steeply to 60.6 in 1987. The decline may have been partly caused by the changes in the registration system. In 1991, the rate again rose to 71.6. Mortality rates for children under five is 84 per 1,000. Maternal mortality is also high at 144 per 100,000 live births, reflecting the high crude birth rate and lack of proper child spacing.

About 40 percent of maternal deaths are caused by delivery and post-delivery complications. This is rather high, considering the good antenatal care and the fact that 98 percent of all deliveries take place in hospitals. Pneumonia causes half the childhood deaths. Diarrheal diseases account for another 25 percent of child mortality, but the rate is declining since the introduction of rehydration therapy.

125. Nutritional standards are generally adequate, i.e., about the same as for middle-income countries. The daily average consumption is 2,800-2,900 calories per capita, much of it from animal sources. The dietary pattern has shifted over the last decades toward greater consumption of potatoes, vegetables, and fruits. While there is no food shortages, Mongolia has micronutrient deficiencies, especially in the Gobi areas, and seasonal shortages of vegetables and fresh milk which it counteracts by importing vitamins, fruits, and selected foods. Overall child nutrition also seems reasonable except for specific deficiencies such as for iron and iodine. The government has recently initiated a milk-supplement program for children under one year (through a national network of milk kitchens) and a food supplement for children attending kindergartens and schools, raising their caloric intake up to 2,400 per day, which exceeds the norms recommended by WHO.

126. Clean drinking water and sanitation facilities are scarce in rural areas, but there is a trend toward urbanization and better facilities in cities. The urban population grew from 44 percent of the total in 1969 to 57 percent in 1989. Half the urban dwellers live in apartments linked to central water/sewage and heating systems. But some 60 percent of the population still live in ghers. Rural gher settlements have scheduled daily deliveries of clean water, but they are not reliable. Their alternatives, for instance salty water naturally available in the Gobi area, are believed to be linked to some illnesses. It is also estimated that some 80 percent lack adequate sanitation facilities. Since 1988, loans for materials to build private houses have been made available at subsidized interest rates.

<u>Structure of Health Services</u>

127. The pre-1990 health system in most respects followed the Soviet model, with treatment largely provided free of charge and a strongly hierarchical organization designed to provide nationwide coverage. The system also emphasized hospital-based curative care over preventive measures as revealed in the structure of health expenditures: city and aimag hospitals account for 60 percent of expenditure, somon hospitals 15 percent, creches 10 percent but rural feldsher posts only 2 percent. In 1990, health expenditures represented about 7 percent of government outlays and 5 percent of GDP.

128. <u>Medical Care</u>. In the 1980s, medical care was provided through clinics and hospitals. The higher the level in the system, the more numerous the medical specialties and the more sophisticated the diagnostic equipment available. Hospital stays are free of charge, but outpatients pay for their medicines at subsidized prices. The structure of services and medical specialties reflect the needs of the young and growing population: the most common specialty is pediatrics, which accounted for 21 percent of all physicians in 1985, followed by general practitioners (15 percent), obstetricians (6 percent), public health specialists (6 percent), and physicians specializing in

the prevention and treatment of epidemic diseases (6 percent). Medical services are provided at five levels:

(a) In the rural areas, medical services are provided at "feldsher" units. These are available throughout the country and number about 1,400. Each feldsher is staffed by a physician assistant (a skilled professional with qualifications between a nurse and a doctor) and serves people within a 30-40 km radius, mostly providing outpatient services. Since it is lowest level in the system, it also screens and refers cases up the hierarchy.

(b) The somon or district level is the first referral step and served by a hospital with 10 to 50 beds and up to five doctors (depending upon the population in the service area). Each doctor supervises about five feldsher physician assistants. There are about 294 such hospitals, each serving a 40-60 km radius and each has an ambulance.

(c) The 32 inter-somon hospitals are the second referral level. As they provide only four specialty areas (therapy, treatment of infections, delivery/gynecology, pediatrics), this level is usually bypassed. These hospitals will be converted soon to somon hospitals since, in practice, they tend to provide services in only one somon.

(d) Aimag level facilities comprise a hospital with 150-200 beds and ten or more doctors. They provide referral services for the somon hospitals. Surgery and dental care are also provided at this level.

(e) The fourth referral level consists of seven specialized centers, four general hospitals and a number of clinics in Ulaanbaatar. These are equipped to perform operations such as heart surgery and research.

129. Sanitary and Epidemiological Services. Services in this area aim at providing the minimum acceptable hygienic conditions for new construction and existing housing stock, workplaces, water and food quality as well as prevention of infectious diseases. These services come under the jurisdiction of the National Inspectorate for Hygiene and Epidemiology, the National Center for Control of Infectious Diseases, and the National Center for Disinfection. Services are provided throughout the country and there are inspectorates and stations for hygiene and epidemiology, and disinfection in somon, aimag, and city centers.

130. Manufacturing and Distribution of Medicines and Medical Hardware. Two central organizations, Mongolemimpex and Medicaltechnick, are responsible for supplying drugs and equipment to health institutions. All medical equipment and 90 percent of medicines are imported. The remaining 10 percent are produced locally using imported raw materials.

131. Medical Education and Research. The Medical University of Ulaanbaatar is the primary institution for professional education and awarding the MD degree. It graduates about 300 students per year. There are also four other medical colleges in Ulaanbaatar, Darkhan, Saynshand, and Altay and a nursing school in Ulaanbaatar. About 1,500 students graduate from these

institutions each year; 400-500 nurses; the remainder, technicians and paramedics. Until 1990, these institutions were managed jointly by the Ministries of Health and Education. However, the Ministry of Health is no longer involved in their administration. It is now only responsible for training at hospitals. Most medical personnel (85 percent) receive their training in Mongolia. There are a number of research and specialized institutions: the Medical Research Institute, the Research Center for Maternal and Child Health, the National Institute of Hygiene, Epidemiology and Microbiology, the Institute of Traditional Medicine, the Methodological Center for Health Education, the Center for Health Statistics and Information.

Reforms

132. Under the reform program, the authorities plan to move from the current system of free health services to one covered by health insurance and user fees. As part of this transition, an experiment is being undertaken in selected somons in which practitioners are given control of budgets but must pay for the cost of hospitalizations they recommend, the intent being to encourage more careful screening. The Ministry of Health is also encouraging decentralization and privatization of services, in line with developments in other sectors. The government has been encouraging private and cooperative practice for doctors since 1990. However, few doctors have opted to set up private practice although it is too early to assess the impact of this policy change.

133. Mongolia has signed the Alma Ata declaration of health cure for all by the year 2000. Improving services for women and children, both in terms of facilities and quality, has been made a priority. In 1987 there was a major policy change in favor of family planning. International organizations are also becoming increasingly involved in the health sector of Mongolia. WHO prepared an initial draft Country Profile in November 1991; it also sent a multidonor (including the World Bank) health sector mission in June 1992.

134. The Ministry of Health has prepared a National Health Development Program covering up to 2025. It aims at a comprehensive restructuring of the sector but its details are not yet available.

Issues

135. As pointed out, health expenditures have been falling since 1988. This suggests that financial restructuring of the sector should be given a priority to guarantee the maintenance of satisfactory health services. Without some form of user fees, the current system does not seem to be sustainable. It also implies that the efficiency of resource use in the sector should be improved and preventive measures emphasized. The Mongolian government recognizes this situation and has some broad ideas about the reforms. For example, to improve financial control, accountability, and management in the sector, the government plans to move to a health insurance system in stages. At the same time the government wants this plan to be flexible enough to reflect Mongolian conditions since part of the population will not be able to pay user fees. However, the details of this program are not yet available, and the government needs technical assistance to design and implement such a plan. This is one area in which assistance from multilateral agencies should

be valuable. A detailed sector study is needed to identify priority areas both in the medium and long term.

136. Another important issue is coordinating the efforts of bilateral donors. Without such coordination, there is a danger that well-intentioned bilateral efforts may focus on centralized and high-technology-intensive curative treatment, rather than supporting the evolution of the system in a more decentralized and preventive direction. The Bank plans to collaborate with WHO in the next steps of the exploratory effort and has allocated funds under the recently approved Technical Assistance Project for follow up sector studies.

137. Mongolia is almost totally dependent upon imports of medicines and pharmaceuticals. Economic crisis has led to shortages of basic medicines, and infant mortality and meningococcal infections rose during 1991. To find a long-term solution to the problem, the government is considering to producing medicines locally and training the necessary staff. The cost effectiveness of this proposal, given Mongolia's small population and the large resources required to bring domestic drug manufacturing up to acceptable standards, should be carefully examined.

138. The logistics of providing health services continue to be problematic. This is further complicated by inadequate communications and transportation means. Ambulances have no wireless; in winter, some areas are hard to reach; and medical personnel have to cover large areas, in some cases 100 km^2.

139. A longer term issue in the health sector is the concentration of physicians in the urban areas. In 1981, Ulaanbaatar had 49 percent of all Mongolia's physicians and an average of 42.9 physicians per 10,000 people. The cities of Darhan and Erdenet had 21.7 and 18.8 physicians per 10,000 people, respectively. On the other hand, the low ratios of 9.5 doctors per 10,000 in Uvs aimag and 10.2 per 10,000 in Hovsgol aimag were also reported. Reforms will have to take this factor into account and devise incentives for physicians to stay in rural areas in sufficient numbers, particularly considering that, with the privatization of agricultural lands and animal stock, a significant percentage of population is expected to go back to the rural areas.

Environment

Overview

140. Mongolia's renewable natural resource endowment is severely limited by its harsh climate. Its limited precipitation (averaging 220 mm per annum) is unevenly distributed, both temporally and geographically, and most of it is lost to evapotranspiration and cross-boundary surface flow. Mongolia's climate is gradually becoming drier. Separated from the ocean's moderating influence, daily and annual temperature fluctuations are great. Because of the country's latitude and high elevation, average temperatures are very low, below freezing for a large part of the country. Winds are intense at the end of winter.

141. Abundant water supplies exist only in certain areas in the north of the country. The rates of humus production, vegetative regeneration and growth, and livestock productivity are very low throughout the country compared to other countries in Asia. Natural ecosystems are relatively fragile, highly susceptible to degradation by human activities, and slow to recover. Desertification is a problem in the south.

142. Given Mongolia's high population growth rate and heavy industrialization during the past few decades, the sustainable rates of use or loss of renewable natural resources, including surface water, ground water, forest, soil, fishery, and rangeland resources, have been exceeded in some areas. The situation is likely to become more widespread if current trends continue, without measures to conserve and manage natural resources. Past policy has not paid sufficient attention to planning natural resource utilization, restoration, and protection. This has led to both the loss and depletion of natural resources and the degradation of environmental quality as seen in contamination of the atmosphere, surface water, and soil mainly around urban areas.

143. In December 1990, the government adopted a strong policy aimed at protecting the environment and encouraging rational use of natural resources, under a general environmental law and five resource specific laws passed earlier.3/ Responsibility for policy implementation rests with the State Committee for Environmental Control (SCEC). The Environmental Monitoring and Meteorological (EMM) program has established monitoring stations capable of basic biological, chemical and physical analysis of water, analysis of soils for the presence of metals, and the collection of meteorological data. Other programs include the development of a capacity within SCEC to receive and process Landsat images in order to analyze and quantify trends in vegetative pattern changes and the implications for natural resources.

144. Nongovernmental organizations such as The Mongolian Association for the Conservation of Nature and the Environment (MACNE), the Green Party, and the Mongolian Women's Federation are active in the environmental field. MACNE has a membership exceeding 600,000 and its goals are to include the preservation of traditional methods of natural resource use, preservation of unique environmental heritage, environmental education and training, environmental research, and mass media advocacy of environmental protection.

Structure of the Sector

145. Water Resources. Of fundamental importance to environmental management is the generally low average precipitation. Rainwater averages 361.1 km^3 per annum of which 90 percent--an extremely high rate compared to other parts of the world--returns to the atmosphere through evapotranspiration. Of the balance, only about 6 percent is available as surface runoff (most of this flowing out of the country) and only about 3 percent infiltrates into the soil to replenish aquifers.

3/ These are the laws for: land resources; air quality protection; water; forestry and hunting; and mining and mineral laws.

146. A rapid rise in demand for water, combined with increased economic activity in key watersheds, has caused a reduction in lake, river flow, and water table levels. Untreated and primary-treated domestic and industrial wastewater discharge has caused significant levels of surface water contamination. The incidence and severity of ground water contamination is unknown. River pollution has already imposed a significant cost to Ulaanbaatar which must draw its water from a course 60 km away, although the Tuula river flows through the city.

147. Addressing these issues will require: comprehensive watershed hydrology and aquifer hydrogeology research; water utilization planning; water quality monitoring system; wastewater discharge elimination programs; and expansion of water storage, distribution, and metering infrastructure.

148. Land Resources. The total land area of 156 million ha comprises the four biogeographic regions: high mountains; forest-steppe (interspersed forests and grasslands); steppe (grasslands); and gobi (arid lands with sparse vegetation). Of the total land area, 79 percent is grassland and arid grassland. Forests and shrublands are estimated to comprise 10 percent; sandy areas 3 percent; settlements, plowed farmland, and infrastructure 2.7 percent; and area covered by water 1 percent. The remainder are glaciated and rocky areas. About 55 percent of the country's forests are considered inaccessible, being on gradients in excess of 22 degrees. Mongolian environmental experts consider most if not all, forest to be critical for watershed protection, and suggest it not be exploited. Some 126 million ha (80 percent of total land area) is devoted to agriculture of which only 1 percent (1.3 million ha) is cultivated, mainly in the north-central part of the country.

149. Overgrazing, deforestation (including loss of forests to fire and insect damage), erosion, and desertification have caused significant degradation of land resources. Crop cultivation has led to soil erosion as Mongolia's climatic conditions make high levels of soil loss associated with soil-tilling almost inevitable. Climatic change, involving a gradual reduction in annual precipitation, contributes to desertification and wind erosion. Other detrimental activities include overland vehicular traffic and improper waste disposal from mining. Given the wide range of factors contributing to land erosion, a multifaceted approach to reversing land resource degradation trends is needed, including in-depth land use planning, infrastructure development, and reforestation.

150. Air Quality. Air pollution is caused by: soft coal-fired cooking and heating stoves of individual dwellings, soft coal-fired thermal electric power plants, industry, and vehicles. The problem is intensified by stationary temperature inversions over the country during the long winter, accompanied by low winds. Measures to address this issue include: fuel and heating technology substitution in individual dwellings; upgrading of the thermal electric power plants; and controls on industrial and vehicular pollutant emissions. Mongolia does not produce CFCs or release significant amounts of ozone-depleting substances. While its per capita rate of greenhouse gas generation is higher than the world average, it is a fraction of that of Europe and North America.

151. Wildlife. Large, relatively undisturbed wildlife areas cover a broad range of habitats. Rich wildlife and biodiversity resources exist, including: 134 species of mammals (59 exploited for commercial purposes), 415 species of birds (128 exploited), 70 species of fish (30 exploited), 9 species of reptiles, 8 species of amphibians, 15,000 species of insects. Of the several thousand species of plants, about 10 percent are considered unique to Mongolia, and many are exploited for nutritional and medicinal purposes. There are 13 nature reserves and parks. Among these, the Great Gobi National Park Reserve has been designated as a Biosphere Reserve under the UNESCO Man-and-Biosphere Program. An extensive program of wildlife research, and a concerted effort to develop a system of reserves based on the results of this research, is greatly needed. Considering Mongolia's many biodiversity resources and their high value to the global community, the considerable finance required to develop a comprehensive program for their protection, and Mongolia's limited funding sources, Mongolia should seek out internationally funded programs aimed at protecting biological diversity.

152. Waste and Toxic Substance Management. All forms of wastes are dumped into open disposal areas with minimal control or site management. Current waste and toxic substance management programs in Mongolia are inadequate to ensure the isolation of contaminants from the environment and human exposure. Development of an effective waste and toxic substance management program is urgent, for both the environment and human health.

Issues

153. The most urgent environmental and natural resource issues are:

(a) protection and better management of the supply and quality of water resources; land resources; atmospheric quality; and biological diversity;

(b) environmentally sound management of wastes and toxic chemicals, including introduction of an environmental pricing policy based on "the polluter pays" principle and marketable pollution rights; and

(c) paying more attention to environmental sustainability of projects, in particular for mining activities and energy plants.

STATISTICAL ANNEX

LIST OF TABLES

Table 1.1: POPULATION AND EMPLOYMENT, 1979-92

(in thousands)

	1979	1981	1982	1983	1984	1985	1986	1987	1988	1989	1990	1991	1992
Total population /a, /b	1,595.0	1,682.0	1,724.7	1,767.5	1,808.9	1,854.3	1,900.6	1,949.7	1,997.0	2,044.0	2,095.6	2,149.3	2,182.3
Males	798.9	842.7	864.1	885.5	906.2	929.0	952.2	976.7	999.5	1,020.7	1,045.9	1,072.3	1,089.0
Females	796.1	839.3	860.6	882.0	902.7	925.3	948.4	973.0	997.5	1,023.3	1,049.7	1,077.0	1,093.3
Urban	817.1	861.2	888.2	919.1	949.7	982.8	1,016.8	1,052.8	1,098.3	1,166.1	1,193.6	1,225.1	1,200.3
Rural	777.9	820.8	836.5	848.4	859.2	871.5	883.8	896.9	898.7	877.9	902.0	924.2	982.0
By age groups /a, /b													
Under 16	746.3	n.a.	n.a.	n.a.	n.a.	n.a.	n.a.	n.a.	n.a.	904.3	920.6	936.9	..
Active age	710.9	n.a.	n.a.	n.a.	n.a.	n.a.	n.a.	n.a.	n.a.	995.1	1,028.2	1,061.9	..
Over active age	137.8	n.a.	n.a.	n.a.	n.a.	n.a.	n.a.	n.a.	n.a.	144.6	146.8	150.5	..

/a At the beginning of the year.
/b Figures for 1979 and 1989 are census data of January 5.

Source: State Statistical Office.

Table 1.2. VITAL STATISTICS, 1940-91
(Per thousand population)

	Crude birth rate	Crude death rate	Natural increase
1940	26.1	21.8	4.3
1951	13.9	9.6	4.3
1960	43.2	10.5	32.7
1970	40.2	12.3	27.9
1980	39.2	10.8	28.4
1985	38.2	10.3	27.9
1988	38.5	9.0	29.5
1989	36.4	8.4	28.0
1990	35.3	8.5	26.8
1991	32.9	8.8	24.1

Sources: National Economy of the MPR for 70 Years (1921-1991), Anniversary Statistical Yearbook, (Several data of 1990 are preliminary), State Statistical Office of the MPR, Ulaanbaatar, 1991, Table 2.8. pp. 18-9. and Asian Development Bank.

Table 1.3: EMPLOYMENT BY SECTOR, 1970-91
(Thousands, yearly average)

	1970	1980	1985	1986	1987	1988	1989	1990	1991*
Total	387.4	511.2	561.6	580.9	598.4	616.1	633.2	651.4	688.1
Sector									
Material	312.3	388.3	413.2	426.6	435.5	443.3	451.4	468.8	492.3
Agriculture	181.9	202.7	187.0	185.8	184.8	183.6	186.0	178.3	180.4
Forestry	1.2	0.9	1.2	1.2	1.2	1.6	2.1	2.6	-
Industry	60.0	81.6	104.6	109.9	115.6	119.2	119.6	135.6	145.3
Construction	22.5	30.7	33.9	35.5	37.2	38.9	41.7	51.4	55.3
Transport	18.0	32.3	38.7	43.4	44.6	47.4	47.0	50.8	53.2
Communications	3.1	4.2	5.5	5.8	6.1	6.1	6.9	7.1	9.0
Trade (retail and wholesale)	25.4	35.0	41.7	44.4	45.4	46.0	47.5	42.4	44.1
Other material production	0.2	0.9	0.6	0.6	0.6	0.5	0.6	0.6	4.5
Nonmaterial	75.1	122.9	148.4	154.3	162.9	172.8	181.8	182.6	195.8
Housing and municipal services	8.0	14.3	20.0	20.9	23.3	24.3	26.4	27.4	29.4
Science, research and development	3.7	9.0	10.3	10.7	11.3	12.9	14.1	12.9	13.6
Education, culture and arts	30.4	49.2	58.7	60.4	63.1	70.5	74.6	69.5	74.2
Health care, social security, sports	20.2	32.0	37.3	39.7	42.2	42.9	44.7	44.1	46.3
Banking, finance, credit, insurance	1.1	1.9	2.1	2.4	2.5	2.6	2.9	3.1	4.0
Government	8.1	11.5	13.9	13.9	13.9	12.8	12.3	20.8	23.0
Other nonmaterial	3.6	5.0	6.1	6.3	6.6	6.8	6.8	4.9	5.3

* - provisional.

Source: State Statistical Office.

Table 1.4: EMPLOYMENT BY ENTERPRISE TYPE, 1989-90
(End of year)

	1989	1990	Percent of Total 1989	Percent of Total 1990
	(Thousands)			
Total labor force	928.0	965.4	100.0	100.0
Of working age /a	905.0	942.9	97.5	97.7
Below working age	2.7	2.2	0.3	0.2
Over working age	16.3	16.3	1.8	1.7
Foreigners	4.0	4.0	0.4	0.4
Total employed /b	764.1	783.6	100.0	
In material sector	549.1	571.4	71.9	72.9
Of which:				
State enterprises	339.1	338.5	44.4	43.2
Cooperatives	188.3	200.0	24.6	25.5
Private part-time	7.9	9.3	1.0	1.2
Unregistered forms	} 13.8	23.6	1.9	3.0
Private enterprises	}			
In nonmaterial sector	215.0	212.5	28.1	27.1
Of which:				
State enterprises	209.7	210.7	27.4	26.9
Cooperatives	4.5	0.6	0.7	0.1
Private enterprises	0.8	1.2	0.1	0.2

/a 16-60 years for men and 16-55 years for women.
/b Average.

Source: State Statistical Office.

Table 1.5: EMPLOYEES IN THE STATE SECTOR, 1989-90
(thousands)

	Tot. No. of Employees 1989	1990	Of Which 1989
Agriculture	44.2	40.1	33.2
Forestry	2.1	2.6	1.0
Industry	107.4	114.6	83.5
Construction	36.4	46.4	27.5
Transport	42.8	42.8	34.2
Communications	6.9	7.1	5.0
Wholesale and retail trade	47.4	40.6	25.5
Other branches of material production	0.6	0.6	0.1
Housing and municipal services	25.7	23.1	n.a.
Science, research and development	14.1	12.9	n.a.
Education, culture and arts	72.5	68.8	n.a.
Public health, social insurance, sport and tourism	43.4	43.6	n.a.
Finance, credit, insurance	2.9	3.0	n.a.
Administration	12.3	12.8	n.a.
Other branches of nonproductive sphere	6.8	4.9	n.a.
Total	465.5	471.9	210.0

Source: State Statistical Office.

Table 2.1: NATIONAL ACCOUNT ESTIMATES AT CURRENT AND CONSTANT PRICES, 1984-90
(Millions of Tugriks)

	1984	1985	1986	1987	1988	1989	1990
1. CURRENT PRICES							
Agriculture	1,361.5	1,353.9	1,663.7	1,568.8	1,683.0	1,831.0	1,820.0
Industry /a	2,578.1	2,767.1	2,974.6	3,245.9	3,482.6	3,680.6	3,549.6
Services	2,914.5	3,078.6	2,992.7	3,230.7	3,505.0	3,455.8	3,627.0
GDP at factor cost	6,854.0	7,199.6	7,631.0	8,045.4	8,670.6	8,968.0	8,996.6
Indirect Taxes	2,699.9	2,735.9	2,295.1	2,281.1	2,217.9	2,406.2	2,087.6
Subsidies (-)	558.2	563.6	616.1	616.9	587.6	643.3	570.1
GDP at market prices	8,995.7	9,371.9	9,310.0	9,709.6	10,300.9	10,730.9	10,514.1
Imports of goods and nonfactor services	4,781.4	5,219.3	5,990.3	5,447.3	5,554.6	6,053.2	5,246.8
Exports of goods and nonfactor services	2,300.0	2,368.8	2,623.5	2,617.9	2,668.7	2,496.5	2,410.3
Resource Gap	2,481.4	2,850.5	3,366.8	2,829.4	2,886.0	3,556.7	2,836.5
Public Consumption	1,869.0	1,961.1	2,272.5	2,383.7	2,474.6	2,491.5	2,562.4
Private Consumption	5,045.8	4,787.6	4,220.5	5,718.0	6,377.8	6,854.8	7,645.9
Total Consumption	6,914.8	6,748.7	6,493.0	8,101.7	8,852.4	9,346.3	10,208.3
Government Investment	..	..	..	..	..	441.8	412.5
Public Enterprise and Private Investment	..	..	..	..	..	4,365.1	2,967.3
Change in Stocks	280.5	839.9	1,421.3	-114.9	-203.4	134.4	-237.5
Total Investment	4,562.3	5,473.7	6,183.8	4,437.3	4,334.5	4,941.3	3,142.3
2. CONSTANT 1990 PRICES							
GDP at market prices	8,279.0	8,664.4	9,380.8	9,803.9	10,304.7	10,735.5	10,514.1
Imports of goods and nonfactor services	6,479.9	7,138.3	7,030.7	6,576.2	6,508.3	5,578.1	5,246.8
Exports of goods and nonfactor services	2,795.5	2,689.7	2,988.8	2,886.7	2,836.4	2,671.5	2,410.3
Resource Gap	3,684.4	4,448.5	4,041.8	3,689.5	3,671.9	2,906.6	2,836.5
Public Consumption	2,045.7	2,275.1	2,648.2	2,726.7	2,760.7	2,452.8	2,562.4
Private Consumption	5,522.8	5,554.1	4,918.3	6,540.9	7,115.2	6,748.2	7,645.9
Total Consumption	7,568.4	7,829.2	7,566.5	9,267.6	9,875.9	9,201.0	10,208.3
Government Investment	..	..	..	..	..	397.1	412.5
Public Enterprise and Private Investment /b	..	..	..	..	..	4,044.0	2,729.8
Total Investment	4,395.0	5,283.7	5,856.1	4,225.8	4,100.7	4,441.1	3,142.3

/a Includes construction.
/b Includes change in stocks.

Sources: State Statistical Office and World Bank estimates.

Table 2.2: COMPOSITION OF GROSS DOMESTIC PRODUCT AT CURRENT FACTOR COST, 1980-90
(Percentages)

	1980	1981	1982	1983	1984	1985	1986	1987	1988	1989	1990
Total GDP at factor cost	100.0	100.0	100.0	100.0	100.0	100.0	100.0	100.0	100.0	100.0	100.0
of which:											
Agriculture	18.6	19.9	20.9	21.2	19.9	18.8	21.8	19.5	19.4	20.4	20.2
Industry	29.2	29.0	29.8	30.9	31.9	32.8	32.8	33.5	33.0	34.1	33.8
Construction	7.1	6.6	6.0	5.6	5.7	5.7	6.2	6.8	7.2	7.0	5.7
Transport	13.6	13.7	13.3	12.9	13.3	13.8	13.5	13.1	12.7	11.6	11.3
Communications	1.3	1.5	1.5	1.6	1.7	1.7	1.7	1.7	1.8	1.8	1.9
Trade and catering	9.7	9.3	9.9	9.7	9.3	9.1	5.3	6.6	7.1	7.1	9.1
Other material sphere	2.0	1.9	1.8	1.7	1.7	1.6	1.8	1.7	1.5	1.6	1.4
Non-material services	18.7	18.3	16.9	16.3	16.5	16.6	17.0	17.1	17.4	16.4	16.5

Source: World Bank staff estimates based on data from the State Statistical Office.

Table 2.3: SOURCES AND USES OF NET MATERIAL PRODUCT, CURRENT PRICES, 1970-91

(in millions of Tugriks)

	1970	1975	1980	1981	1982	1983	1984	1985	1986	1987	1988	1989	1990	1991
Sources	3,135.2	4,511.7	5,576.9	6,150.6	6,825.7	7,325.3	7,378.1	7,636.5	7,247.6	7,478.7	7,889.9	8,646.0	8,327.5	11,598.8
Agriculture	793.0	1,012.3	838.3	1,007.7	1,219.5	1,320.1	1,250.2	1,237.7	1,520.7	1,405.5	1,510.0	1,722.9	1,686.9	2,944.1
Industry	708.9	1,112.3	1,634.6	1,806.8	2,110.6	2,358.2	2,383.6	2,493.3	2,442.8	2,519.5	2,639.1	2,919.8	2,915.1	4,792.0
Construction	182.3	245.7	342.1	342.3	346.1	352.6	367.5	382.0	423.1	503.8	563.1	617.2	462.3	530.0
Distribution & warehousing	1,144.3	1,632.1	2,024.5	2,210.9	2,307.9	2,400.4	2,436.4	2,516.3	1,865.2	2,036.2	2,129.8	2,327.4	2,280.5	202.8
Other sectors	306.7	509.3	737.4	782.9	841.6	894.0	940.4	1,007.2	995.8	1,013.7	1,047.9	1,058.7	982.7	1,310.9
Uses	3,386.9	4,415.8	5,414.6	6,028.6	6,613.7	7,164.7	7,162.5	7,420.1	7,083.2	7,098.4	7,492.1	8,521.8	7,869.4	-
Personal consumption	1,960.6	2,712.3	3,500.5	3,647.1	3,856.4	4,068.1	4,262.5	4,429.5	4,618.7	4,844.4	5,066.7	5,348.3	5,746.1	-
Public consumption	420.3	728.4	1,128.6	1,388.5	1,446.0	1,543.2	1,632.3	1,739.5	1,928.5	1,997.0	2,147.9	2,174.8	2,040.3	-
Accumulation	1,156.0	2,081.0	2,615.3	3,640.5	3,629.3	3,857.8	3,618.8	4,140.8	4,105.5	3,214.3	3,115.3	3,590.0	2,283.9	-
Fixed investment	1,143.7	1,662.4	2,882.5	2,358.4	2,642.6	2,544.4	4,298.5	4,759.0	2,505.8	3,213.3	2,824.9	3,195.5	806.6	-
Change in stocks	195.3	484.3	169.1	381.1	533.9	645.1	392.4	655.7	581.6	(114.9)	(203.4)	134.4	205.6	-
Changes in incomplete projects	(183.0)	(65.7)	(436.3)	901.0	452.8	668.3	(1,072.1)	(1,273.9)	1,018.1	115.9	493.8	260.1	1,271.7	-
Net exports	(150.0)	(1,105.9)	(1,829.8)	(2,647.5)	(2,318.0)	(2,304.4)	(2,351.1)	(2,889.7)	(3,569.5)	(2,957.3)	(2,837.8)	(2,591.3)	(2,200.9)	-
Exports /a	459.2	784.5	1,343.2	1,583.4	1,923.6	2,082.1	2,343.5	2,237.2	2,508.6	2,670.4	2,616.7	2,309.2	2,238.9	-
Imports /b	609.2	1,890.4	3,173.0	4,230.9	4,241.6	4,386.5	4,694.6	5,126.9	6,078.1	5,627.7	5,454.5	4,900.5	4,439.8	-
Statistical discrepancy /c	(251.7)	95.9	162.3	122.0	212.0	160.6	215.6	216.4	164.4	380.3	397.8	124.2	458.1	-

/a Exports measured at domestic prices.

/b Imports include turnkey projects.

/c Includes production losses.

Source: State Statistical Office.

Table 2.4: SOURCES OF NET MATERIAL PRODUCT, CONSTANT (1986) PRICES, 1970–91
(in millions of Tugriks)

	1970	1975	1980	1981	1982	1983	1984	1985	1986	1987	1988	1989	1990	1991 /a
Sources	2,726.1	3,774.1	4,939.8	5,353.3	5,802.1	6,157.7	6,434.0	6,776.7	7,153.5	7,400.7	7,712.6	8,461.9	8,147.9	6,223.2
Agriculture	903.0	1,083.1	1,004.9	1,111.9	1,268.9	1,280.7	1,232.4	1,348.1	1,426.6	1,335.7	1,367.1	1,556.3	1,525.6	1,420.2
Industry	534.8	967.2	1,575.2	1,714.3	1,897.9	2,085.8	2,267.7	2,390.0	2,442.8	2,511.3	2,604.6	2,902.3	2,892.8	2,537.1
Construction	182.3	245.7	342.1	342.3	346.1	352.6	367.5	382.0	423.1	503.8	563.1	617.2	454.4	323.0
Distribution & warehousing	829.6	1,023.0	1,365.0	1,493.3	1,545.8	1,649.5	1,737.6	1,770.8	1,865.2	2,036.2	2,129.9	2,327.4	2,280.5	1,145.0
Other sectors	276.4	455.1	652.6	691.5	743.4	789.1	828.8	885.8	995.8	1,013.7	1,047.9	1,058.7	994.6	797.9

/a Provisional.

Source: State Statistical Office.

Table 2.5 COMPOSITION OF NET MATERIAL PRODUCT AND GROSS DOMESTIC PRODUCT, 1980-91
(Millions of tugriks at Current Prices)

	1980	1981	1982	1983	1984	1985	1986	1987	1988	1989	1990	1991 /a
A. Net material product (A1+A2)	5,576.9	6,150.6	6,825.7	7,325.3	7,378.1	7,636.5	7,247.6	7,478.7	7,889.9	8,646.0	8,327.5	11,598.8
A1. Primary income of the population	2,123.8	2,186.0	2,330.7	2,498.9	2,539.6	2,641.5	2,806.6	2,884.1	2,989.7	3,201.2	3,269.0	
a. Wages and salaries of employees in non-material sphere	692.2	737.0	758.0	786.4	810.1	847.3	880.6	923.5	989.4	1,044.5	1,077.9	
b. Income from personal and subsidiary plots of the population	262.7	277.6	289.3	311.5	329.1	353.9	371.3	410.4	440.9	449.2	489.7	
c. Employers contributions to social security in	155.5	164.1	169.5	178.5	187.6	198.2	209.0	219.5	231.6	242.1	246.1	
c1. material sphere	113.1	118.7	123.8	134.4	140.4	148.2	162.8	167.0	170.2	180.2	185.7	
non-material sphere	42.4	45.4	45.7	44.1	47.2	50.0	46.2	52.5	61.4	61.9	60.4	
d. Business travel expenses	20.2	21.3	30.9	37.9	42.9	42.1	44.3	46.1	53.0	50.2	49.6	
material sphere	20.2	21.3	30.9	37.9	42.9	42.1	44.3	46.1	53.0	50.2	49.6	
non-material sphere	n.a.	n.a.	n.a.	n.a.	n.a.	n.a.	n.a.	n.a.	n.a.	n.a.	n.a.	
B1. Compensation of employees (A1+a-b+c-d)	2,688.6	2,788.2	2,938.0	3,114.4	3,165.3	3,291.0	3,480.6	3,570.6	3,716.8	3,988.4	4,053.7	
A2. Primary income of the enterprises	3,453.1	3,964.6	4,495.0	4,826.4	4,838.5	4,995.0	4,441.0	4,594.6	4,900.2	5,444.8	5,058.5	
e. Operating surplus and taxes of non-budgetary units in non-material sphere	100.0	120.0	142.3	150.0	165.0	177.5	200.1	227.7	247.5	223.2	188.7	
f. Purchase of non-material services in material sphere	59.8	79.3	92.1	96.1	100.9	112.0	103.3	111.6	93.3	84.0	80.7	
g. Expenditure in connection with the provision of cultural etc. facilities in material sphere	n.a.	n.a.	n.a.	n.a.	n.a.	n.a.	n.a.	n.a.	n.a.	n.a.	n.a.	
h. Losses in stocks	730.8	771.8	805.1	830.5	853.3	895.0	762.0	805.3	850.3	1,261.0	1,298.8	
B2. Operating surplus including net indirect taxes (A2+e+b-c1-f-g-h)	2,912.1	3,392.4	3,905.6	4,226.9	4,238.0	4,371.2	3,984.3	4,148.8	4,474.8	4,592.0	4,171.7	
B3. Consumption of fixed capital /b	1,154.2	1,245.7	1,361.7	1,427.1	1,592.4	1,709.7	1,845.1	1,990.4	2,109.4	2,150.5	2,288.7	2,332.2
B. Gross domestic product (B1+B2+B3)	6,754.9	7,426.3	8,205.3	8,768.4	8,995.7	9,371.9	9,310.0	9,709.8	10,301.0	10,730.9	10,514.1	15,071.0

/a Provisional.
/b Including undepriciated value of scrapped fixed assets.

Source: State Statistical Office.

Table 2.6 COMPOSITION OF NATIONAL PRODUCT BY SECTOR, 1980-91
(Million tugriks at Current Prices)

	1980	1981	1982	1983	1984	1985	1986	1987	1988	1989	1990	1991p
						TOTAL MATERIAL SECTORS						
National product	10,915.4	11,952.7	13,084.9	14,081.6	14,624.7	15,561.3	16,911.0	17,646.1	18,360.5	19,261.7	18,193.8	28,780.3
Material input	5,338.5	5,802.1	6,259.2	6,756.3	7,246.6	7,924.8	9,663.4	10,167.4	10,470.6	10,615.7	9,866.3	17,181.5
of which: depreciation	986.1	1,056.8	1,154.5	1,214.5	1,367.5	1,460.9	1,567.4	1,697.0	1,771.1	1,833.0	1,973.7	--
National income (NI)	5,576.9	6,150.6	6,825.7	7,325.3	7,378.1	7,636.5	7,247.6	7,478.7	7,889.9	8,646.0	8,327.5	11,598.8
of which:												
Wages and salaries	1,959.3	2,018.8	2,138.7	2,297.2	2,356.0	2,464.9	2,617.0	2,753.7	2,842.9	3,041.1	3,149.7	--
Other income	212.8	231.2	365.9	394.7	495.5	461.1	125.9	150.9	178.9	345.7	379.4	--
Turnover tax	1,990.4	2,183.7	2,245.6	2,362.9	2,428.7	2,435.7	1,936.6	1,916.6	1,897.9	2,106.6	2,016.3	--
Profits/losses	1,301.3	1,598.2	1,951.7	2,136.1	1,957.5	2,126.6	2,405.3	2,490.5	2,800.0	2,972.4	2,596.4	--
Social security contributions	113.1	118.7	123.8	134.4	140.4	148.2	162.8	167.0	170.2	180.2	185.7	--
Memo items: NI - Turnover tax	3,586.5	3,966.9	4,580.1	4,962.4	4,949.4	5,200.8	5,311.0	5,562.1	5,992.0	6,539.4	6,311.2	--
NI + depreciation - Turnover tax	4,572.6	5,023.7	5,734.6	6,176.9	6,316.9	6,661.7	6,878.4	7,259.1	7,763.1	8,372.4	8,284.9	--
						Industry						
National product	4,636.2	5,162.8	5,775.1	6,316.1	6,704.9	7,213.6	8,195.2	8,542.2	8,797.8	9,243.7	8,887.4	14,567.8
Material input	3,001.6	3,356.0	3,664.5	3,957.9	4,321.3	4,720.3	5,752.4	6,022.7	6,158.7	6,323.9	5,972.3	9,775.8
of which: depreciation	449.6	451.4	498.1	529.4	649.1	688.9	702.0	788.7	822.1	906.9	994.6	--
National income (NI)	1,634.6	1,806.8	2,110.6	2,358.2	2,383.6	2,493.3	2,442.8	2,519.5	2,639.1	2,919.8	2,915.1	4,792.0
of which:												
Wages and salaries	483.4	490.9	519.8	569.2	606.9	644.5	685.2	745.5	717.5	819.2	819.4	--
Other income	53.5	67.5	83.6	115.0	88.7	76.9	64.1	61.3	58.0	50.8	39.1	--
Turnover tax	445.6	473.3	554.2	606.0	620.4	565.4	428.0	372.1	360.7	412.3	554.1	--
Profits/losses	610.0	730.4	905.9	1,016.1	1,012.2	1,147.7	1,203.6	1,275.7	1,435.5	1,561.6	1,427.4	--
Social security contributions	42.1	44.7	47.1	51.9	55.4	58.8	61.9	64.9	67.4	75.9	75.1	--
Memo items: NI - Turnover tax	1,189.0	1,333.5	1,556.4	1,752.2	1,763.2	1,927.9	2,014.8	2,147.4	2,278.4	2,507.5	2,361.0	--
NI + depreciation - Turnover tax	1,638.6	1,784.9	2,054.5	2,281.6	2,412.3	2,616.8	2,716.8	2,936.1	3,100.5	3,414.4	3,355.6	--
						Construction						
National product	1,148.2	1,201.7	1,253.7	1,310.7	1,321.5	1,475.1	1,768.9	1,869.1	2,082.7	2,222.6	1,793.3	1,870.0
Material input	806.1	859.4	907.6	958.1	954.0	1,093.1	1,345.8	1,365.3	1,519.6	1,605.4	1,331.0	1,340.0
of which: depreciation	57.6	60.5	65.8	63.5	67.4	70.3	88.8	92.8	111.9	80.5	98.8	--
National income (NI)	342.1	342.3	346.1	352.6	367.5	382.0	423.1	503.8	563.1	617.2	462.3	530.0
of which:												
Wages and salaries	212.7	201.0	211.2	226.9	231.0	249.0	247.4	271.2	295.2	309.9	298.8	--
Other income	29.6	23.6	25.1	29.3	25.6	22.8	18.9	21.3	30.0	28.2	31.1	--
Turnover tax	--	--	--	--	--	--	--	--	--	--	--	--
Profits/losses	83.4	101.6	93.8	79.1	92.4	89.7	129.3	185.6	212.5	256.4	105.0	--
Social security contributions	16.4	16.1	16.0	17.3	18.5	20.5	27.5	25.7	25.4	22.7	27.4	--
Memo items: NI - Turnover tax	342.1	342.3	346.1	352.6	367.5	382.0	423.1	503.8	563.1	617.2	462.3	--
NI + depreciation - Turnover tax	399.7	402.8	411.9	416.1	434.9	452.3	511.9	596.6	675.0	697.7	561.1	--

p = Provisional.
(Continued)

Table 2.6 COMPOSITION OF NATIONAL PRODUCT BY SECTOR, 1980-91 (continued)
(Million tugriks at Current Prices)

	1980	1981	1982	1983	1984	1985	1986	1987	1988	1989	1990	1991p
Agriculture												
National product	1,624.2	1,790.6	2,041.5	2,222.9	2,225.7	2,279.9	2,720.8	2,750.3	2,847.8	2,967.3	2,858.4	5,165.2
Material input	785.9	782.9	822.0	902.8	975.5	1,042.2	1,200.1	1,344.8	1,337.8	1,244.4	1,171.5	2,221.1
of which: depreciation	204.8	216.5	221.7	241.8	253.4	263.9	285.2	301.9	314.5	323.5	321.3	--
National income (NI)	838.3	1,007.7	1,219.5	1,320.1	1,250.2	1,237.7	1,520.7	1,405.5	1,510.0	1,722.9	1,686.9	2,944.1
of which:												
Wages and salaries	865.1	897.6	962.5	1,035.1	1,054.0	1,080.0	1,174.1	1,188.5	1,252.2	1,315.4	1,373.1	--
Other income	(116.2)	(95.5)	(59.6)	(66.8)	62.1	64.3	(71.3)	(103.3)	(57.0)	17.3	(11.5)	--
Turnover tax	--	--	--	--	--	--	--	--	--	--	--	--
Profits/losses	71.6	186.7	296.1	328.8	111.6	70.1	392.5	294.9	288.9	364.8	297.6	--
Social security contributions	17.8	18.9	20.5	23.0	22.5	23.3	25.4	25.4	25.9	25.4	27.7	--
Memo items: NI - Turnover tax	838.3	1,007.7	1,219.5	1,320.1	1,250.2	1,237.7	1,520.7	1,405.5	1,510.0	1,722.9	1,686.9	--
NI + depreciation - Turnover tax	1,043.1	1,224.2	1,441.2	1,561.9	1,503.6	1,501.6	1,805.9	1,707.4	1,824.5	2,046.4	2,008.2	--
Transport												
National product	1,127.6	1,199.3	1,284.8	1,367.3	1,452.8	1,566.4	1,783.7	1,829.2	1,865.5	1,833.0	1,697.5	2,332.0
Material input	565.0	604.7	650.6	697.2	743.7	795.7	1,042.9	1,078.4	1,079.2	1,058.7	993.8	1,422.0
of which: depreciation	216.5	262.2	296.9	299.1	316.5	345.0	385.5	401.1	403.7	392.3	420.9	--
National income (NI)	562.6	594.6	634.2	670.1	709.1	770.7	740.8	750.8	786.3	774.3	703.7	910.0
of which:												
Wages and salaries	217.6	236.7	247.5	251.5	256.9	274.9	284.4	285.8	283.2	281.3	281.0	--
Other income	23.5	16.4	16.8	26.7	23.9	16.2	25.3	22.3	44.0	37.8	16.2	--
Turnover tax	17.4	17.5	14.6	15.1	16.4	17.1	7.4	9.0	--	--	--	--
Profits/losses	284.6	303.4	333.9	354.6	388.8	438.7	398.6	406.8	433.5	429.4	380.7	--
Social security contributions	19.5	20.6	21.4	22.2	23.1	23.8	25.1	26.9	25.6	25.8	25.8	--
Memo items: NI - Turnover tax	545.2	577.1	619.6	655.0	692.7	753.6	733.4	741.8	786.3	774.3	703.7	--
NI + depreciation - Turnover tax	761.7	839.3	916.5	954.1	1,009.2	1,098.6	1,118.9	1,142.9	1,190.0	1,166.6	1,124.6	--
Communications												
National product	97.4	118.1	132.9	148.3	158.8	172.7	196.0	207.5	219.8	235.2	236.9	335.4
Material input	36.0	43.8	49.5	51.7	54.5	63.2	91.6	97.2	100.2	105.7	99.3	140.6
of which: depreciation	15.0	20.6	25.1	26.6	27.7	34.7	42.0	44.4	46.4	51.4	53.2	--
National income (NI)	61.4	74.3	83.4	96.6	104.3	109.5	104.4	110.3	119.6	129.5	137.6	194.8
of which:												
Wages and salaries	19.0	21.0	22.6	23.5	24.2	25.3	26.8	28.2	29.6	31.5	33.6	--
Other income	1.5	2.1	2.1	2.3	1.5	1.8	1.4	1.4	1.4	1.8	3.5	--
Turnover tax	4.7	5.0	5.4	5.6	6.1	6.6	7.1	7.5	--	--	--	--
Profits/losses	34.4	44.2	51.2	63.0	70.1	73.4	66.5	70.5	85.8	93.2	97.3	--
Social security contributions	1.8	2.0	2.1	2.2	2.4	2.4	2.6	2.7	2.8	3.0	3.2	--
Memo items: NI - Turnover tax	56.7	69.3	78.0	91.0	98.2	102.9	97.3	102.8	119.6	129.5	137.6	--
NI + depreciation - Turnover tax	71.7	89.9	103.1	117.6	125.9	137.6	139.3	147.2	166.0	180.9	190.8	--

(Continued)

Table 2.6 COMPOSITION OF NATIONAL PRODUCT BY SECTOR, 1980-91 (continued)
(Million tugriks at Current Prices)

	1980	1981	1982	1983	1984	1985	1986	1987	1988	1989	1990	1991p
						Trade and catering						
National product	2,153.4	2,348.8	2,457.9	2,572.3	2,614.2	2,708.0	2,073.9	2,270.5	2,374.4	2,571.7	2,515.7	4,203.9
Material input	128.9	137.9	150.0	171.9	177.8	191.7	208.7	234.3	244.6	244.3	235.2	2,182.1
of which: depreciation	42.3	45.6	46.7	54.0	53.3	57.9	63.8	68.0	72.0	77.7	82.9	--
National income (NI)	2,024.5	2,210.9	2,307.9	2,400.4	2,436.4	2,516.3	1,865.2	2,036.2	2,129.8	2,327.4	2,280.5	2,021.8
of which:												
Wages and salaries	156.8	164.8	168.9	184.7	176.0	183.6	191.4	221.7	246.8	264.8	309.3	--
Other income	114.9	108.2	182.5	168.9	176.0	162.3	(52.9)	11.2	(15.8)	83.6	202.3	--
Turnover tax	1,522.7	1,687.9	1,671.4	1,736.2	1,785.8	1,846.6	1,494.1	1,528.0	1,537.2	1,694.3	1,462.2	--
Profits/losses	214.8	233.9	268.7	293.1	280.5	304.8	212.7	254.4	338.9	257.7	280.5	--
Social security contributions	15.3	16.1	16.4	17.5	18.1	19.0	19.9	20.9	22.7	27.0	26.2	--
Memo items: NI - Turnover tax	501.8	523.0	636.5	664.2	650.6	669.7	371.1	508.2	592.6	633.1	818.3	--
NI + depreciation - Turnover tax	544.1	568.6	683.2	718.2	703.9	727.6	434.9	576.2	664.6	710.8	901.2	--
						Other material sphere						
National product	128.4	131.4	139.0	144.0	146.8	145.6	172.5	177.3	172.5	188.2	204.6	306.0
Material input	15.0	17.4	15.0	16.7	19.8	18.6	21.9	24.7	30.5	33.3	63.2	100.0
of which: depreciation	0.3	--	0.2	0.1	0.1	0.2	0.1	0.1	0.5	0.7	2.0	--
National income (NI)	113.4	114.0	124.0	127.3	127.0	127.0	150.6	152.6	142.0	154.9	141.4	106.0
of which:												
Wages and salaries	4.7	6.8	6.2	6.3	7.0	7.6	7.7	12.8	18.4	19.0	34.5	--
Other income	106.0	108.9	115.4	119.3	117.7	116.8	140.4	136.7	118.3	126.2	98.7	--
Turnover tax	--	--	--	--	--	--	--	--	--	--	--	--
Profits/losses	2.5	(2.0)	2.1	1.4	1.9	2.2	2.1	2.6	4.9	9.3	7.9	--
Social security contributions	0.2	0.3	0.3	0.3	0.4	0.4	0.4	0.5	0.4	0.4	0.3	--
Memo items: NI - Turnover tax	113.4	114.0	124.0	127.3	127.0	127.0	150.6	152.6	142.0	154.9	141.4	--
NI + depreciation - Turnover tax	113.7	114.0	124.2	127.4	127.1	127.2	150.7	152.7	142.5	155.6	143.4	--
						NON-MATERIAL SPHERE						
National product	--	..	--	--	--	--	2,856.5	3,023.5	3,271.2	--	--	--
Material input	--	..	--	--	--	--	1,706.9	1,790.3	1,942.4	--	--	--
of which: depreciation	168.1	188.9	207.2	212.6	224.9	248.8	277.7	293.4	338.3	317.5	315.0	--
National income (NI)	884.1	937.9	964.8	992.2	1,032.0	1,079.2	1,149.6	1,233.2	1,328.8	1,363.1	1,353.0	--
of which:												
Wages and salaries	692.2	737.0	758.0	786.4	810.1	847.3	880.6	923.5	989.4	1,044.5	1,077.9	--
Other income	--	..	--	--	--	--	--	--	--	--	--	--
Turnover tax	3.6	3.8	3.9	3.9	4.2	4.4	22.7	29.5	30.5	33.5	26.0	--
Profits/losses	145.9	151.8	157.2	157.8	170.5	177.5	200.1	227.7	247.5	223.2	188.7	--
Social security contributions	42.4	45.4	45.7	44.1	47.2	50.0	46.2	52.5	61.4	61.9	60.4	--
Memo items: NI - Turnover tax	880.5	934.2	960.9	988.3	1,027.8	1,074.8	1,126.9	1,203.7	1,298.3	1,329.6	1,327.0	--
NI + depreciation - Turnover tax	1,048.6	1,123.1	1,168.1	1,200.9	1,252.7	1,323.6	1,404.6	1,497.1	1,636.6	1,647.1	1,642.0	--

(Continued)

Table 2.6 COMPOSITION OF NATIONAL PRODUCT BY SECTOR, 1980-91 (concluded)
(Million tugriks at Current Prices)

	1980	1981	1982	1983	1984	1985	1986	1987	1988	1989	1990
TOTAL MATERIAL and NON-MATERIAL SECTORS											
National product	..	..	..	..	..	..	19,767.5	20,669.6	21,631.7	..	..
Material input	..	..	..	..	..	..	11,370.3	11,957.7	12,413.0	..	..
of which: depreciation	1,154.2	1,245.7	1,361.7	1,427.1	1,592.4	1,709.7	1,845.1	1,990.4	2,109.4	2,150.5	2,288.7
National income (NI)	6,461.0	7,088.5	7,790.5	8,317.5	8,410.1	8,715.7	8,397.2	8,711.9	9,218.7	10,009.1	9,680.5
of which:											
Wages and salaries	2,651.5	2,755.8	2,896.7	3,083.6	3,166.1	3,312.2	3,497.6	3,677.2	3,832.3	4,085.6	4,227.6
Other income	212.8	231.2	365.9	394.7	495.5	461.1	125.9	150.9	178.9	345.7	379.4
Turnover tax	1,994.0	2,187.5	2,249.5	2,366.8	2,432.9	2,440.1	1,959.3	1,946.1	1,928.4	2,140.1	2,042.3
Profits/losses	1,447.2	1,750.0	2,108.9	2,293.9	2,128.0	2,304.1	2,605.4	2,718.2	3,047.5	3,195.6	2,785.1
Social security contributions	155.5	164.1	169.5	178.5	187.6	198.2	209.0	219.5	231.6	242.1	246.1
Memo Items:											
NI - Turnover tax	4,467.0	4,901.1	5,541.0	5,950.7	5,977.2	6,275.6	6,437.9	6,765.8	7,290.3	7,869.0	7,638.2
NI + depreciation - Turnover tax (GDPfc)	5,621.2	6,146.8	6,902.7	7,377.8	7,569.6	7,985.3	8,283.0	8,756.2	9,399.7	10,019.5	9,926.9
National income + depreciation	7,615.2	8,334.2	9,152.2	9,744.6	10,002.5	10,425.4	10,242.3	10,702.3	11,328.1	12,159.6	11,969.2
Subsidies total	860.3	907.9	946.9	976.2	1,006.8	1,053.5	932.3	992.7	1,027.1	1,428.7	1,455.1
NI+depreciation-subsidies (GDP)	6,754.9	7,426.3	8,205.3	8,768.4	8,995.7	9,371.9	9,310.0	9,709.6	10,301.0	10,730.9	10,514.1
Net factor income from abroad	(1,037.4)	(1,073.9)	(1,098.9)	(1,131.5)	(1,168.3)	(1,216.6)	(1,257.9)	(1,358.9)	(1,287.9)	(1,186.0)	(1,218.8)
Gross National Product	5,717.5	6,352.4	7,106.4	7,636.9	7,827.4	8,155.3	8,052.1	8,350.7	9,013.1	9,544.9	9,295.3

Sources: State Statistical Office and The World Bank.

Table 3.1: THE CONSOLIDATED BALANCE OF PAYMENTS, 1980-91
(Millions of USDollars)

	1980	1981	1982	1983	1984	1985	1986	1987	1988	1989	1990	1991
Trade balance	-274.4	-331.0	-370.4	-451.0	-342.2	-436.6	-587.3	-542.1	-628.7	-743.8	-314.4	-80.0
Merchandise exports fob	402.5	438.0	518.6	556.7	596.2	566.9	740.8	816.9	829.1	795.8	444.8	346.5
of which barter	388.1	426.2	500.3	543.0	566.0	536.8	704.7	772.9	774.2	720.9	427.7	289.4
Merchandise imports cif	-676.9	-769.0	-889.0	-1007.7	-938.5	-1003.4	-1328.1	-1359.0	-1457.8	-1539.6	-759.3	-426.5
of which barter	-658.6	-751.7	-868.3	-985.3	-917.4	-980.8	-1293.9	-1312.3	-1410.7	-1470.8	-673.6	-286.2
Turnkey projects 1/	-185.1	-470.8	-463.5	-354.6	-370.3	-362.3	-510.7	-468.4	-391.9	-374.0	-264.5	-74.7
Services balance	-31.2	-5.2	-12.4	-19.1	-27.4	-14.4	37.6	20.1	-12.2	-116.6	-72.6	0.2
Receipts	40.8	38.6	49.5	56.2	53.6	71.7	84.3	89.1	94.5	43.9	53.1	26.5
Shipment	9.0	11.0	7.6	9.7	11.3	15.6	22.9	24.1	29.0	21.3	22.3	--
Travel	1.9	3.3	3.6	3.6	3.6	3.2	3.5	4.7	4.8	4.4	5.0	--
Interest income	0.2	0.2	0.2	--	0.1	0.1	0.1	0.2	0.2	7.5	5.1	--
Others	29.7	24.2	38.2	42.9	38.6	52.8	57.8	60.1	60.6	10.6	20.8	--
Expenditures	-72.1	-43.9	-61.9	-75.4	-81.0	-86.2	-46.7	-69.0	-106.8	-160.5	-121.2	26.3
Shipment	-16.0	-16.7	-16.7	-17.2	-13.6	-13.9	-17.3	-22.5	-24.9	-21.5	-14.6	--
Travel	-0.2	-0.1	-0.2	-0.2	-0.2	-0.2	-0.3	-0.3	-0.5	-0.4	-1.2	--
Interest payments	34.5	11.1	20.6	31.1	39.1	45.1	1.8	11.5	34.4	56.4	48.7	--
Others	-21.4	-16.0	-24.4	-26.9	-28.1	-27.0	-27.3	-34.6	-46.9	-82.2	-56.8	--
Unrequited transfers	146.5	-0.1	-0.1	-0.1	-0.1	-0.1	-0.1	-0.3	-0.3	3.9	7.4	43.6
Private	-0.1	-0.1	-0.1	-0.1	-0.1	-0.1	-0.1	-0.3	-0.3	--	--	--
Official	146.6	--	--	--	--	--	--	--	--	3.9	7.4	--
Current account before off. transfers	-490.8	-807.1	-846.4	-824.8	-740.0	-813.4	-1060.6	-990.7	-1033.1	-1234.5	-651.0	-110.8
Capital account	344.1	807.1	850.0	821.7	756.2	844.2	1060.4	1024.9	1037.9	1236.6	590.5	106.9
Direct foreign investment	--	--	--	--	--	--	--	--	--	--	--	--
Medium- and long-term capital	418.1	806.7	859.2	740.5	746.0	753.9	1051.0	1113.2	1102.7	1228.2	516.8	130.3
Disbursements	437.0	845.6	900.9	781.2	785.0	791.7	1067.1	1130.1	1120.0	1250.5	537.1	139.3
Repayments	-19.0	-38.9	-41.6	-40.7	-39.1	-37.8	-16.1	-16.9	-17.3	-22.3	-20.3	-9.0
Short-term capital 2/	--	0.7	7.7	0.9	-0.2	3.6	30.6	-20.0	-76.5	-33.3	66.8	-23.4
Net errors and omissions	-73.9	-0.3	-17.0	80.3	10.4	86.7	-21.2	-68.4	11.7	41.7	6.8	-43.9
Overall balance	-0.1	0.0	3.5	-3.1	16.1	30.8	-0.2	34.2	4.8	6.0	-53.1	-47.8 3/
Financing	0.1	0.0	-3.5	3.1	-16.1	-30.8	0.2	-34.2	-4.8	-6.0	53.1	47.8 3/
Net change in reserves (increase -)	0.1	0.0	-3.5	3.1	-16.1	-30.8	0.2	-34.2	-4.8	-6.0	53.1	31.2
Memorandum items:												
Net official reserves end year	-0.1	-0.1	3.4	0.3	16.5	47.3	57.3	91.5	96.3	102.3	49.2	18.0
In weeks of total imports	0.0	0.0	0.2	0.0	0.9	2.4	2.2	3.5	3.4	3.5	3.3	2.2
In weeks of non-barter imports	-0.3	-0.4	8.6	0.7	40.7	108.4	87.0	102.0	106.3	77.3	22.7	6.7

1/ Includes both goods and services; data are not available for disaggregation.
2/ Includes changes in the balances of nonconvertible currency deposits held by nonresidents, net borrowing from IBEC and other clearing accounts as reported by the State Bank.
3/ Includes arrears of US$16.6 million incurred by the end of 1991.

Sources: Government of Mongolia, IMF and World Bank staff estimates.

Table 3.2a: THE BALANCE OF PAYMENTS WITH THE CMEA AREA, 1980-90
(Millions of transferable rubles)

	1980	1981	1982	1983	1984	1985	1986	1987	1988	1989	1990
Current account after official transfers	-224.5	-579.9	-619.2	-610.7	-602.8	-695.6	-775.6	-657.6	-690.7	-852.0	-622.1
Trade balance	-176.6	-233.9	-268.5	-328.7	-280.2	-371.0	-422.0	-351.1	-414.3	-506.7	-258.6
Merchandise exports fob	253.5	306.2	365.1	403.6	451.2	448.6	504.7	503.1	503.9	487.1	449.9
Merchandise imports cif	-430.2	-540.1	-633.7	-732.3	-731.5	-819.5	-926.7	-854.2	-918.2	-993.8	-708.5
Equipment 1/	-83.3	-80.3	-129.1	-112.1	-99.3	-106.0	-126.7	-144.0	-202.8	-385.7	-126.2
Other	-346.9	-459.8	-504.5	-620.3	-632.2	-713.6	-800.0	-710.2	-715.4	-608.1	-582.3
Turnkey projects 2/	-120.9	-338.2	-338.2	-263.6	-295.2	-302.7	-365.8	-304.9	-255.1	-252.7	-278.2
Services balance	-22.6	-7.7	-12.4	-18.4	-27.2	-21.9	12.3	-1.4	-21.1	-92.6	-85.3
Receipts	22.4	22.3	30.5	35.6	34.8	47.0	44.0	41.8	45.2	9.3	20.5
Shipment	5.0	7.1	5.4	5.3	5.3	5.7	6.4	6.5	10.0	5.1	4.7
Travel	0.5	0.7	0.7	0.8	1.0	0.8	0.8	0.9	0.9	0.6	0.6
Interest income	0.1	0.1	0.1	--	0.1	0.0	--	--	--	--	--
Others	16.8	14.5	24.4	29.5	28.4	40.5	36.8	34.4	34.3	3.6	15.2
Expenditures	-45.0	-30.0	-42.9	-53.9	-62.0	-68.8	-31.7	-43.2	-66.3	-101.9	-105.8
Shipment	-10.4	-12.0	-12.0	-12.7	-10.7	-11.4	-12.3	-14.6	-16.1	-14.4	-14.5
Travel	-0.1	-0.1	-0.1	-0.1	-0.2	-0.1	-0.2	-0.2	-0.3	-0.3	-0.6
Interest payments	-22.5	-7.9	-15.0	-23.1	-31.2	-37.7	-1.3	-7.5	-22.4	-38.1	-51.2
Others	-12.0	-10.0	-15.7	-18.0	-20.0	-19.7	-17.9	-20.9	-27.5	-49.1	-39.5
Unrequited transfers	95.7	-0.1	-0.1	-0.1	-0.1	-0.1	-0.1	-0.2	-0.2	0.0	0.0
Private	-0.1	-0.1	-0.1	-0.1	-0.1	-0.1	-0.1	-0.2	-0.2	0.0	0.0
Official	95.7	--	--	--	--	--	--	--	--	--	--
Current account	224.5	580.2	619.8	611.5	603.9	696.5	775.6	657.4	690.6	852.0	622.2
Medium- and long-term capital	273.1	579.6	627.0	550.4	593.5	628.6	755.1	726.5	720.2	832.7	550.2
Disbursements	285.5	607.6	657.4	580.6	624.6	660.2	762.6	734.1	727.9	843.8	565.4
Trade loans	81.3	189.0	190.0	205.0	230.2	251.5	270.1	285.2	270.0	205.4	161.0
Turnkey projects	120.9	338.2	338.2	263.6	295.2	302.7	365.8	304.9	255.1	252.7	278.2
Equipment 1/	83.3	80.3	129.1	112.1	99.3	106.0	126.7	144.0	202.8	385.7	126.2
Repayments	-12.4	-28.0	-30.4	-30.3	-31.2	-31.6	-7.5	-7.6	-7.7	-11.1	-15.2
Short-term capital 3/	--	0.5	5.6	0.7	-0.2	3.0	21.9	-13.0	-49.8	-22.5	70.3
Net errors and omissions	-48.6	0.2	-12.8	60.4	10.6	64.9	-1.4	-56.1	20.2	41.8	1.7
Overall balance	0.0	0.3	0.5	0.7	1.1	0.9	0.0	-0.2	-0.1	0.0	0.1
Financing	0.0	-0.3	-0.5	-0.7	-1.1	-0.9	0.0	0.2	0.1	0.0	-0.1
Change in reserves	0.0	-0.6	-0.5	-0.7	-1.1	-0.9	0.0	0.2	0.1	0.0	-0.1

1/ Imports of equipment constituting technical assistance financed by the USSR.
2/ Includes both goods and services; data are not available for disaggregation.
3/ Includes changes in the balances of nonconvertible currency deposits held by nonresidents, net borrowing from IBEC and other clearing accounts as reported by the State Bank

Sources: Government of Mongolia and IMF staff estimates.

Table 3.2b: THE BALANCE OF PAYMENTS WITH COUNTRIES OF BILATERAL CLEARING ARRANGEMENTS, 1980–90
(Millions of USDollars)

	1980	1981	1982	1983	1984	1985	1986	1987	1988	1989	1990
Current account after official transfers	-0.5	-0.4	-1.0	1.2	1.5	1.9	15.8	-3.0	8.4	5.9	-5.3
Trade balance	-1.7	-1.6	-1.1	-1.2	-3.1	-6.6	2.0	-16.7	-4.8	-3.1	-16.4
Merchandise exports fob	7.7	5.5	9.5	8.7	9.9	7.0	18.4	12.5	20.8	22.3	16.3
Merchandise imports 1/	-9.4	-7.1	-10.6	-9.8	-13.0	-13.5	-16.4	-29.2	-25.6	-25.4	-32.7
Services balance	1.3	1.2	0.2	2.4	4.6	8.5	13.8	13.7	13.2	9.0	10.6
Receipts	1.5	1.3	0.4	2.6	4.8	8.8	14.0	14.0	13.5	13.0	16.6
Shipment	1.3	1.2	0.2	2.5	4.6	8.8	13.8	13.8	13.1	12.8	16.3
Travel	0.0	—	—	0.0	—	—	—	—	—	—	—
Interest income	—	—	—	—	—	—	—	—	—	—	—
Others	0.1	0.2	0.1	0.1	0.2	0.1	0.2	0.2	0.4	0.2	0.3
Expenditures	-0.2	-0.1	-0.2	-0.2	-0.2	-0.3	-0.2	-0.3	-0.3	-4.0	-6.0
Shipment	—	—	-0.1	-0.1	-0.1	-0.2	-0.1	—	—	—	—
Travel	—	—	—	0.0	0.0	—	—	—	—	—	—
Interest payments	—	—	—	—	—	—	—	—	—	—	—
Others	-0.2	-0.1	-0.1	-0.1	-0.1	-0.1	-0.1	-0.3	-0.3	-4.0	-6.0
Urequited transfers	—	—	—	—	—	—	—	—	—	—	—
Private	—	—	—	—	—	—	—	—	—	—	—
Official	—	—	—	—	—	—	—	—	—	—	—
Capital account	0.5	0.4	1.0	-1.2	-1.5	-1.9	-15.7	3.0	-8.4	-5.9	5.8
Medium- and long-term capital	—	—	—	—	—	—	-5.6	-5.2	-5.5	-5.9	-5.8
Disbursements	—	—	—	—	—	—	—	—	—	—	—
Repayments 2/	—	—	—	—	—	—	-5.6	-5.2	-5.5	-5.9	-5.8
Short-term capital	—	—	—	—	—	—	—	—	—	—	—
Net errors and omissions	0.5	0.4	1.0	-1.2	-1.5	-1.9	-10.1	8.2	-2.9	—	11.6
Overall balance	0.0	0.0	0.0	0.0	0.0	0.0	0.0	0.0	0.0	0.0	0.0
Financing	0.0	0.0	0.0	0.0	0.0	0.0	0.0	0.0	0.0	0.0	0.0
Net change in foreign exchange reserves	0.0	0.0	0.0	0.0	0.0	0.0	0.0	0.0	0.0	0.0	0.0

Note: Arrangements cover trade with the People's Republic of China, the Democratic People's Republic of Korea and Yugoslavia.

1/ Imports on cif as well as fob basis.

2/ Repayments to the People's Republic of China of debts contracted in the 1960s.

Sources: Government of Mongolia and International Monetary Fund.

Table 3.2c: THE BALANCE OF PAYMENTS WITH CONVERTIBLE CURRENCY AREA, 1980-90
(Millions of USDollars)

	1980	1981	1982	1983	1984	1985	1986	1987	1988	1989	1990
Current account after official transfers	-0.1	0.4	3.1	-4.3	14.5	17.1	6.5	22.6	19.6	24.5	-46.3
Trade balance	-2.2	-3.9	-1.3	-7.5	12.3	13.9	-0.1	14.0	12.6	9.2	-56.1
Merchandise exports fob	6.7	6.3	8.7	5.0	20.3	23.1	17.7	31.5	34.1	52.6	24.1
Merchandise imports 1/	-8.9	-10.2	-10.0	-12.5	-8.0	-9.2	-17.8	-17.5	-21.5	-41.6	-76.5
Grants in kind	---	---	---	---	---	---	---	---	---	-1.8	-3.7
Services balance	2.1	4.3	4.4	3.2	2.2	3.2	6.7	8.6	7.0	11.4	2.4
Receipts	5.1	6.3	7.3	5.8	5.2	6.7	8.9	10.9	11.6	17.1	17.0
Shipment	0.0	0.0	0.0	0.1	0.1	0.1	0.2	0.3	0.5	1.0	1.5
Travel	1.1	2.3	2.6	2.6	2.3	2.2	2.4	3.3	3.4	3.5	4.4
Interest income	0.1	0.1	0.1	---	---	0.1	0.1	0.2	0.2	7.5	5.1
Others	3.8	3.8	4.6	3.2	2.9	4.3	6.2	7.1	7.5	5.1	6.0
Expenditures	-2.9	-2.0	-2.9	-2.6	-3.2	-3.5	-2.2	-2.3	-4.6	-5.7	-14.6
Shipment	-0.1	-0.1	-0.2	-0.1	-0.1	-0.1	0.0	-0.1	-0.2	-0.2	-0.8
Travel	---	---	---	---	---	---	---	---	---	---	-0.6
Interest payments	---	---	---	---	---	---	---	---	---	---	---
Others	-2.9	-2.0	-2.7	-2.5	-3.0	-3.4	-2.2	-2.2	-4.4	-5.5	-13.2
Urequited transfers	---	---	---	---	---	---	---	---	---	3.9	7.4
Private	---	---	---	---	---	---	---	---	---	---	---
Official	---	---	---	---	---	---	---	---	---	3.9	7.4
Capital account	---	-0.9	-0.3	0.2	0.3	12.6	-6.8	11.9	-14.7	-18.5	-6.9
Medium- and long-term capital	---	---	---	---	1.6	1.6	2.3	2.3	1.7	1.7	-0.5
Disbursements	---	---	---	---	1.6	1.6	2.3	2.3	1.7	1.7	-0.5
Repayments	---	---	---	---	---	---	---	---	---	---	---
Short-term capital	---	---	---	---	---	---	---	---	---	---	---
Net errors and omissions 2/	---	-0.9	-0.3	0.2	-1.3	11.0	-9.1	9.6	-16.4	-20.2	-6.4
Overall balance	-0.1	-0.5	2.8	-41.0	14.8	29.7	-0.3	34.5	4.9	6.0	-53.2
Financing	0.1	0.5	-2.8	4.1	-14.8	-29.7	0.3	-34.5	-4.9	-6.0	53.2
Net change in foreign exchange reserves	0.1	0.5	-2.8	4.1	-14.8	-29.7	0.3	-34.5	-4.9	-6.0	53.2
Memorandum item:											
Net official reserves and year	14.9	14.4	17.1	13.1	27.8	57.5	57.3	91.8	96.7	102.7	49.5

1/ Imports on cif as well as fob basis.

2/ Includes valuation adjustment.

Sources: Government of Mongolia and IMF staff estimates.

Table 3.3: FOREIGN TRADE BY MARKETS, 1980-92
(in millions of USDollars)

	1980	1985	1986	1987	1988	1989	1990	1991	Jan-May 1992
Exports	402.8	689.1	716.1	717.9	739.1	721.5	660.7	346.5	114.1
Socialist or former Socialist countries	396.6	662.2	692.4	688.7	699.4	671.9	622.7	317.7	87.4
Nonsocialist countries	6.2	26.9	23.7	29.2	39.7	49.6	38.0	28.8	26.7
Imports	547.8	1095.5	1139.7	1104.6	1113.6	964.0	923.9	391.5	121.8
Socialist or former Socialist countries	387.3	709.4	743.3	732.1	740.7	725.4	846.3	325.7	60.9
Nonsocialist countries	160.5	386.1	396.4	372.5	372.9	238.6	77.6	65.8	60.9
Trade balance	-145.0	-406.4	-423.6	-386.7	-374.5	-242.5	-263.2	-45.0	-7.7
Socialist or former Socialist countries	9.3	-47.2	-50.9	-43.4	-41.3	-53.5	-223.6	-8.0	26.5
Nonsocialist countries	-154.3	-359.2	-372.7	-343.3	-333.2	-189.0	-39.6	-37.0	-34.2

Source: State Statistical Office.

Table 3.4: COMPOSITION OF EXPORTS TO AND IMPORTS FROM SOCIALIST COUNTRIES, 1970-90

(in percent of total at current prices; CMEA classification)

	1970	1975	1980	1985	1986	1987	1988	1989	1990
Exports	100.0	100.0	100.0	100.0	100.0	100.0	100.0	100.0	100.0
Foodstuffs	9.6	21.4	19.0	9.4	11.0	10.6	8.1	8.7	6.6
Consumer goods	5.9	9.1	9.6	16.8	15.4	15.8	15.7	17.5	20.0
Fuels, mineral and metals	5.4	6.5	26.4	42.2	40.1	39.7	41.7	42.8	49.7
Chemicals	0.0	0.1	-	-	-	-	0.1	-	0.6
Building materials	0.9	0.3	0.4	0.7	4.0	4.5	3.4	4.0	3.9
Agricultural goods	19.5	27.4	13.4	6.1	9.4	7.6	8.1	6.5	5.3
Other	58.7	35.2	31.2	24.8	20.1	21.8	22.9	20.5	13.9
Imports	100.0	100.0	100.0	100.0	100.0	100.0	100.0	100.0	100.0
Fuels, mineral and metals	12.8	10.3	24.1	28.7	28.3	30.8	33.5	27.3	27.2
Consumer goods	36.3	33.4	20.9	17.2	19.1	18.4	18.5	21.9	21.6
Chemicals	5.1	5.2	6.3	5.9	5.5	6.1	5.6	6.3	5.3
Agricultural goods	-	-	-	-	-	0.1	0.2	0.1	0.0
Engineering goods	25.9	35.8	33.1	36.3	36.1	32.2	30.2	29.6	31.1
Other	19.9	15.3	15.6	11.9	11.0	12.4	12.0	14.8	14.8

Source: State Statistical Office.

Table 3.5.: COMPOSITION OF EXPORTS TO AND IMPORTS FROM NONSOCIALIST COUNTRIES, 1970-90

(in percent of total at current prices: CMEA classification)

	1970	1975	1980	1985	1986	1987	1988	1989	1990
Exports	100.0	100.0	100.0	100.0	100.0	100.0	100.0	100.0	100.0
Fuels, minerals and metals	-	-	-	-	-	-	-	-	7.9
Foodstuffs	-	-	-	0.0	1.8	0.5	-	-	0.1
Raw materials	100.0	100.0	97.8	97.7	93.8	93.5	94.2	94.2	55.9
Consumer goods	-	-	2.2	2.3	4.4	6.0	5.8	5.5	35.5
Other	-	-	-	-	-	-	-	0.3	0.6
Imports	100.0	100.0	100.0	100.0	100.0	100.0	100.0	100.0	100.0
Raw materials	...	1.1	1.3	30.3	24.1	21.2	21.3	19.3	9.3
Chemicals	55.5	29.2	14.0	17.1	14.0	12.4	12.3	13.9	14.0
Consumer goods	33.3	47.3	33.4	5.3	9.6	5.3	5.1	20.3	24.8
Foodstuffs	-	0.5	0.3	3.9	16.3	13.3	11.6	8.2	10.6
Other	11.2	21.9	51.0	43.4	36.0	47.8	49.7	38.3	41.3

Source: State Statistical Office.

Table 3.6a: COMPOSITION OF EXPORTS BY END-USE, 1980-90
(in millions of transferable rubles)

	1980	1981	1982	1983	1984	1985	1986	1987	1988	1989	1990
Total	269.9	314.0	376.4	408.6	453.9	461.7	479.8	481.0	495.2	483.4	442.7
CMEA	260.4	303.7	363.6	396.7	426.6	436.0	451.7	451.1	455.8	436.7	402.5
Non-CMEA	9.5	10.3	12.8	11.9	27.3	25.7	28.1	29.9	39.4	46.7	40.2
Capital goods	0.7	0.7	0.5	0.7	0.7	0.7	0.2	0.1	0.5	0.1	-
CMEA	0.7	0.7	0.5	0.7	0.7	0.7	0.2	0.1	0.5	0.1	-
Non-CMEA	-	-	-	-	-	-	-	-	-	-	-
Fuel, minerals and metals	71.3	107.9	147.0	160.2	187.4	195.0	192.4	189.3	206.5	206.7	213.0
CMEA	71.1	107.6	146.6	159.5	187.0	194.1	191.3	188.2	205.2	206.7	208.5
Non-CMEA	0.2	0.3	0.4	0.7	0.4	0.9	1.1	1.1	1.3	-	4.5
Chemical fertilizers and rubber	-	-	-	0.0	-	0.1	-	-	0.3	-	2.6
CMEA	-	-	-	0.0	-	0.1	-	-	0.3	-	0.6
Non-CMEA	-	-	-	-	-	-	-	-	-	-	2.0
Building materials and elements	1.1	1.6	1.9	3.4	4.6	3.0	19.2	21.9	17.0	19.5	17.1
CMEA	1.1	1.6	1.9	3.4	4.6	3.0	17.6	21.9	17.0	19.5	17.1
Non-CMEA	-	-	-	-	-	-	1.6	-	-	-	-
Animals (live)	-	-	-	0.4	-	-	-	-	-	-	-
CMEA	-	-	-	0.4	-	-	-	-	-	-	-
Non-CMEA	-	-	-	-	-	-	-	-	-	-	-
Raw materials for food industry	36.3	30.0	31.3	34.8	39.3	28.3	45.1	36.7	39.9	31.4	23.4
CMEA	36.3	30.0	31.1	34.6	38.5	27.7	44.0	35.2	39.2	30.6	22.9
Non-CMEA	-	-	0.2	0.2	0.8	0.6	1.1	1.5	0.7	0.8	0.5
Other raw materials	83.4	86.3	99.7	104.5	107.2	113.5	96.3	106.0	113.0	99.1	68.6
CMEA	74.6	77.4	88.2	94.8	82.3	90.9	78.1	84.6	80.3	58.8	48.0
Non-CMEA	8.8	8.9	11.5	9.7	24.9	22.6	18.2	21.4	32.7	40.3	20.6
Food	51.4	53.5	49.5	49.5	52.1	43.4	52.6	51.0	40.1	42.1	29.2
CMEA	51.3	53.0	49.3	49.3	52.1	43.2	47.7	47.4	38.2	40.3	27.7
Non-CMEA	0.1	0.5	0.2	0.2	-	0.2	4.9	3.6	1.9	1.8	1.5
Other consumer goods	25.7	34.0	46.5	55.1	62.6	77.7	74.0	76.0	77.9	84.5	88.8
CMEA	25.3	33.4	46.0	54.0	61.4	76.3	72.8	73.7	75.1	80.7	77.7
Non-CMEA	0.4	0.6	0.5	1.1	1.2	1.4	1.2	2.3	2.8	3.8	11.1

Source: State Statistical Office.

Table 3.6b: COMPOSITION OF IMPORTS BY END-USE, 1980-90
(in millions of transferable rubles)

	1980	1981	1982	1983	1984	1985	1986	1987	1988	1989	1990
Total	367.0	471.5	529.9	621.9	653.4	734.0	763.6	740.1	746.1	645.4	619.0
CMEA	355.4	459.3	514.4	605.7	636.6	715.4	738.7	707.7	713.7	597.1	542.6
Non-CMEA	11.6	12.2	15.5	16.2	16.8	18.6	24.9	32.4	32.4	48.3	76.4
Capital goods	121.4	164.7	187.7	221.0	223.4	266.1	275.7	238.6	225.5	191.3	192.4
CMEA	117.9	162.3	184.7	216.7	220.0	261.7	270.2	232.1	218.4	179.9	172.2
Non-CMEA	3.5	2.4	3.0	4.3	3.4	4.4	5.5	6.5	7.1	11.4	20.2
Fuel, minerals and metals	88.3	115.2	152.2	183.7	195.5	210.5	216.5	227.8	250.0	176.4	168.2
CMEA	88.3	115.2	152.2	183.6	195.5	210.5	216.5	227.8	250.0	176.4	168.2
Non-CMEA	-	-	-	0.1	-	-	-	-	-	-	-
Chemical fertilizers and rubber	23.1	23.7	30.2	28.2	36.7	43.1	41.5	45.4	41.7	40.4	32.5
CMEA	22.3	21.9	28.0	25.7	34.5	41.3	39.3	43.5	39.6	36.0	25.0
Non-CMEA	0.8	1.8	2.2	2.5	2.2	1.8	2.2	1.9	2.1	4.4	7.5
Building materials and elements	6.8	7.8	7.4	6.9	10.1	10.6	9.7	14.4	10.7	14.8	11.9
CMEA	6.8	7.8	7.4	6.9	9.8	10.5	9.6	13.2	8.8	13.0	7.3
Non-CMEA	-	-	-	-	0.3	0.1	0.1	1.2	1.9	1.8	4.6
Animals (live)	-	-	-	-	-	-	0.5	0.8	1.4	0.6	0.1
CMEA	-	-	-	-	-	-	0.5	0.8	1.4	0.6	0.1
Non-CMEA	-	-	-	-	-	-	-	-	-	-	-
Raw materials for food industry	10.6	23.1	9.6	10.1	7.7	10.5	7.9	9.9	0.7	5.3	1.6
CMEA	10.6	23.1	9.6	10.1	7.7	10.5	7.9	8.9	0.7	5.3	0.8
Non-CMEA	-	-	-	-	-	-	-	1.0	-	-	0.8
Other raw materials	8.8	9.5	10.7	11.8	15.0	20.7	17.9	18.8	24.8	25.9	23.7
CMEA	8.7	9.3	10.1	11.6	12.4	17.0	13.5	16.2	19.1	18.1	16.0
Non-CMEA	0.1	0.2	0.6	0.2	2.6	3.7	4.4	2.6	5.7	7.8	7.7
Food	31.0	35.8	38.7	42.5	42.0	46.0	48.3	48.0	53.5	49.4	54.7
CMEA	30.1	35.0	36.8	40.6	39.5	43.7	44.4	43.4	49.6	45.0	47.0
Non-CMEA	0.9	0.8	1.9	1.9	2.5	2.3	3.9	4.6	3.9	4.4	7.7
Other consumer goods	77.0	91.7	93.4	117.7	123.0	126.5	145.6	136.4	137.8	141.3	133.9
CMEA	70.7	84.7	85.6	110.5	117.2	120.2	136.8	121.8	126.1	122.8	106.0
Non-CMEA	6.3	7.0	7.8	7.2	5.8	6.3	8.8	14.6	11.7	18.5	27.9

Sources: State Statistical Office and The World Bank.

Table 3.7: ORIGIN OF IMPORTS AND DESTINATION OF EXPORTS, 1970–92
(in percent of total at current prices)

	1970	1975	1980	1985	1986	1987	1988	1989	1990	1991	Jan–May 1992
Exports	100.0	100.0	100.0	100.0	100.0	100.0	100.0	100.0	100.0	100.0	100.0
Socialist or former Socialist countries	98.2	99.3	98.4	96.1	96.7	95.9	94.3	93.1	94.2	91.7	76.6
Of which: CMEA	93.5	96.4	96.5	94.4	94.2	93.8	92.0	90.3	90.9	-	-
Nonsocialist countries	1.8	0.7	1.6	3.9	3.3	4.1	5.7	6.9	5.8	8.3	23.4
Industrial countries	-	-	-	-	-	3.8	5.4	6.7	5.6	-	-
Of which: Germany	-	0.0	0.4	0.2	0.2	0.2	0.2	0.2	2.0	-	-
Japan	-	-	-	-	-	-	-	-	1.2	-	-
Developing countries	-	-	-	-	-	0.3	0.2	0.2	0.2	-	-
Imports	100.0	-	100.0	100.0	100.0	100.0	100.0	100.0	100.0	100.0	100.0
Socialist or former Socialist countries	99.2	-	98.5	99.0	98.3	98.3	97.9	95.6	91.6	83.2	50.0
Of which: CMEA	96.9	-	96.8	97.5	96.7	95.6	95.7	92.5	87.7	-	-
Nonsocialist countries	0.8	-	1.5	1.0	1.7	1.7	2.1	4.4	8.4	16.8	50.0
Industrial countries	-	-	-	-	-	1.6	2.1	4.1	7.9	-	-
Of which: Germany	-	-	0.4	0.3	0.3	0.4	0.4	0.4	4.1	-	-
Japan	-	-	-	-	-	-	-	-	1.1	-	-
Developing countries	-	-	-	-	-	0.1	0.0	0.3	0.5	-	-

Source: State Statistical Office.

Table 3.8: EXPORT AND IMPORT VALUES, VOLUMES AND DEFLATORS, 1980-90

	1980	1981	1982	1983	1984	1985	1986	1987	1988	1989	1990
	(In millions of transferable rubles; index of deflators 1980=100) /b										
Exports (Current prices) /a	269.9	314.0	376.4	408.6	453.9	461.7	479.8	481.0	495.2	483.4	442.7
Centrally planned	265.7	308.0	370.4	406.1	433.8	443.7	463.9	461.4	468.6	450.1	427.0
Other	4.2	6.0	6.0	2.5	20.1	18.0	15.9	19.6	26.6	33.3	15.7
Exports (1980 prices)	269.9	295.6	324.3	369.3	383.2	368.7	409.7	395.7	388.8	366.2	330.4
Centrally planned	265.7	290.6	320.5	367.3	364.5	354.1	393.4	380.5	368.4	341.0	318.6
Other	4.2	5.0	3.8	2.0	18.7	14.6	16.3	15.2	20.4	25.2	11.8
Export price deflator	100	106	116	111	118	125	117	122	127	132	134
Centrally planned	100	106	116	111	119	125	118	121	127	132	134
Other	100	120	158	125	107	123	98	129	130	132	133
Imports (Current prices) /a	367.0	471.5	529.9	621.9	653.4	734.0	763.6	740.1	746.1	646.1	619.0
Centrally planned	361.6	464.3	522.6	612.5	646.8	726.4	750.8	727.8	730.3	617.7	582.6
Other	5.4	7.2	7.3	9.4	6.6	7.6	12.8	12.3	15.8	28.4	36.4
Imports (1980 prices)	367.0	439.8	428.1	487.9	457.7	504.2	496.6	464.5	459.7	394.0	370.6
Centrally planned	361.6	432.6	420.8	478.6	451.1	496.6	483.9	455.4	447.5	372.3	343.0
Other	5.4	7.2	7.3	9.3	6.6	7.6	12.7	9.1	12.2	21.7	27.6
Import price deflator	100	107	124	127	143	146	154	159	162	164	167
Centrally planned	100	107	124	128	143	146	155	160	163	166	170
Other	100	100	100	101	100	100	101	135	130	131	132
Terms of trade	100	99	94	87	83	86	76	76	78	80	80
Centrally planned	100	99	93	86	83	86	76	76	78	80	79
Other	100	120	158	124	107	123	97	95	101	101	101
	(Annual percentage change) /c										
Export prices	1.7	6.2	9.3	-4.7	7.1	5.7	-6.5	3.8	4.8	3.6	1.5
Centrally planned	1.7	6.0	9.0	-4.3	7.6	5.3	-5.9	2.8	4.9	3.8	1.5
Other	5.9	20.0	31.6	-20.8	-14.0	14.7	-20.9	32.2	1.1	1.3	0.7
Import prices	10.0	7.2	15.5	3.0	12.0	2.0	5.6	3.6	1.9	1.0	1.9
Centrally planned	10.4	7.3	15.7	3.0	12.0	2.0	6.1	3.0	2.1	1.7	2.4
Other	-18.0	0.0	0.0	1.1	-1.1	0.0	0.8	34.1	-4.2	1.1	0.8
Terms of trade	-7.5	-0.9	-5.4	-7.4	-4.4	3.7	-11.5	0.2	2.9	2.6	-0.3
Centrally planned	-7.9	-1.2	-5.8	-7.2	-3.9	3.2	-11.3	-0.2	2.7	2.1	-0.8
Other	29.1	20.0	31.6	-21.7	-13.1	14.7	-21.5	-1.4	5.5	0.3	-0.1

/a Centrally planned economies include CMEA members, Yugoslavia, China, and the Democratic People's Republic of Korea, while "other" refers to countries in the convertible currency area; components may not add to totals because of rounding.
/b Trade under bilateral clearing arrangements and with the convertible currency area is converted into transferable rubles at the official rate of exchange.
/c For 1980, the rates of growth are averages for the previous five years.

Sources: Ministry of Trade and Industry, International Monetary Fund and The World Bank.

Table 3.9: INDICES OF EXPORT AND IMPORT PRICES, 1970-90

(In transferable rubles)

	Exports	Imports	Terms of trade
		(1970 = 100)	
1970	100.0	100.0	100.0
1976	169.3	119.7	141.4
1977	169.5	143.6	118.0
1978	172.9	156.0	110.8
1979	173.2	165.3	104.8
		(1980 = 100)	
1980	100.0	100.0	100.0
1981	106.2	107.2	99.1
1982	116.1	123.8	93.8
1983	110.6	127.5	86.7
1984	118.4	141.8	83.5
1985	125.2	145.6	86.0
1986	117.1	153.8	76.1
1987	121.6	159.3	76.3
1988	127.3	162.5	78.3
1989	132.0	164.0	80.5
1990	134.0	167.0	80.2

Sources: State Statistical Office and International Monetary Fund.

Table 3.10.: EXPORT COMMODITIES, 1970-90

	1970	1975	1980	1985	1990
Copper concentrate ('000 tons)	n.a.	n.a.	n.a.	n.a.	347.5
Fluorspar ('000 tons)	n.a.	n.a.	n.a.	n.a.	116.6
Coal ('000 tons)	-	-	-	225.0	490.2
Cement ('000 tons)	23.6	33.9	6.8	-	95.4
Timber ('000 cubic meters)	42.3	127.7	87.7	58.7	19.9
Sawn wood ('000 cubic meters)	10.9	59.8	125.9	136.1	42.5
Scoured wool ('000 tons)	8.0	9.3	8.9	5.7	2.8
Sheep and lamb wool ('000 tons)	2.1	1.9	1.9	2.0	0.5
Camel wool ('000 tons)	3.2	2.9	3.0	2.6	1.9
Goat down ('000 tons)	0.9	1.1	1.2	0.6	0.4
Horse mane ('000 ton)	0.9	0.6	0.7	0.6	0.5
Horse skins ('000 tons)	12.1	121.0	65.0	58.0	105.2
Sheep skins ('000 pieces)	5.1	64.0	261.0	280.2	130.0
Goat skins ('000 pieces)	4.2	72.0	315.1	526.2	113.2
Goat leather ('000 pieces)	224.6	341.6	175.0	236.6	172.0
Chevrette ('000 pieces)	394.6	517.2	123.1	411.0	24.1
Leather clothes (mln Tugrik)	14.2	30.2	54.7	88.4	87.0
Skin goods (mln Tugrik)	-	9.9	17.8	44.4	51.6
Carpets (million square meters)	-	0.3	0.4	1.5	1.7
Woolen fabrics ('000 m)	230.3	205.3	31.9	34.6	-
Woolen blankets ('000 pieces)	37.6	143.0	330.8	313.9	336.4
Goat down goods ('000 pieces)	-	-	38.9	236.5	275.7
Camel woolen goods ('000 pieces)	-	-	6.2	16.1	23.2
Marmot skins ('000 pieces)	907.8	715.2	520.0	578.8	73.0
Wheat ('000 tons)	1.5	-	-	6.2	-
Vodka ('000 liters)	-	-	130.0	350.0	186.4
Meat ('000 tons)	20.9	35.7	45.9	36.8	24.3
Livestock ('000 tons)	51.0	50.2	36.1	24.7	20.8
Horses ('000 head)	67.5	61.8	76.3	63.1	42.3

Source: State Statistical Office.

Table 3.11: IMPORT COMMODITIES, 1970-90

	1970	1975	1980	1985	1990
Machines, equipment & transport vehicles (mln Tugrik)	125.3	304.9	539.6	1,182.7	855.0
Energy generating equipment (mln Tugrik)	4.9	11.1	23.1	49.8	48.4
Diesel generators (pieces)	10	19	3	11	5
Cranes (pieces)	53	55	64	102	31
Excavators (pieces)	27	29	191	121	76
Tractors & self-propelled mechanisms (pieces)	493	490	383	375	390
Trucks (pieces)	288	1071	1186	1670	927
Buses (pieces)	63	139	214	224	246
Cars (pieces)	388	356	625	557	300
Fuel, raw materials, metals (mln Tugrik)	61.8	88.0	392.4	935.6	746.8
Gas oil ('000 tons)	74.3	129.2	213.3	312.2	364.3
Gasoline ('000 tons)	151.0	191.9	284.5	315.2	341.2
Fuel oil ('000 tons)	6.4	7.8	38.9	67.8	63.4
Lubricants ('000 tons)	17.4	26.3	22.8	22.8	20.9
Chemical products, fertilizers, rubber (mln Tugrik)	24.9	44.9	102.7	191.6	144.3
Nitrogenous fertilizers ('000 tons)	1.9	7.7	28.6	22.1	9.1
Phosphatic fertilizers ('000 tons)	0.6	1.5	22.8	13.8	19.9
Building/construction materials (mln Tugrik)	8.4	22.2	30.2	47.1	52.9
Cement ('000 tons)	18.7	28.1	36.4	107.4	38.5
Window glass ('000 square meters)	293.5	669.0	759.7	657.0	477.4
Nonfood raw materials & reprocessing products (mln Tugrik)	9.8	12.4	39.1	92.0	105.8
Paper ('000 tons)	4.4	6.3	9.4	9.6	8.5
Food, raw materials (mln Tugrik)	1.3	25.8	47.1	46.7	7.1
Wheat ('000 tons)	-	20.1	31.3	17.1	-
Foodstuffs (mln Tugrik)	61.3	62.7	137.8	204.4	243.0
Oil ('000 tons)	0.7	-	1.5	2.1	2.1
Sugar ('000 tons)	14.7	19.9	36.1	34.2	47.6
Fresh fruits ('000 tons)	1.3	2.5	3.1	1.4	3.5
Industrial consumer goods (mln Tugrik)	152.4	284.0	342.2	562.2	595.1
Cotton fabrics (mln Tugrik)	13.6	41.3	51.3	56.3	57.1
Woolen fabrics (mln m)	0.7	1.3	1.3	1.6	0.9
Silk (mln Tugrik)	4.4	5.1	5.5	7.0	3.8
Ready-made garments (mln Tugrik)	20.7	62.2	51.1	92.9	53.6
Knitted garments (mln Tugrik)	13.3	34.7	10.2	12.0	22.6
Furniture (mln Tugrik)	8.0	4.0	8.0	15.1	3.0
Sewing machines ('000 pieces)	-	3.2	5.0	10.0	7.0
Refrigerators ('000 pieces)	0.4	2.8	4.0	17.3	1.0
Washing machines ('000 pieces)	2.0	4.0	3.7	5.0	5.7
Television sets ('000 pieces)	5.1	2.0	0.4	10.1	19.1

Sources: State Statistical Office and The World Bank.

Table 3.12. EXPORTS BY COUNTRY OF DESTINATION, 1960-90

(Million Tugriks at current prices)

	1960	1970	1980	1985	1990
Total exports	289.6	337.6	1,199.5	2,052.0	1,967.4
Bulgaria	4.9	13.5	26.7	39.1	49.9
Viet Nam	-	-	3.1	4.9	0.8
German Democratic Republic	10.8	17.2	39.1	68.4	-
USSR	219.8	230.9	951.9	1,580.3	1,540.7
Cuba	-	0.6	2.7	3.6	3.8
Poland	7.4	13.4	25.8	56.4	33.2
Romania	1.1	7.2	17.8	47.1	30.2
Hungary	6.2	9.1	23.1	44.0	41.1
Czechoslovakia	22.3	24.4	67.1	93.8	89.1
People's Republic of China	13.1	6.9	11.6	8.0	33.7
Yugoslavia	0.2	0.5	4.0	9.8	8.3
United States	-	-	0.4	0.4	2.7
Austria	-	0.4	-	0.9	0.1
Germany, Federal Republic of	-	-	4.4	4.0	40.7
United Kingdom	-	3.3	8.4	8.4	9.0
Netherlands	-	-	0.9	20.4	4.5
Italy	-	-	0.9	2.7	16.4
France	-	-	1.3	0.9	8.2
Switzerland	0.7	0.5	-	19.6	3.5
Japan	0.2	1.4	2.2	22.7	22.7
India	-	-	-	-	0.1
Others	2.9	8.3	8.1	16.6	28.7

Source: State Statistical Office.

Table 3.13. ORIGIN OF IMPORTS BY COUNTRY, 1960-90

(Million Tugriks at current prices)

	1960	1970	1980	1985	1990
Total imports	387.1	482.8	1,631.2	3,262.2	2,751.1
Bulgaria	3.8	9.4	25.7	32.5	50.7
Viet Nam	-	-	5.3	7.9	6.8
German Democratic Republic	16.2	18.5	36.9	79.2	-
USSR	235.5	390.3	1,399.2	2,833.9	2,132.4
Cuba	-	-	2.6	2.6	1.2
Poland	10.3	10.3	17.8	45.4	39.2
Romania	1.0	9.3	16.0	53.8	18.6
Hungary	5.9	10.0	19.1	38.2	61.2
Czechoslovakia	20.8	19.8	57.0	86.2	101.1
People's Republic of China	87.7	3.9	10.6	14.7	66.3
Yugoslavia	0.3	-	7.1	18.7	26.0
Austria	-	-	6.2	9.3	29.7
Germany, Federal Republic of	-	-	5.8	9.3	111.5
United Kingdom	0.1	0.7	2.7	2.2	7.3
Netherlands	-	-	-	-	0.3
Italy	-	-	-	0.4	10.8
France	-	-	0.5	1.3	7.1
Switzerland	0.8	1.6	5.8	4.0	17.5
Japan	-	1.7	1.8	5.3	29.1
Singapore	-	-	-	-	2.0
Others	4.7	7.3	11.1	17.3	32.3

Source: State Statistical Office.

Table 4.1: INTERNATIONAL RESERVES, 1986-92
(Millions of dollars; end of year)

	1986	1987	1988	1989	1990	1991	(Mar.) 1992
Net reserves	57.3	91.7	96.6	102.5	49.2	18.0	7.7
Gross reserves	72.2	148.5	149.2	278.9	177.3	126.7	102.4
of which: foreign exchange	53.5	128.4	130.3	260.1	122.6	74.9	50.6
gold 1/	18.7	20.1	18.9	18.8	54.7	51.8	51.8
Liabilities	14.9	56.8	52.6	176.4	128.1	108.7	94.7

Note: 1/ Gold was valued for 1986-89 and 1990 at about $185 per troy ounce and world price of $385 per troy ounce respectively.

Source: Mongolbank.

Table 4.2: EXCHANGE RATES, 1980–92

	1980	1981	1982	1983	1984	1985	1986	1987	1988	1989	1990	1991	1992 /a
Commercial rates:													
Tugrik/dollar (period average)	2.90	3.19	3.24	3.30	3.54	3.71	3.18	2.89	2.89	3.00	4.67	25.86	40.00
Tugrik/dollar (end of year)	2.96	3.11	3.31	3.41	3.79	3.40	3.06	2.84	3.00	3.00	5.33	40.00	40.00
Tugrik/transferable ruble (period average and end of year)	4.44	4.44	4.44	4.44	4.44	4.44	4.44	4.44	4.44	4.44	4.44	4.44	..
Noncommercial rates:													
Tugrik/dollar (period average)	..	..	..	..	..	..	..	..	20.00	20.00	20.00	40.00	40.00
Tugrik/dollar (end of year)	..	..	..	..	..	..	..	..	20.00	20.00	20.00	40.00	40.00
Tugrik/transferable ruble (end of year)	..	..	..	..	..	..	6.69	6.69	6.69	6.69	6.69	..	
Barter rate:													
Tugrik/dollar (end of year)	..	..	..	..	..	..	..	..	..	..	..	7.10 /b	40.00

/a The barter exchange rate was eliminated on March 23, 1992, leading to a unified exchange rate at $1=Tug.40.
/b The barter exchange rate was $1=Tug.15 between November 1991 and March 1992.

Source: Mongolbank.

Table 5.1: SUMMARY OPERATIONS OF STATE BUDGET, 1980-91
(Millions of Tugriks)

	1980	1981	1982	1983	1984	1985	1986	1987	1988	1989	1990	1991 /d
Total revenue	3452.6	3720.2	4182.3	4477.7	4680.4	4918.0	4360.4	4540.4	4680.7	5243.3	5328.8	9013.7
Tax	3125.3	3397.7	3818.3	4120.0	4296.8	4486.3	3939.5	4073.6	4242.0	4765.6	4392.4	8067.1
Nontax	327.3	322.5	364.0	357.7	383.6	431.7	420.9	466.8	438.7	477.7	936.4	946.6
Total expenditure	3988.6	4145.6	4622.2	4991.5	5244.6	5560.6	6005.4	6359.6	6690.6	7008.0	6744.6	11050.4
Current /a	3337.0	3572.1	3960.2	4195.6	4467.8	4625.1	4874.0	5067.0	5175.8	5378.5	5468.5	9918.3
Capital /b	651.6	573.5	662.0	795.9	776.8	935.5	1131.4	1292.6	1514.8	1629.5	1276.1	1132.1
Overall balance	-536.0	-425.4	-439.9	-513.8	-564.2	-642.6	-1645.0	-1819.2	-2009.9	-1764.7	-1415.8	2036.7
Financing	536.0	425.4	439.9	513.8	564.2	642.6	1645.0	1819.2	2009.9	1764.7	1415.8	2036.7
Foreign	565.6	524.8	512.5	543.8	612.0	682.7	1699.7	1852.3	2015.7	1603.9	1513.3	1825.7
Disbursements	620.7	649.1	647.0	678.3	750.5	823.0	1750.5	1901.3	2066.8	1658.3	1567.7	1839.7
Commodity lending	240.0	306.7	222.2	244.4	311.1	360.0	1200.0	1266.7	1200.0	912.9	768.9	--
Investment lending	380.7	342.4	424.8	433.9	439.4	463.0	550.5	634.6	866.8	745.4	798.8	--
Amortization /a	55.1	124.3	134.5	134.5	138.5	140.3	50.8	49.0	51.1	54.4	54.4	14.0
Domestic	-29.6	-99.4	-72.6	-30.0	-47.8	-40.1	-54.7	-33.1	-5.8	160.8	-97.5	211.0
Compensation account /c	488.3	654.2	815.9	929.8	1022.6	1063.8	--	--	--	--	--	--
Soviet aid	424.4	533.3	622.2	666.7	711.1	755.6	--	--	--	--	--	--
Export price differential	63.9	120.9	193.7	263.1	311.5	308.2	--	--	--	--	--	--

/a The disaggregation of debt service between interest and amortization is parially estimated.
/b Excludes geological feasibility studies, some equipment, classified as current expenditure.
/c Includes the Soviet loans and grants channeled through the compensation account and remittances from export price differentials on goods shipped to the USSR through 1986.
/d Preliminary

Sources: Government of Mongolia, IMF and World Bank staff estimates.

Table 5.2: STATE BUDGET REVENUES, 1980-91
(Millions of Tugriks)

	1980	1981	1982	1983	1984	1985	1986	1987	1988	1989	1990	1991 /a
Total revenue	3452.6	3720.2	4182.3	4477.7	4680.4	4918.0	4360.4	4540.4	4680.7	5243.3	5328.8	9013.7
Of which: Local government	1061.9	1063.5	1153.5	1257.9	1393.0	1380.4	1451.3	1502.2	2033.0	2549.5	1823.5	n.a.
Tax revenue	3125.3	3397.7	3818.3	4120.0	4296.8	4486.3	3939.5	4073.6	4242.0	4765.6	4392.4	8067.1
Turnover taxes	2092.9	2277.4	2465.3	2633.2	2699.9	2735.9	2261.3	2269.2	2246.0	2410.8	2314.4	2178.3
Import price differential	1501.2	1586.1	1629.6	1667.9	1669.5	1744.1	1547.1	1570.0	1570.9	1739.1	1570.7	-
Domestic turnover taxes /b	591.7	691.3	835.7	965.3	1030.4	991.8	714.2	699.2	675.1	671.7	743.7	-
Profit taxes	968.6	1056.9	1291.9	1425.5	1533.2	1686.0	1608.2	1736.2	1921.1	2276.0	2011.5	2602.0
Production taxes	30.9	29.0	25.1	24.0	24.1	22.6	25.7	21.9	26.4	24.6	16.2	-
Taxes on individuals	32.9	34.4	36.0	37.3	39.6	41.8	44.3	46.3	48.5	54.2	50.3	-
Customs duties	-	-	-	-	-	-	-	-	-	-	-	294.7
Windfall gains	-	-	-	-	-	-	-	-	-	-	-	2082.9
Nontax revenue	327.3	322.5	364.0	357.7	383.6	431.7	420.9	466.8	438.7	477.7	936.4	1812.7
From state enterprises	13.8	24.2	27.9	32.8	31.5	28.5	32.0	32.9	33.4	32.4	30.5	-
From cooperatives	42.2	42.4	49.3	47.6	46.5	41.3	47.3	53.6	48.8	55.1	31.3	-
Social security premia	158.5	169.3	176.7	185.5	198.6	206.0	218.6	229.0	242.1	253.0	243.3	866.1
Other	112.8	86.6	110.1	91.8	107.0	155.9	123.0	151.3	114.4	137.2	631.3	-
Duty taxes	-	-	-	-	-	-	-	-	-	-	-	-

/a Preliminary
/b Including, from 1986, taxes arising from the differential in export contract prices.

Sources: Government of Mongolia, IMF and World Bank staff estimates.

Table 5.3: STATE BUDGET EXPENDITURES, 1980-91
(Millions of Tugriks)

	1980	1981	1982	1983	1984	1985	1986	1987	1988	1989	1990	1991 /c
Total expenditures	3988.6	4145.6	4622.2	4991.5	5244.6	5560.6	6005.4	6359.6	6690.6	7008.0	6744.6	11050.4
Of which: Local government	1521.5	1541.8	1625.0	1727.3	1866.0	1969.8	2416.9	2805.5	3143.9	3437.7	3365.7	n.a.
Current expenditures	3337.0	3572.1	3960.2	4195.6	4467.8	4625.1	4874.0	5067.0	5175.8	5378.5	5468.3	9918.3
Of which: Wages and salaries	680.2	736.7	747.4	797.6	843.9	888.8	901.2	903.2	953.8	975.6	904.3	1862.6
National development	1204.3	1251.4	1539.4	1659.1	1816.4	1843.8	1924.0	1968.1	1916.1	2087.6	2101.2	--
Interest payments /a	105.6	40.2	77.7	113.4	138.6	167.5	5.8	33.3	99.6	169.2	229.1	--
Export subsidies	342.7	386.9	476.3	528.0	558.2	563.6	483.0	459.7	401.8	432.3	333.6	--
Other	756.0	824.3	985.4	1017.7	1119.6	1112.7	1435.2	1475.1	1414.7	1486.1	1538.5	--
Social and cultural	1494.9	1612.2	1723.7	1819.3	1903.5	1999.4	2095.3	2228.6	2371.6	2445.7	2612.1	--
Free food and medicine	157.1	171.7	182.2	229.8	247.6	244.1	246.6	245.9	269.9	297.1	294.7	--
Social security payments	129.1	136.6	138.8	146.2	154.3	174.3	177.4	207.4	241.0	220.6	235.9	2165.7
Pensions	293.6	313.2	333.5	358.3	380.5	401.8	425.4	456.1	481.7	508.8	557.3	--
Material expenditure	453.6	500.2	553.9	514.3	528.2	555.7	610.9	672.5	676.1	698.3	802.9	--
Other	461.5	490.5	515.3	570.7	592.9	623.5	635.0	546.7	702.9	720.9	721.3	--
Administration and defense	581.5	631.5	641.5	664.5	691.6	712.6	790.2	792.5	813.2	777.0	680.6	--
Other	56.3	77.0	55.6	52.7	56.3	69.3	64.5	77.8	74.9	68.2	74.6	--
Investments /b	651.6	573.5	662.0	795.9	776.8	935.5	1131.4	1292.6	1514.8	1629.5	1276.1	1132.1
Material sectors	225.1	168.6	197.3	252.1	252.9	318.4	473.9	530.1	696.6	785.5	863.6	--
Nonmaterial sectors	426.5	404.9	464.7	543.8	523.9	617.1	657.5	762.5	818.2	844.0	412.5	--

/a Partially estimated from debt-service data.

/b Excludes geological feasibility studies, some equipment, classified as current expenditure.

/c Preliminary.

Sources: Government of Mongolia, IMF and World Bank staff estimates.

Table 5.4.: TRANSFERS TO PUBLIC ENTERPRISES AND SUBSIDIES, 1986-91

(Millions of Tugriks)

	1986	1987	1988	1989	1990	1991 Budget
Total transfers and subsidies	1,693.9	1,656.0	1,618.2	1,754.9	1,698.4	1,092.6
Agriculture	497.9	515.8	457.2	502.0	528.4	30.0
Price incentives to increase production	168.9	122.4	159.1	148.8	113.4	30.0
Farmgate price subsidy	57.1	102.8	100.1	102.9	-	-
Transportation of fodder for winter	151.1	143.1	149.0	140.1	179.3	-
Crop cultivation in state farms	-	-	-	-	156.0	-
Current assets shortfall compensation	93.6	100.2	7.0	79.5	70.0	-
Compensation for anticipated losses /a	15.7	30.5	26.5	29.2	1.2	-
Other subsidies	11.5	16.8	15.5	6.5	8.5	-
Industry	240.8	263.3	303.3	339.7	447.2	609.8
Electric and heating energy production /b	53.8	75.2	84.4	97.2	165.5	437.8
Clothing, shoes, boots etc for children	69.7	85.5	96.2	103.8	107.5	135.3
Subsidiezed cow milk supply in Ulaanbaatar	23.6	22.4	29.1	38.7	36.2	36.7
Bread production	-	-	-	8.8	8.3	-
Meat storage	12.8	20.0	30.8	33.2	43.0	-
Wood transport to processing factories	6.1	6.3	20.0	20.7	18.0	-
Coal mines	30.1	35.3	29.0	29.2	40.5	-
Sheep wool boots	-	-	-	-	13.5	-
Newspaper printing /c	-	-	-	-	3.8	-
Compensation for anticipated losses /a	27.7	10.9	3.2	2.3	3.9	-
Current assets shortfall compensation	13.4	3.5	5.9	-	2.7	-
Glass production	3.6	4.2	4.7	5.8	4.3	-
Construction	51.8	25.4	18.0	15.8	17.8	18.0
Subsidy to the Mapping Office	14.3	15.0	15.3	15.8	16.8	18.0
Current assets shortfall compensation	29.9	2.5	1.4	-	1.0	-
Compensation for anticipated losses /a	7.6	7.9	1.3	-	-	-
Transport	28.6	29.7	33.4	23.2	31.6	25.3
Public transport /d	27.0	29.3	29.7	23.2	31.6	25.3
Current assets shortfall compensation	0.5	0.3	-	-	-	-
Compensation for anticipated losses /a	1.1	0.1	3.7	-	-	-
Trade	594.2	526.1	469.0	477.6	347.0	-
Export subsidies	483.0	459.7	401.8	432.3	333.6	-
Export quality premia (incentives)	55.7	32.1	34.1	22.6	5.7	-
Current assets shortfall compensation	21.0	-	-	-	-	-
Petroleum price difference compensation	20.8	20.2	22.3	5.8	-	-
Other subsidies	13.7	14.1	10.8	16.9	7.7	-
Housing	69.5	72.6	117.9	172.9	101.8	71.2
Private sector home building	-	-	-	3.3	6.1	31.2
Compensation for increase in interest rates	69.5	72.6	117.9	169.6	95.7	40.0
Other services	211.1	223.1	219.4	223.7	224.6	338.3
Geologic research	138.2	145.5	134.2	135.8	144.7	200.0
Veterinary services	72.9	77.6	85.2	87.9	79.9	138.3

/a Compensation for anticipated losses during a transitional period.

/b For electric energy production by diesel generators in aimaks not connected to the central energy system. In some aimaks production of heating energy is also subsidized.

/c Compensation for price differentials.

/d Auto- and trolleybus services in Ulaan Baatar.

Sources: Ministry of Finance and The World Bank.

Table 6.1: MONETARY SURVEY, 1986-91
(Millions of Tugriks, end of year)

	1986	1987	1988	1989	1990	1991 /b
Net foreign reserves	181.9	275.1	289.8	307.5	270.2	761.5
Other foreign assets, net /a	-529.9	-472.2	-250.9	-41.2	-364.1	-802.8
Net domestic assets	5520.3	5433.0	4735.3	4821.2	6460.7	9994.6
Domestic credit	5520.3	5433.0	5786.1	5903.1	6573.9	11195.5
Government	-2385.3	-2431.6	12209.0	-2050.0	-1454.2	-1666.8
Public enterprises	7608.5	7558.7	7606.2	7562.4	7549.7	10454.4
Private	297.1	305.9	388.9	390.7	478.4	2407.9
of which: cooperatives	—	—	353.1	324.7	351.2	n.a.
Other items, net	-962.4	-861.4	-1050.8	-1081.9	-113.2	-1200.5
Liabilities (M2)	4199.9	4374.5	4774.2	5087.5	6366.8	9953.6
Money	2738.1	2835.3	3021.7	3509.6	4658.8	7286.5
Currency in circulation	439.9	490.0	526.1	581.1	642.7	1695.5
Current accounts	2298.2	2345.3	2495.6	2928.5	4016.1	5591.0
Quasi-money	1461.8	1539.2	1752.5	1577.9	1708.0	2667.1

Note: Data for 1990 presented according to new classification system; to the extent possible, figures for 1988-89 have been revised accordingly.

/a Includes net balances held at IBEC, net borrowing from IBEC, and borrowing in rubles from the Foreign Trade Bank in Moscow, and capital subscriptives to IBRD and AsDB.

/b Preliminary.

Sources: Mongolbank, IMF and World Bank staff estimates.

Table 7.1: GROSS OUTPUT IN AGRICULTURE, 1991
(Thousand Tugriks)

	Current prices					Constant (1986) prices		
	Gross Output	Net input + depreciation	Net material product	Of which Wages	Profits	Gross output	Net input + depreciation	Net material product
Agricultural Production Cooperatives	1,980,785.3	669,663.7	1,311,721.6	809,975.2	501,146.4	928,779.0	310,709.8	618,069.2
Livestock	1,809,174.6	551,931.0	1,257,243.6	760,386.4	496,857.2	856,952.1	261,433.3	595,518.8
Crop farming	171,610.7	117,732.7	53,878.0	49,588.8	4,289.2	71,826.9	49,276.5	22,550.4
State Farms	1,279,226.3	729,836.9	549,389.4	345,541.1	203,848.3	606,655.3	343,620.1	263,035.2
Livestock	544,104.3	325,619.9	218,484.4	156,258.1	62,226.3	206,685.8	123,691.3	82,994.5
Crop farming	735,122.0	404,217.0	330,905.0	189,283.0	141,622.0	399,969.5	219,928.8	180,040.7
Intercooperative organizations A /a	7,020.8	2,931.9	4,088.9	3,048.1	1,040.8	4,651.1	1,907.9	2,743.2
Livestock	5,613.5	2,220.4	3,393.1	2,482.5	910.6	4,032.3	1,595.0	2,437.3
Crop farming	1,407.3	711.5	695.8	565.6	130.2	618.8	312.9	305.9
Intercooperative organizations B /b	27,651.2	15,217.7	12,433.5	7,432.3	5,001.2	10,166.8	5,985.8	4,181.0
Livestock	11,658.8	8,346.4	3,312.4	2,780.3	532.1	5,651.2	4,045.6	1,605.6
Crop farming	15,992.4	6,871.3	9,121.1	4,652.0	4,469.1	4,515.6	1,940.2	2,575.4
Scientific institutions	15,087.6	4,863.9	10,223.7	5,826.0	4,397.7	13,244.9	3,792.7	9,452.2
Livestock	6,090.8	1,118.6	4,972.2	2,685.2	2,287.0	7,397.8	1,358.6	6,039.2
Crop farming	8,996.8	3,745.3	5,251.5	3,140.8	2,110.7	5,847.1	2,434.1	3,413.0
State-owned enterprises	45,004.4	--	45,004.4	--	45,004.4	24,378.7	--	24,378.7
Livestock	28,926.5	--	28,926.5	--	28,926.5	12,870.8	--	72,870.8
Crop farming	16,077.9	--	16,077.9	--	16,077.9	11,507.9	--	11,507.9
Households	1,520,505.7	--	1,520,505.7	1,520,505.7	--	774,940.5	--	774,940.5
Livestock	1,495,709.7	--	1,495,709.7	1,495,709.7	--	749,548.8	--	749,548.8
Crop farming	24,796.0	--	24,796.0	24,796.0	--	25,391.7	--	25,391.7
TOTAL	4,875,281.3	1,422,514.1	3,452,767.2	2,692,328.4	760,438.8	2,362,816.2	666,016.2	1,696,800.0
Livestock	3,901,278.2	889,236.3	3,012,041.9	2,420,302.2	591,739.7	1,843,138.8	392,123.8	1,451,015.0
Crop farming	974,003.1	533,277.8	440,725.3	272,026.2	168,699.1	519,677.4	273,892.4	245,785.0

/a There is one intercooperative organization type A in each aimak. Main activities are in construction and transport.
/b Activities of intercooperative organizations type B are mainly in crop production.

Source: State Statistical Office.

Table 7.2: **AGRICULTURAL PRODUCTION, FIXED (1986) PRICES, 1970–91**
(in millions of Tugrik)

	1970	1975	1980	1981	1982	1983	1984	1985	1986	1987	1988	1989	1990	1991
Total gross agricultural production	1,622.6	1,995.0	1,746.1	1,959.4	2,176.9	2,209.7	2,140.0	2,464.5	2,552.5	2,468.7	2,536.2	2,650.7	2,551.8	2,491.5
Crop production	258.0	458.8	319.5	397.8	576.9	797.7	701.9	816.2	816.5	749.1	761.0	802.0	700.2	531.9
Of which:														
Grains	185.5	314.6	168.5	209.4	335.8	530.9	391.9	523.2	436.8	346.9	410.9	422.6	362.1	302.8
Fodder and rootcrops	37.7	78.1	82.0	105.5	120.9	129.3	145.7	144.5	202.6	202.8	187.8	68.1	77.6	23.1
Potatoes	17.5	34.1	31.8	33.9	63.0	81.7	105.6	95.4	111.3	119.0	86.5	130.5	109.8	81.7
Vegetables	16.0	27.0	35.1	36.2	48.4	47.8	46.1	48.4	56.1	62.8	73.1	78.0	59.3	36.0
Fruits	0.9	1.3	1.6	1.2	2.2	1.7	1.3	1.2	1.9	1.1	1.1	1.2	2.2	2.7
Animal production	1,364.6	1,536.2	1,426.6	1,561.6	1,600.0	1,412.0	1,438.1	1,648.3	1,736.0	1,719.6	1,775.2	1,848.7	1,851.6	1,959.7
Of which:														
Livestock for slaughter	830.0	1,086.5	1,112.7	1,160.0	1,146.7	1,132.7	1,147.8	1,178.8	1,058.0	1,039.9	1,007.2	1,074.4	1,121.9	1,286.5
Of which:														
Cattle	238.2	275.3	348.5	339.1	317.8	330.6	330.8	330.3	365.5	352.5	355.6	353.2	321.0	401.6
Smaller cattle	412.0	571.2	524.4	574.9	596.4	560.9	573.0	526.8	557.1	547.7	510.2	553.3	594.3	687.2
Pigs	3.0	6.2	11.3	15.3	14.2	16.3	20.3	23.9	26.1	32.8	40.7	59.4	85.0	56.8
Poultry	0.6	1.0	1.5	1.5	1.5	1.3	1.6	1.7	1.9	2.0	2.5	2.2	1.9	1.7
Milk	129.5	130.4	129.0	130.9	137.6	127.5	148.0	162.7	298.8	302.0	303.4	322.4	315.4	316.0
Eggs	2.8	9.1	10.5	9.4	9.3	10.8	11.4	12.7	13.3	14.1	15.2	17.6	18.6	12.9
Material inputs	384.5	615.8	741.2	777.5	828.0	812.0	907.6	1,116.4	1,125.9	1,133.0	1,168.6	1,094.4	1,026.2	1,071.3
Of which:														
Crop production	30.2	129.2	346.6	368.3	441.2	437.9	520.3	503.4	535.2	567.8	559.3	573.0	518.5	541.2
Animal production	354.3	486.6	394.6	409.2	386.8	374.1	387.3	613.0	590.7	565.2	609.3	521.4	507.7	530.1
Net material product	1,072.4	1,050.4	1,004.9	1,181.9	1,349.1	1,347.2	1,232.4	1,348.1	1,426.6	1,335.7	1,367.1	1,556.3	1,525.6	1,420.2
Of which:														
Crop production	(227.8)	(329.6)	(27.1)	29.5	135.7	309.3	181.6	312.8	281.3	181.3	201.2	1,327.3	181.7	169.1
Animal production	1,300.2	1,380.0	1,032.0	1,152.4	1,213.4	1,037.9	1,050.8	1,035.3	1,145.3	1,154.4	1,165.9	229.0	1,343.9	1,251.1

Source: State Statistical Office.

Table 7.3: PRODUCTION AND AVERAGE YIELD OF MAJOR AGRICULTURAL CROPS, 1970–91

	1970	1975	1980	1981	1982	1983	1984	1985	1986	1987	1988	1989	1990	1991
Production (thousand tons)														
Wheat	288.1	413.0	229.8	295.5	440.1	647.6	460.4	688.5	663.7	543.3	672.2	686.9	596.2	538.3
Maize /a	6.6	44.3	15.7	38.6	55.6	35.4	24.6	1.3	9.5	-	-	-	-	-
Barley	10.1	67.5	35.2	32.8	67.6	88.8	87.4	132.4	146.0	102.0	100.2	108.5	88.9	48.0
Oats	26.3	52.4	19.4	13.0	34.0	57.2	38.3	52.6	49.3	37.8	37.4	38.2	30.2	7.2
Sunflower seed /a	-	48.4	23.9	76.4	90.5	141.9	166.0	306.2	246.3	204.2	148.5	222.7	246.3	131.5
Potatoes	20.8	40.7	37.9	40.4	75.1	97.5	126.0	113.9	132.8	147.6	103.0	155.5	131.1	97.5
Average yield (tons/ha)														
Wheat	8.3	13.1	5.6	7.2	10.2	14.6	10.0	14.3	14.2	11.6	10.5	13.0	11.2	10.1
Maize /a	27.0	76.0	41.2	69.8	87.8	84.5	124.5	6.4	23.3	-	-	-	-	-
Barley	6.7	12.5	3.8	4.2	12.0	11.9	10.2	13.9	14.5	10.2	9.9	10.9	10.1	8.1
Oats	5.1	8.9	4.0	2.7	10.2	10.8	6.9	12.0	10.0	8.1	8.8	10.3	10.4	3.5
Sunflower seed /a	-	12.4	37.4	90.3	98.6	133.3	132.7	202.8	130.5	120.3	87.8	102.3	126.3	107.7
Potatoes	72.5	94.4	50.9	86.1	99.7	102.1	130.0	110.1	119.1	118.8	78.3	123.2	107.7	96.6

/a For the years 1987–91, sunflower seeds and maize figures are combined.

Source: State Statistical Office.

Table 7.4: NET PRODUCT OF AGRICULTURE, 1980–91

(millions of Tugriks)

	1980	1981	1982	1983	1984	1985	1986	1987	1988	1989	1990	1991
Current prices												
Total	838.2	1,007.7	1,219.5	1,320.2	1,250.2	1,237.8	1,520.7	1,405.5	1,510.0	1,722.9	1,686.9	3,452.7
State farms	(35.8)	20.9	84.5	223.5	138.7	165.8	221.9	148.6	203.3	231.7	241.3	559.6
Cooperatives	532.9	622.9	739.9	664.4	651.2	563.6	729.3	670.2	664.6	805.8	757.7	1,327.6
Personal plots and private farms	341.1	363.9	395.1	432.3	460.3	508.4	569.5	586.7	642.1	685.4	687.9	1,565.5
1986 Constant prices												
Total	1,004.9	1,181.9	1,348.9	1,347.7	1,232.4	1,348.1	1,426.6	1,335.7	1,367.1	1,556.3	1,525.6	1,696.8
State farms	(44.7)	15.8	89.8	270.4	150.9	227.2	195.0	182.1	173.5	196.3	189.5	272.5
Cooperatives	661.3	749.6	806.5	623.9	605.5	640.2	681.9	637.5	622.2	755.3	710.8	625.0
Personal plots and private farms	388.3	416.5	452.6	453.4	476.0	480.7	549.7	516.1	571.4	604.7	625.3	799.3

Source: State Statistical Office.

Table 7.5: IMPLICIT PRODUCER PRICE INDICES IN AGRICULTURE, 1991
(1986=1)

	Gross output	Net input + depreciation	Net material product
Agricultural production cooperatives	2.133	2.155	2.121
Livestock	2.111	2.111	2.111
Crop farming	2.389	2.389	2.389
State farms	2.109	2.124	2.089
Livestock	2.632	2.632	2.632
Crop farming	1.838	1.838	1.838
Intercooperative organizations A /a	1.509	1.537	1.491
Livestock	1.392	1.392	1.392
Crop farming	2.274	2.274	2.274
Intercooperative organizations B /b	2.720	2.542	2.974
Livestock	2.063	2.063	2.063
Crop farming	3.542	3.542	3.542
Scientific institutions	1.139	1.282	1.082
Livestock	0.833	0.823	0.823
Crop farming	1.539	1.539	1.539
State-owned enterprises	1.846	0	1.846
Livestock	2.247	0	2.247
Crop farming	1.397	0	1.397
Households	1.962	0	1.962
Livestock	1.995	0	1.995
Crop farming	0.976	0	0.976
TOTAL	2.063	2.136	2.035
Livestock	2.117	2.268	2.076
Crop farming	1.874	1.947	2.170

/a There is one intercooperative organization type A in each aimak. Main activities are in construction and transport.
/b Activities of intercooperative organizations type B are mainly in crop production.

Source: State Statistical Office.

Table 7.6a GROSS OUTPUT IN THE LIVESTOCK SECTOR, 1991

(Tons unless stated otherwise)

	Total	Agricultural production cooperatives	State farms	Intercooperative organizations A a/	Intercooperative organizations B b/	Scientific institutions	State-owned enterprises	Households
Meat - Total	577,837	326,622	64,460	603	1,211	213	4,384	180,344
Camel	41,391	23,773	583	-	15	9	57	16,955
Horse	72,744	28,177	9,354	32	60	33	8	35,084
Cattle	167,503	62,307	24,164	164	387	47	1,556	78,879
Sheep	234,870	167,553	27,437	345	622	42	1,752	37,119
Goat	53,911	42,969	1,294	57	103	82	39	9,366
Pig	6,414	1,080	1,405	6	24	1	961	2,939
Poultry	391	152	224	-	-	-	11	4
Others	612	612	-	-	-	-	-	-
Milk - Total	311,284	102,714	46,361	462	1,653	108	5,022	154,964
Camel	916	645	-	-	-	-	1	269
Horse	21,120	7,038	599	21	16	-	301	13,145
Cattle	257,427	77,931	45,336	403	1,624	85	4,399	127,649
Sheep	17,906	9,407	348	34	11	-	229	7,878
Goat	13,915	7,693	78	5	2	23	92	6,022
Wool - Total	28,624	17,460	2,232	58	279	192	256	8,147
Sheep	2,446	1,860	17	18	25	6	21	499
Camel	21,493	13,321	2,077	36	53	37	194	5,744
Goat hair	1,645	914	29	1	1	87	17	597
Goat cashmere	898	450	12	1	93	51	6	284
Horse, yak and cattle cashmere	1,304	542	66	2	95	11	10	579
Horse, yak and cattle hair	840	373	31	1	13	-	8	414
Poultry eggs ('000 pieces)	25,492	330	25,122	14	25	-	-	-
Poultry feathers (kg)	4,700	4,700	-	-	-	-	-	-
Honey	36	1	5	-	-	30	-	-
Deer antlers (kg)	456	-	456	-	-	-	-	-
Fur skins - Total ('000 pieces)								
Karakul ('000 pieces)	32	9	23	-	-	-	-	-
Black fox (piece)	3,320	-	3,320	-	-	-	-	-
Marsh beaver (piece)	1,128	-	1,128	-	-	-	-	-
Other livestock products	1,250	245	220	-	-	-	-	785

a/ There is one intercooperative organization type A in each aimak. Main activities are in construction and transport.
b/ Activities of intercooperative organizations type B are mainly in crop production.

Source: State Statistical Office.

Table 7.6b GROSS OUTPUT IN THE LIVESTOCK SECTOR, 1990

(Million tugriks at current prices)

	Total	Agricultural production cooperatives	State farms	Intercooperative organizations A a/	Intercooperative organizations B b/	Scientific institutions	State-owned enterprises	Households
Meat - Total	2,455.5	1,300.5	305.5	2.7	5.8	1.0	24.8	815.2
Camel	106.5	50.6	2.6	-	0.1	0.1	0.3	52.8
Horse	279.5	120.0	33.5	0.1	0.2	0.1	0.0	125.7
Cattle	816.9	309.3	108.3	0.7	1.9	0.2	7.5	389.1
Sheep	1,025.7	684.9	140.2	1.7	3.2	0.2	8.0	187.5
Goat	160.1	120.2	3.9	0.2	0.2	0.5	0.1	35.0
Pig	58.5	9.8	14.5	0.1	0.2	0.0	8.8	25.1
Poultry	3.5	0.9	2.5	0.0	0.0	-	0.1	0.0
Others	4.8	4.8	-	-	0.0	-	-	-
Milk - Total	651.3	155.7	143.3	0.9	5.4	0.3	7.4	338.3
Camel	2.4	1.6	-	-	-	-	0.0	0.7
Horse	51.9	18.4	1.1	0.1	0.1	-	0.8	31.5
Cattle	545.7	110.7	141.6	0.7	5.4	0.3	6.2	280.8
Sheep	29.1	13.3	0.5	0.1	0.0	-	0.3	15.0
Goat	22.3	11.8	0.1	0.0	0.0	0.0	0.1	10.2
Wool - Total	710.2	448.8	38.3	0.6	0.4	1.7	7.0	213.5
Sheep	110.9	88.8	0.7	0.0	0.0	0.0	1.1	20.2
Camel	210.0	125.6	30.2	0.3	0.2	0.0	1.6	52.0
Goat hair	376.4	227.7	6.9	0.2	0.2	1.7	4.1	135.7
Goat cashmere	4.8	3.0	0.0	0.0	0.0	0.0	0.0	1.7
Horse, yak and cattle cashmere	4.4	2.1	0.2	0.0	0.0	0.0	0.0	2.0
Horse, yak and cattle hair	3.8	1.6	0.2	0.0	0.0	0.0	0.0	1.9
Poultry eggs	33.1	0.5	32.5	0.0	0.0	-	-	-
Poultry feathers	-	-	-	-	-	-	-	-
Honey	3.6	0.1	0.4	-	0.0	3.1	-	-
Deer antlers	4.3	-	4.3	-	-	-	-	-
Fur skins - Total	28.0	1.1	26.9	-	-	-	0.0	0.0
Karakul	1.4	1.1	0.2	-	-	-	-	-
Black fox	7.3	-	7.3	-	-	-	-	-
Marsh beaver	1.0	-	1.0	-	-	-	-	-
Increase in principal livestock c/	-20.4	-110.7	-22.3	1.4	-	-	-	111.1
Increase in other livestock	-57.3	-6.5	-11.0	-	-	-	-10.2	-29.6
Other animal production	93.1	19.6	26.4	-	-	-	-	47.1
Total Livestock Production	3,901.3	1,809.2	544.1	5.6	11.7	6.1	28.9	1,495.7

a/ There is one intercooperative organization type A in each aimak. Main activities are in construction and transport.
b/ Activities of intercooperative organizations type B are mainly in crop production.
c/ Camel, horse, cattle, sheep and goat.

Source: State Statistical Office.

Table 7.6c GROSS OUTPUT IN THE LIVESTOCK SECTOR, 1990

(Million tugriks at constant 1986 prices)

	Total	Agricultural production cooperatives	State farms	Intercooperative organizations A a/	Intercooperative organizations B b/	Scientific institutions	State-owned enterprises	Households
Meat - Total	1,220.0	676.5	145.5	1.3	2.8	0.4	14.1	379.4
Camel	51.5	29.6	0.7	-	0.0	0.0	0.1	21.1
Horse	101.6	39.3	13.1	0.0	0.1	0.0	0.0	49.0
Cattle	406.4	151.2	58.6	0.4	0.9	0.1	3.8	191.4
Sheep	517.2	369.0	60.4	0.8	1.4	0.1	3.9	81.7
Goat	99.2	79.1	2.4	0.1	0.2	0.2	0.1	17.2
Pig	41.5	7.0	9.1	0.0	0.2	0.0	6.2	19.0
Poultry	2.1	0.8	1.2	0.0	0.0	-	0.1	0.0
Others	0.7	0.7	-	-	-	-	-	-
Milk - Total	310.7	99.4	48.8	0.6	1.7	0.1	5.1	154.9
Camel	0.7	0.5	-	-	-	-	-	0.2
Horse	17.1	5.7	0.5	0.0	0.0	-	0.2	10.7
Cattle	273.3	82.7	48.1	0.6	1.7	0.1	4.7	135.4
Sheep	11.1	5.8	0.2	0.0	0.0	-	0.1	4.9
Goat	8.6	4.7	0.0	0.0	0.0	0.0	0.1	3.7
Wool - Total	345.3	192.0	23.5	0.6	1.1	6.1	4.0	117.9
Sheep	76.9	38.5	0.3	0.3	0.2	0.1	1.5	36.1
Camel	151.8	89.8	20.9	0.2	0.3	0.2	1.3	38.9
Goat hair	107.4	59.7	1.9	0.1	0.0	5.7	1.1	39.0
Goat cashmere	2.3	1.2	0.0	0.0	0.2	0.1	0.0	0.7
Horse, yak and cattle cashmere	3.3	1.4	0.2	0.0	0.2	0.0	0.0	1.5
Horse, yak and cattle hair	3.6	1.6	0.1	0.0	0.1	0.0	0.0	2.0
Poultry eggs	12.5	0.2	12.3	0.0	0.0	-	-	-
Poultry feathers	-	-	-	-	-	-	-	-
Honey	0.9	0.0	0.1	-	0.0	0.8	-	-
Deer antlers	0.3	-	0.3	-	-	-	-	-
Fur skins - Total	6.2	1.0	5.2	-	-	-	0.0	0.0
Karakul	3.7	1.0	2.6	-	-	-	-	-
Black fox	0.6	-	0.6	-	-	-	-	-
Marsh beaver	0.1	-	0.1	-	-	-	-	-
Increase in principal livestock c/	-20.4	-110.7	-22.3	1.4	-	-	-	111.1
Increase in other livestock	-57.3	-6.5	-11.0	-	-	-	-10.2	-29.6
Other animal production	25.0	4.9	4.4	-	-	-	-	15.7
Total Livestock Production	1,843.1	857.0	206.7	4.0	5.7	7.4	12.9	749.5

a/ There is one intercooperative organization type A in each aimak. Main activities are in construction and transport.
b/ Activities of intercooperative organizations type B are mainly in crop production.
c/ Camel, horse, cattle, sheep and goat.

Source: State Statistical Office.

Table 7.6d: IMPLICIT PRODUCER PRICES IN THE LIVESTOCK SECTOR, 1990
(Tugrik/kg unless stated otherwise)

	Total	Agricultural production cooperatives	State farms	Intercooperative organizations A a/	Intercooperative organizations B b/	Scientific institutions	State-owned enterprises	House-holds
Meat - Total	2.41	2.22	3.47	2.13	2.20	2.46	3.42	2.47
Camel	1.46	1.50	1.99	1.70	1.25	5.38	2.30	1.23
Horse	1.59	1.53	1.86	1.56	1.42	1.12	1.38	1.65
Cattle	2.65	2.54	2.95	2.45	3.00	3.11	3.08	2.66
Sheep	2.42	2.36	3.15	2.05	1.92	2.34	2.84	2.28
Goat	1.90	1.91	1.90	1.16	1.62	1.16	1.43	1.92
Pig	7.48	7.32	9.11	7.70	3.40	7.52	6.81	6.81
Poultry	7.20	16.43	5.62	7.73	6.23	12.56	6.00	6.00
Milk - Total	1.21	0.82	1.96	1.12	1.86	1.17	1.28	1.20
Camel	1.11	1.06	2.24	-	-	-	-	1.25
Horse	0.98	1.03	1.16	0.68	1.05	1.45	1.44	0.92
Cattle	1.28	0.83	1.98	1.19	1.90	1.19	1.25	1.28
Sheep	0.67	0.63	0.86	0.74	0.99	0.95	-	0.73
Goat	0.75	0.69	1.04	0.80	0.74	0.97	-	0.83
Wool - Total	12.27	12.77	14.15	6.65	9.01	64.36	8.58	10.58
Sheep	7.33	6.92	13.43	5.76	6.13	3.98	6.09	6.02
Camel	22.75	22.49	22.21	17.00	3.33	-	18.60	24.49
Goat hair	1.40	1.21	1.59	2.57	2.33	4.00	0.59	1.78
Goat cashmere	86.89	93.93	103.19	49.93	113.60	160.31	64.87	72.04
Horse, yak and cattle cashmere	2.58	2.50	3.44	1.28	2.78	3.00	1.86	2.63
Horse, yak and cattle hair	3.48	3.14	4.77	2.27	5.00	2.33	3.66	3.77
Poultry egg (Tugrik/piece)	0.60	0.94	0.58	-	0.68	1.13	0.80	0.80
Poultry feathers	29.93	7.23	33.79	-	-	-	-	-
Honey	39.82	29.07	36.14	-	35.17	47.20	-	-
Fur skins - Total (Tugrik/piece)	194.30	77.81	248.45	-	-	-	16.00	16.02
Karakul (Tugrik/piece)	140.08	86.24	197.91	-	-	-	-	-
Black fox (Tugrik/piece)	574.63	-	574.63	-	-	-	-	-
Marsh beaver (Tugrik/piece)	300.00	-	300.00	-	-	-	-	-
Other livestock products	64.21	105.17	59.83	-	-	-	-	47.34

a/ There is one intercooperative organization type A in each aimak. Main activities are in construction and transport.
b/ Activities of intercooperative organizations type B are mainly in crop production.

Source: WOrld Bank staff calculations based on data from the State Statistical Office.

Table 7.6e: IMPLICIT PRODUCER PRICE INDICES IN LIVESTOCK SECTOR, 1990 (1986=1)

	Total	Agricultural production cooperatives	State farms	Intercooperative organizations A a/	Intercooperative organizations B b/	Scientific institutions	State-owned enterprises	House-holds
Meat - Total	1.100	1.070	1.337	0.971	0.935	1.098	1.160	1.080
Camel	1.174	1.203	1.596	1.363	1.005	4.321	1.849	0.989
Horse	1.137	1.093	1.335	1.118	1.017	0.802	0.987	1.183
Cattle	1.091	1.047	1.214	1.009	1.235	1.283	1.270	1.096
Sheep	1.098	1.071	1.431	0.932	0.872	1.063	1.290	1.037
Goat	1.035	1.036	1.031	0.630	0.881	0.633	0.777	1.044
Pig	1.157	1.132	1.408	1.191	0.525	1.163	1.053	1.053
Poultry	1.351	3.081	1.054	1.449	1.169	2.355	1.125	1.125
Milk - Total	1.207	0.844	1.860	1.112	1.782	1.177	1.247	1.204
Camel	1.450	1.383	2.934	-	-	-	-	1.639
Horse	1.204	1.265	1.436	0.837	1.300	1.792	1.772	1.137
Cattle	1.210	0.782	1.868	1.117	1.794	1.120	1.180	1.208
Sheep	1.082	1.027	1.386	1.192	1.605	1.534	-	1.180
Goat	1.209	1.121	1.681	1.295	1.199	1.576	-	1.340
Wool - Total	1.132	1.133	1.832	0.794	1.027	2.193	0.901	0.981
Sheep	1.036	0.978	1.899	0.815	0.866	0.562	0.861	0.851
Camel	1.100	1.088	1.074	0.822	0.161	-	0.899	1.184
Goat hair	0.548	0.474	0.621	1.005	0.912	1.564	0.231	0.698
Goat cashmere	1.331	1.438	1.580	0.765	1.740	2.455	0.993	1.103
Horse, yak and cattle cashmere	1.025	0.994	1.366	0.508	1.104	1.192	0.741	1.047
Horse, yak and cattle hair	0.802	0.724	1.102	0.525	1.154	0.539	0.845	0.869
Poultry eggs	1.226	1.925	1.189	-	1.398	2.296	1.629	1.629
Poultry feathers	2.993	0.723	3.379	-	-	-	-	-
Honey	1.564	1.142	1.419	-	1.381	1.854	-	-
Deer antlers	1.969	-	1.969	-	-	-	-	-
Fur skins - Total	1.964	0.793	2.443	-	-	-	1.000	1.001
Karakul	1.229	0.757	1.736	-	-	-	-	-
Black fox	2.993	-	2.993	-	-	-	-	-
Marsh beaver	1.000	-	1.000	-	-	-	-	-
Increase in principal livestock c/	1.000	1.000	1.000	1.000	1.000	-	-	1.000
Increase in other livestock	1.000	1.000	1.000	-	-	-	1.000	1.000
Other livestock products	1.000	1.000	1.000	-	-	-	-	1.000
Total Livestock Production	1.125	1.055	1.511	0.981	1.131	1.598	1.203	1.091

a/ There is one intercooperative organization type A in each aimak. Main activities are in construction and transport.
b/ Activities of intercooperative organizations type B are mainly in crop production.
c/ Camel, horse, cattle, sheep and goat.

Source: World Bank staff calculations based on data from the State Statistical Office.

Table 8.1: INDUSTRIAL PRODUCTION, FIXED (1986) PRICES, 1970-91
(In Thousands of Tugriks)

	1970	1975	1980	1985	1986	1987	1988	1989	1990	1991
Power	152,583.2	247,908.9	410,936.2	724,128.4	795,523.4	830,314.7	890,299.1	919,822.1	914,967.2	866,558.6
Fuel	74,647.3	101,538.9	163,394.1	242,990.8	263,393.2	289,488.4	320,406.6	299,912.7	266,813.4	266,759.7
Nonferrous ores	6,908.5	11,892.0	370,580.6	890,565.0	922,172.0	930,559.4	941,392.0	901,484.6	909,011.6	687,976.4
Iron	59,838.9	94,714.4	150,482.4	240,307.5	249,322.0	277,046.5	280,346.4	280,946.3	238,229.9	219,745.8
Chemicals	38,049.5	97,490.1	164,993.7	213,565.8	247,474.6	266,849.4	317,515.1	326,654.8	309,426.9	267,420.7
Construction materials	121,069.6	199,687.9	305,176.2	503,848.7	716,275.5	799,946.0	835,879.5	834,469.2	803,702.2	480,971.7
Wood	230,878.7	323,176.2	449,510.3	523,308.5	543,349.2	539,146.6	536,212.8	543,589.9	447,170.1	333,174.1
Glass	7,355.2	13,002.6	13,364.4	23,669.2	24,335.6	26,390.6	29,710.4	32,829.2	27,067.0	35,117.6
Textiles	169,080.8	270,746.9	342,818.9	778,638.7	825,118.5	846,095.9	839,123.2	948,670.3	852,681.6	675,831.0
Clothing	100,997.1	194,646.7	296,127.0	330,056.2	349,122.5	337,682.4	342,620.5	384,826.7	349,183.5	376,373.3
Leather	289,441.7	353,771.1	477,212.5	649,399.1	646,740.8	703,390.3	727,532.2	756,132.5	790,362.9	657,265.4
Print	25,225.2	34,675.2	50,251.4	51,858.7	59,921.5	63,391.1	65,998.9	68,717.0	59,440.4	57,884.1
Food	560,073.8	842,574.2	975,354.2	1,340,829.5	1,380,835.7	1,405,209.3	1,437,806.2	1,476,800.0	1,353,337.8	1,478,522.5
Other	12,516.3	48,650.0	38,630.9	79,858.8	86,338.2	99,078.3	103,744.2	100,656.0	105,533.4	157,046.5
Statistical discrepancy	(30,105.6)	(12,486.3)	8,417.8	(616.4)	--	--	--	--	--	--
Total	1,818,560.2	2,821,988.8	4,217,250.5	6,592,408.5	7,109,922.7	7,414,588.9	7,668,587.1	7,875,511.3	7,426,927.7	6,560,197.4

Source: State Statistical Office.

Table 8.2: NET INDUSTRIAL PRODUCTION, CURRENT PRICES, 1980-90
(in thousands of Tugriks)

	1980	1981	1982	1983	1984	1985	1986	1987	1988	1989	1990
Power	189,687.1	216,917.7	264,735.2	277,113.8	258,038.1	338,359.0	280,359.7	294,095.3	274,368.5	294,616.8	192,070.1
Fuel	83,117.8	77,387.0	99,970.8	86,397.0	87,067.5	92,866.8	84,599.6	103,558.4	119,044.7	84,694.8	64,709.5
Nonferrous ores	96,555.5	130,989.1	298,528.1	353,334.0	390,857.8	406,924.0	402,327.4	426,272.5	398,592.9	411,405.0	436,110.3
Iron	61,136.2	60,181.6	64,737.9	70,785.2	64,964.3	82,234.9	83,308.4	93,795.3	96,531.4	101,193.4	127,945.5
Chemicals	66,361.2	64,371.8	62,965.0	69,170.4	71,103.7	68,159.0	81,255.2	92,141.7	107,157.0	127,132.0	127,252.4
Construction materials	79,776.9	83,952.8	101,911.8	117,307.9	108,562.6	113,493.3	168,425.5	187,412.1	197,735.0	208,637.0	153,479.5
Wood	135,746.9	137,101.7	136,514.7	166,834.5	153,724.9	170,618.8	161,286.7	158,068.5	155,694.0	169,483.8	130,962.0
Glass	3,742.2	6,456.8	7,398.3	8,920.4	8,686.2	9,944.3	9,322.6	9,285.8	13,992.6	16,676.2	12,233.5
Textiles	82,999.9	94,363.7	101,689.3	144,487.6	154,889.5	178,054.3	251,335.7	283,218.0	292,475.8	334,099.2	429,787.0
Clothing	99,875.7	103,255.7	106,113.2	109,186.9	111,759.8	117,889.5	107,670.7	109,465.7	116,786.8	154,973.1	140,236.5
Leather	139,447.9	154,868.9	140,942.7	176,595.9	161,011.8	158,758.3	184,262.3	197,908.3	234,766.3	301,169.5	302,560.3
Print	42,706.5	44,833.3	46,332.9	47,828.3	51,863.7	50,672.2	35,355.1	36,540.3	38,780.5	43,094.6	44,520.5
Food	537,509.3	614,165.9	651,269.9	704,296.0	727,977.7	679,956.5	566,699.2	502,239.4	505,908.8	629,396.6	691,111.4
Other	15,951.6	17,918.5	27,484.0	25,971.6	33,108.0	25,411.5	26,598.4	25,417.0	29,435.7	43,190.6	53,973.9
Total	1,634,614.7	1,806,764.5	2,110,593.8	2,358,229.5	2,383,615.6	2,493,342.4	2,442,806.5	2,519,418.3	2,581,270.0	2,919,762.6	2,906,952.4

Source: State Statistcal Office.

Table 8.3: ENERGY SECTOR STATISTICS, 1980-90

	1980	1981	1982	1983	1984	1985	1986	1987	1988	1989	1990
1. Electric Power Subsector											
Fixed assets (Tugrik million)	1,627	1,753	1,856	1,945	3,468	3,071	3,756	4,227	4,483	4,631	5,243
As percentage of total industry (%)	25.8	23.5	23.2	3.0	30.4	27.5	30.3	31.7	32.9	30.9	35.1
Gross output (Tugrik million)	410	453	445	493	601	724	796	830	890	920	925
As percentage of total industry (%)	8.8	8.8	7.7	7.8	9.0	10.0	9.7	9.7	10.1	10.0	10.4
Number of employees	4,900	5,400	5,900	6,200	6,800	7,000	7,600	8,200	9,800	8,400	8,930
Public sector (MW)	430	430	430	422	522	650	656	668	772	852	932
Self-producers (MW)	40	44	45	44	47	47	49	50	51	52	52
Total installed capacity (MW)	470	474	475	466	569	697	705	718	823	904	984
Coal-fired generation (GWh)	1,311	1,321	1,271	1,450	1,957	2,480	2,817	2,992	3,185	3,090	3,068
Oil-fired generation (GWh)	255	242	247	318	307	363	353	369	359	480	398
Total generation (GWh)	1,566	1,563	1,518	1,768	2,264	2,843	3,170	3,361	3,544	3,570	3,466
Electricity imports (GWh)	263	476	774	694	417	153	87	70	75	158	228
Total electricity supply (GWh)	1,829	2,041	2,292	2,462	2,681	2,998	3,257	3,431	3,619	3,728	3,694
Industry and construction (GWh)	873	1,052	1,175	1,221	1,263	1,633	1,799	1,837	1,871	1,911	1,803
Transport and communications (GWh)	68	81	84	88	89	145	161	178	182	185	174
Agriculture (GWh)	98	95	91	98	112	85	91	102	103	123	116
Communal housing & public services (GWh)	325	375	433	445	484	327	343	351	358	370	349
Other sectors (GWh)	75	55	108	172	190	190	205	206	267	293	290
Total energy consumption (GWh)	1,437	1,658	1,891	2,024	2,136	2,380	2,599	2,674	2,781	2,882	2,732
(Annual growth rate (%))	-	15.4	14.1	7.0	5.6	11.3	9.2	2.9	4.0	3.6	-5.2
Electricity consumption per capita (kWh)	865	973	1,063	1,132	1,167	1,268	1,350	1,355	1,376	1,392	1,287
Electricity consumption per employee (MWh)	293	307	321	326	314	340	342	326	284	343	306
Electricity exports (GWh)	-	-	-	-	2	53	38	26	58	-77	-76
Transmission and distribution losses (GWh)	125	110	123	134	155	174	181	248	278	280	323
As percentage of total supply (%)	6.8	5.4	5.4	5.4	5.8	5.8	5.6	7.2	7.7	7.5	8.7
Own use of power station (GWh)	267	273	276	304	388	443	477	509	560	566	563
As percentage of total supply (%)	14.6	13.4	12.1	12.3	14.5	14.8	14.6	14.8	15.5	15.2	15.2
Industrial and public tariff (Tugrik/kWh)	0.18	0.18	0.18	0.18	0.18	0.18	0.18	0.18	0.18	0.18	0.18
Residential tariff (Tugrik/kWh)	0.35	0.35	0.35	0.35	0.35	0.35	0.35	0.35	0.35	0.35	0.35
Diesel for industrial sector (Tugrik/kWh)	0.48	0.48	0.48	0.48	0.48	0.48	0.48	0.48	0.48	0.48	0.48
2. Coal subsector											
Fixed assets (Tugrik million)	405	413	429	453	661	870	908	1,008	1,077	1,189	1,208
As percentage of total industry (%)	6.4	5.5	5.4	5.4	5.8	7.8	7.3	7.6	7.9	7.9	8.1
Gross output (Tugrik million)	163	160	184	187	203	243	263	290	320	300	267
As percentage of total industry (%)	3.5	3.1	3.2	3.0	3.0	3.4	3.2	3.4	3.6	3.2	3.0
Number of employees	3,300	3,300	3,300	3,400	4,300	3,900	3,700	4,100	4,300	4,100	4,370

(Continued)

Table 8.3: ENERGY SECTOR STATISTICS, 1980-90 (continued)

	1980	1981	1982	1983	1984	1985	1986	1987	1988	1989	1990
Coal production ('000 tons)	4,376	4,303	4,921	4,975	5,425	6,516	6,962	7,762	8,606	8,040	7,156
Coal imports ('000 tons)	2	34	1	2	12	0	0	0	73	77	73
Change in stocks ('000 tons) /a	-62	244	58	73	395	-129	50	48	-38	-94	-90
Total coal supply ('000 tons)	4,316	4,581	4,980	5,050	5,832	6,387	7,012	7,810	8,641	8,023	7,139
Thermal power stations ('000 tons)	2,184	2,211	2,353	2,520	3,468	3,679	3,904	4,243	4,542	4,311	4,324
Industry and construction ('000 tons)	712	810	793	816	766	1,232	912	1,329	1,137	1,066	948
Agriculture ('000 tons)	322	348	349	353	381	401	465	517	429	202	206
Communal housing & public services ('000 tons)	671	775	772	740	666	702	784	439	737	1,248	723
Other sectors ('000 tons)	427	437	441	420	251	148	647	680	751	420	426
Total coal consumption ('000 tons)	4,316	4,581	4,706	4,849	5,532	6,162	6,712	7,208	7,596	7,247	6,627
(Annual growth rate (%))	-	6.1	2.8	3.0	14.1	11.4	8.9	7.4	5.4	-4.6	-8.6
Coal exports ('000 tons)	0	0	259	201	300	225	300	600	1,045	776	512
Coal price (Tugrik/ton)	34.1	34.3	35.3	35.1	35.0	35.8	36.0	36.4	37.0	37.6	n.a.
3. Oil Subsector											
Motor gasoline ('000 tons)	n.a.	n.a.	n.a.	n.a.	n.a.	n.a.	n.a.	n.a.	370	360	364
Aviation fuel ('000 tons)	n.a.	n.a.	n.a.	n.a.	n.a.	n.a.	n.a.	n.a.	39	34	40
Diesel oil ('000 tons)	n.a.	n.a.	n.a.	n.a.	n.a.	n.a.	n.a.	n.a.	347	344	356
Residential fuel oil ('000 tons)	n.a.	n.a.	n.a.	n.a.	n.a.	n.a.	n.a.	n.a.	58	60	68
Others ('000 tons)	n.a.	n.a.	n.a.	n.a.	n.a.	n.a.	n.a.	n.a.	47	42	36
Total oil imports ('000 tons)	n.a.	n.a.	n.a.	n.a.	n.a.	n.a.	n.a.	n.a.	861	840	866
Motor gasoline price (Tugrik/liter)	0.90	n.a.	n.a.	n.a.	n.a.	n.a.	n.a.	n.a.	1.25	1.25	1.25
Diesel oil price (Tugrik/liter)	0.54	n.a.	n.a.	n.a.	n.a.	n.a.	n.a.	n.a.	1.13	1.13	1.13
Residential fuel oil price (Tugrik/liter)	n.a.	n.a.	n.a.	n.a.	n.a.	n.a.	n.a.	n.a.	0.60	0.60	0.60
4. Heating Subsector											
Central region (Teal)	3,419	3,652	3,808	4,028	4,374	4,702	5,070	5,166	5,046	5,460	5,565
Rural areas (Teal)	55	58	56	60	101	109	149	331	980	982	1,545
Total heating supply (Teal)	3,474	3,710	3,864	4,088	4,475	4,811	5,219	5,497	6,026	6,442	7,110
5. Macroeconomic Indicators											
Population (yearly average, thousand)	1,661	1,703	1,746	1,788	1,832	1,877	1,925	1,973	2,021	2,070	2,122
Industrial fixed assets (Tugrik million)	6,306	7,460	7,999	8,448	11,404	11,180	12,395	13,327	13,626	14,989	14,931
Gross industrial output (Tugrik million)	4,636	5,163	5,775	6,316	6,705	7,214	8,195	8,542	8,798	9,244	8,887

/a A minus sign indicates an increase in stocks.

Sources: Ministry of Energy, State Statistical Office, The World Bank.

Table 8.4. ELECTRICITY PRODUCTION AND CONSUMPTION, 1970-90

(GWh)

	1970	1975	1980	1985	1990
Production	548.3	817.9	1,566	2,843	3,466
Imports	--	--	263	153	228
Losses	50.5	65.0	125	174	323
Domestic consumption	354.7	622.3	1,437	2,380	2,732
Of which:					
Industry	204.7	334.1	873	1,633	1,803
Agriculture	20.9	34.5	96	85	116
Households	109.3	149.7	325	327	349

Sources: State Statistical Office and Ministry of Energy.

Table 8.5: COAL BALANCE SHEET, 1975–91
(Thousand tons)

	1975	1980	1985	1990	1991
Sources	3,013.1	5,107	6,537	7,413	7,335.3
Stocks at the beginning of the year	285.3	729	21	184	274.0
Production	2,726.2	4,376	6,516	7,156	7,061.3
Imports	1.6	2	0	73	—
Uses	3,013.1	5,107	6,537	7,413	7,335.3
For electric power stations	1,762.8	2,184	3,679	4,324	4,983.7
Consumption	989.9	2,132	2,483	2,303	1,970.7
Industry	391.5	712	1,232	948	798.3
Agriculture	76.7	322	401	206	101.0
Households	210.5	671	702	723	610.8
Other	311.2	427	148	426	460.6
Losses	15.0	0	0	0	0
Exports	—	0	225	512	118.6
Stocks at the end of the year	245.5	791	150	274	262.3

Sources: State Statistical Office and Ministry of Energy.

Table 8.6: ELECTRICITY GENERATION AND CONSUMPTION IN THE CENTRAL ENERGY SYSTEM, 1980-90

(GWh)

Year	Gross generation (A)	Station use (B)	As percentage of gross generation (C=B/A)	Net generation (D=A-B)	Electricity imports (E)	Electricity exports (F)	Total supply (G=D+E-F)	Transmission and distribution losses (H)	As percentage of total supply (I=H/G)	Electricity consumption (J=G-H)
1980	1,311	258	19.7	1,053	263	-	1,316	112	8.5	1,204
1981	1,320	260	19.7	1,060	505	-	1,565	97	6.2	1,468
1982	1,271	270	21.2	1,001	760	-	1,761	110	6.2	1,651
1983	1,479	294	19.9	1,185	679	-	1,864	123	6.6	1,741
1984	1,958	378	19.3	1,580	410	4	1,986	146	7.4	1,840
1985	2,480	430	17.3	2,050	169	53	2,166	169	7.8	1,997
1986	2,830	460	16.3	2,370	87	38	2,419	234	9.7	2,185
1987	2,991	494	16.5	2,497	72	32	2,537	195	7.7	2,342
1988	3,169	525	16.6	2,644	75	58	2,661	234	8.8	2,427
1989	3,090	519	16.8	2,571	158	77	2,652	242	9.1	2,410
1990	2,966	538	18.1	2,428	228	76	2,580	323	12.5	2,257

Source: Ministry of Energy.

Table 8.7: ELECTRICITY CONSUMPTION IN THE CENTRAL ENERGY SYSTEM

(1989 - 1990)

A. By Consumer Category

Consumer category	Electricity consumption 1989 GWh	%	1990 GWh	%
Residential	109.3	4.5	95.8	4.3
Industrial	2,103.3	87.3	2,009.4	89.0
Public	197.2	8.2	151.5	6.7
Total	2,409.8	100.0	2,256.7	100.0

B. By Region

District (aimak)	Main population centers	1990 consumption (GWh)	(%)
Central	Ulaan Baatar	880.7	39.0
Bulgan Arhangay Ovorhangay	Erdenet, Bulgan Tsetserleg Arvayhaar	770.3	34.1
Selenge	Darhan, Suhbaatar	364.7	16.2
Dornogovi	Baganur, Sayanshand	241.0	10.7
Total		2,256.7	100.0

Source: Ministry of Energy.

Table 8.8: POWER STATIONS IN THE CENTRAL ENERGY SYSTEM, 1990

Power station	Unit no.	Installed capacity (MW)	Dependable capacity (MW)	Commissioning date
Ulaan	1	6		Dec 1961
Baatar	2	6		Dec 1961
No. 2	3	12		Dec 1969

		24	18	
Ulaan	1	12		Aug 1973
Baatar	2	12		Dec 1973
No. 3	3	12		Jun 1974
	4	12		Dec 1975
	5	25		Dec 1977
	6	25		Oct 1978
	7	25		Dec 1978
	8	25		Jun 1979

		148	125	
Ulaan	1	80		Oct 1983
Baatar	2	100		Nov 1984
No. 4	3	100		Dec 1985
	4	100		Dec 1986
	5	80		Feb 1990
	6	80		/a

		540	480	
Darhan	1	12		Oct 1965
	2	12		Oct 1965
	3	12		Oct 1965
	4	12		Jan 1966

		48	36	
Erdenet	1	12		Sep 1987
	2	8		Dec 1988
	3	8		Sep 1988

		28	20	
Total		788	679	
-----		---	---	

/a Under construction; scheduled for commissioning in late 1991.

Source: Ministry of Energy.

Table 8.9: INCOME STATEMENT OF THE CENTRAL ENERGY SYSTEM, 1988-91

(Million tugrik)

	1988	1989	1990	1991 /a
Revenues from electricity	508.7	479.3	452.8	190.7
Revenues from heat	296.5	311.1	318.1	163.5
Other revenues	0.0	0.0	8.1	3.2
Total Revenues	805.2	790.4	779.0	357.4
Coal	197.4	183.8	185.0	89.2
Fuel oil	21.3	19.2	30.2	17.6
Own use of electricity	9.8	9.0	9.4	4.3
Electricity imports	16.2	26.4	31.9	2.0
Water	13.7	13.9	14.4	6.0
Maintenance materials	5.6	3.5	5.8	2.0
Salaries and wages	32.1	27.4	33.4	21.0
Technical personnel	37.6	28.8	34.3	14.5
Administration	9.4	7.5	7.7	3.1
Insurance	3.0	2.6	3.2	2.7
Depreciation	219.5	210.6	215.9	61.9
Bank charges	52.7	0.0	49.9	0.0
Total Costs	618.3	532.7	621.1	224.3
Operating profit	186.9	257.7	157.9	133.1
Other profit	2.3	2.6	2.4	1.9
Total Profit	189.2	260.3	160.3	135.0

/a First quarter.

Source: Ministry of Energy.

Table 8.10: OPERATIONAL STATISTICS OF THE NO. 4 POWER STATION

(October 1990 to March 1991)

Unit No.	Normal operation		Planned maintenance		Forced outage		Demand constraint		Total period	
	Hours	%	Hours	%	Hours	%	Hours	%	Hours	%
1	3,185	73	408	9	775	18	-	-	4,368	100
2	3,706	85	-	-	662	15	-	-	4,368	100
3	3,839	88	240	5	289	7	-	-	4,368	100
4	3,216	74	744	17	398	9	10	-	4,368	100
5	2,166	49	-	-	1,519	35	683	16	4,368	100
Average	3,222	74	278	6	729	17	139	3	4,368	100

Source: Ministry of Energy.

Table 9.1: INDICIES OF AVERAGE RETAIL PRICES BY COMMODITY GROUPS, 1985-92

(1980=100)							Jan. 16, 1991=100.0	
	1985	1986	1987	1988	1989	1990	1991	March 1992
Total	103.0	102.0	102.0	102.0	102.0	102.0	152.7	230.8
Foodstuff	104.0	103.0	104.0	104.0	104.0	104.0	131.0	235.0
Nonfood	101.0	101.0	100.0	100.0	100.0	100.0	173.5	226.8

Source: State Statistical Office.

Table 9.2: THE AVERAGE ANNUAL WAGE BY INDUSTRY, 1989-90

Branches and enterprises	1989	1990 (Tugriks)	Index of 1990 (1989=100)
Coal industry	8,266	8,294	100.3
Energy industry	7,582	7,015	92.5
Mining industry	9,964	9,872	99.1
Construction corporation of Ulaan Baatar	7,571	9,067	119.8
Wood processing company	7,707	7,167	93.0
Auto repair corporation	8,903	6,949	78.1
Food processing industry			
Meat processing factory	9,485	10,862	114.5
Alcohol and beer producing factory	6,170	6,491	105.2
Bread and bakery goods producing factory	6,976	6,469	92.7
Milk factory	7,144	6,866	96.1
Bakery	6,697	6,874	102.6
Light industry			
Clothing factory	7,440	8,513	114.4
Shoe manufacturing	7,262	7,874	108.4
Leather processing factory	6,244	7,271	116.4
Carpet manufacturing factory	6,858	7,102	103.6
Chrome plant	8,029	8,520	106.1
Factory of woolen products	7,883	7,920	100.5
Construction materials plant	10,501	9,619	91.6
Ferro-concrete plant	8,340	8,640	103.6
Transportation companies (total)	8,114	7,708	95.0
22nd transportation depot	8,697	8,559	98.4
Transportation company of Ulaan Baatar	8,433	7,880	93.4
Transportation corporation	6,965	7,599	109.1

Source: Ministry of Labor.

Table 10.1: COMPOSITION OF INVESTMENT, 1977-90

	Total investment	Building and installation works	Machines, equipment, tools	Other	Building and installation works	Machines, equipment, tools	Other
	(Million tugrik)				(Percent of total)		
1977	3,009.9	1,896.4	954.9	158.6	63.0	31.7	5.3
1978	3,724.2	2,236.3	1,256.3	231.6	60.0	33.7	6.2
1979	2,600.0	1,704.9	719.1	176.0	65.6	27.7	6.8
1980	3,104.0	2,060.8	806.2	237.0	66.4	26.0	7.6
1981	4,288.9	2,556.7	1,209.5	522.7	59.6	28.2	12.2
1982	4,646.1	2,804.2	1,287.4	554.5	60.4	27.7	11.9
1983	3,924.3	2,200.0	1,269.4	454.9	56.1	32.3	11.6
1984	4,281.8	2,405.9	1,324.0	551.9	56.2	30.9	12.9
1985	4,633.8	2,740.0	1,409.4	484.4	59.1	30.4	10.5
1981-85	21,774.9	12,706.8	6,499.7	2,568.4	58.4	29.8	11.8
1986	4,762.5	2,627.8	1,525.4	609.3	55.2	32.0	12.8
1987	4,552.2	2,361.3	1,523.1	667.8	51.9	33.5	14.7
1988	4,537.9	2,492.3	1,358.8	686.8	54.9	29.9	15.1
1989	4,806.8	2,639.7	1,528.0	639.1	54.9	31.8	13.3
1990	3,379.8	2,227.1	810.0	342.7	65.9	24.0	10.1

Source: State Statistical Office.

Table 10.2: COMPOSITION OF INVESTMENTS BY INDUSTRY, 1977-90

	1977	1978	1979	1980	1981	1982	1983	1984	1985	1986	1987	1988	1989	1990
							(Million tugrik)							
Industry	1,423.0	1,689.5	907.4	1,254.3	1,767.2	2,614.5	1,740.9	1,668.3	1,583.3	1,870.1	1,397.8	1,246.5	1,401.0	936.1
Agriculture	425.8	483.6	391.2	408.6	488.2	563.2	552.2	691.6	671.0	615.6	601.2	687.5	731.6	337.2
Forestry	4.1	3.1	4.6	4.6	4.5	-	0.6	1.5	4.7	2.9	14.8	8.2	7.0	-
Construction	87.7	174.7	255.3	60.5	242.7	208.8	147.8	213.7	357.7	138.1	237.7	318.4	213.7	142.7
Transportation	213.0	270.8	153.1	165.8	223.2	262.6	280.7	288.1	293.1	445.3	461.7	552.3	515.0	341.2
Communications	32.5	96.5	122.3	157.4	131.7	56.2	62.7	109.8	89.3	102.2	58.9	51.6	65.0	26.2
Trade	85.0	43.9	41.8	52.6	82.1	63.3	27.3	43.5	58.7	100.9	122.2	127.5	162.0	95.7
Education, culture, art	174.7	134.4	108.3	117.7	164.9	207.3	167.8	317.1	251.0	210.3	241.0	220.3	274.0	257.6
Science, health, sports	55.7	64.5	72.5	81.4	133.8	102.8	100.3	98.6	102.2	136.6	140.7	108.0	141.7	154.7
Personal services	102.5	98.6	109.9	97.7	86.0	141.0	108.8	114.7	107.3	205.3	238.4	226.0	267.0	} 991.9
Housing	344.1	617.3	372.0	487.5	702.8	772.8	447.4	490.1	796.0	608.0	746.4	753.3	857.0	}
Other	61.8	48.3	61.6	215.4	261.8	252.0	292.8	246.8	319.5	327.2	291.4	236.4	169.2	95.2
Total	3,009.9	3,724.2	2,600.0	3,104.0	4,288.9	5,242.5	3,924.3	4,281.8	4,633.8	4,762.5	4,552.2	4,536.0	4,804.2	2,386.6
							(Percent of total)							
Industry	47.3	45.4	34.9	40.4	41.2	49.9	44.4	39.0	34.2	39.3	30.7	27.5	29.2	39.2
Agriculture	14.1	13.0	15.0	13.2	11.4	10.7	14.1	16.2	14.5	12.9	13.2	15.2	15.2	14.1
Forestry	0.1	0.1	0.2	0.1	0.1	0.0	0.0	0.0	0.1	0.1	0.3	0.2	0.1	0.0
Construction	2.9	4.7	9.8	1.9	5.7	3.9	3.8	5.0	7.7	2.9	5.2	7.0	4.4	6.0
Transportation	7.1	7.3	5.9	5.3	5.2	5.0	7.2	6.7	6.3	9.4	10.1	12.2	10.7	14.3
Communications	1.1	2.6	4.7	5.1	3.1	1.1	1.6	2.6	1.9	2.1	1.3	1.1	1.4	1.1
Trade	2.8	1.2	1.6	1.7	1.9	1.2	0.7	1.0	1.3	2.1	2.7	2.8	3.4	4.0
Education, culture, art	5.8	3.6	4.2	3.8	3.8	4.0	4.3	7.4	5.4	4.4	5.3	4.9	5.7	10.8
Science, health, sports	1.9	1.7	2.8	2.6	3.1	2.0	2.6	2.3	2.2	2.9	3.1	2.4	2.9	6.5
Personal services	3.4	2.6	4.2	3.1	2.0	2.7	2.6	2.7	2.3	4.3	5.2	5.0	5.6	0.0
Housing	11.4	16.6	14.3	15.7	16.4	14.7	11.4	11.4	17.2	12.8	16.4	16.6	17.8	0.0
Other	2.1	1.3	2.4	6.9	6.1	4.8	7.5	5.8	6.9	6.9	6.4	5.2	3.5	4.0
Total	100.0	100.0	100.0	100.0	100.0	100.0	100.0	100.0	100.0	100.0	100.0	100.0	100.0	100.0

Source: State Statistical Office.

Table 10.3: INVESTMENT BY MATERIAL/NONMATERIAL SPHERES

	Total	Material sphere	Nonmaterial sphere	Material sphere	Nonmaterial sphere
	------ (Million tugrik) ------			- (Percent of total) -	
1940	17.2	9.9	7.3	57.6	42.4
1941	26.5	15.3	11.2	57.7	42.3
1942	18.6	11.1	7.5	59.7	40.3
1943	17.4	10.4	7.0	59.8	40.2
1944	22.6	6.6	16.0	29.2	70.8
1945	26.3	11.5	14.8	43.7	56.3
1946	43.8	14.3	29.5	32.6	67.4
1947	47.0	11.1	35.9	23.6	76.4
1948	40.6	13.9	26.7	34.2	65.8
1949	31.7	9.6	22.1	30.3	69.7
1950	41.1	19.9	21.2	48.4	51.6
1951	40.7	14.8	25.9	36.4	63.6
1952	49.5	28.6	20.9	57.8	42.2
1953	60.2	37.8	22.4	62.8	37.2
1954	88.5	62.9	25.6	71.1	28.9
1955	123.9	92.6	31.3	74.7	25.3
1956	185.2	135.1	50.1	72.9	27.1
1957	341.6	267.1	74.5	78.2	21.8
1958	377.7	260.8	116.9	69.0	31.0
1959	510.7	355.5	155.2	69.6	30.4
1960	579.4	388.7	190.7	67.1	32.9
1961	639.4	391.6	247.8	61.2	38.8
1962	794.1	531.0	263.1	66.9	33.1
1963	872.4	667.4	205.0	76.5	23.5
1964	532.6	508.7	23.9	95.5	4.5
1965	814.9	490.0	324.9	60.1	39.9
1966	846.3	422.0	424.3	49.9	50.1
1967	1,018.2	690.4	327.8	67.8	32.2
1968	1,195.4	908.8	286.6	76.0	24.0
1969	1,168.4	897.4	271.0	76.8	23.2
1970	1,061.9	794.1	267.8	74.8	25.2
1971	1,149.2	833.1	316.1	72.5	27.5
1972	1,146.5	871.6	274.9	76.0	24.0
1973	1,236.3	853.6	382.7	69.0	31.0
1974	1,596.0	1,159.1	436.9	72.6	27.4
1975	1,882.5	1,174.0	708.5	62.4	37.6
1976	2,575.3	1,744.3	831.0	67.7	32.3
1977	3,009.9	2,271.1	738.8	75.5	24.5
1978	3,724.2	2,761.1	963.1	74.1	25.9
1979	2,600.0	1,875.7	724.3	72.1	27.9
1980	3,104.0	2,104.3	999.7	67.8	32.2
1981	4,288.9	2,939.6	1,349.3	68.5	31.5
1982	4,646.1	3,170.2	1,475.9	68.2	31.8
1983	3,924.3	2,812.2	1,112.1	71.7	28.3
1984	4,281.8	3,016.5	1,265.3	70.4	29.6
1985	4,633.8	3,057.8	1,576.0	66.0	34.0
1986	4,762.5	3,275.1	1,487.4	68.8	31.2
1987	4,552.2	2,894.3	1,657.9	63.6	36.4
1988	4,537.9	2,992.0	1,545.9	65.9	34.1
1989	4,806.8	3,097.0	1,709.8	64.4	35.6
1990	3,379.8	1,880.4	1,499.4	55.6	44.4

Source: State Statistical Office.

Table 10.4: INVESTMENT IN INDUSTRY BY SUBSECTORS a/, 1977-90
(Million tugrik)

	Generation of electric energy and heating	Petroleum refineries	Engineering	Nonferrous metals	Metal working	Chemicals	Building materials	Wood processing	Textiles	Glass	Clothing	Leather, fur	Printing	Food	Other	Total
1977	328.2	97.2	96.4	611.9	88.3	1.3	181.8	46.6	19.9	-	1.2	29.3	0.3	14.3	2.7	1,519.4
1978	188.0	202.9	142.8	783.5	48.9	67.3	133.1	105.4	86.8	-	0.1	32.3	1.5	16.6	23.1	1,832.3
1979	110.7	240.9	224.2	135.6	25.5	1.8	79.5	56.6	175.4	-	1.6	45.5	0.9	22.3	11.1	1,131.6
1980	81.2	207.0	207.0	168.2	58.2	29.4	381.6	56.6	167.6	3.3	-	31.6	0.3	29.5	40.6	1,462.1
1981	412.6	274.7	-	76.7	15.1	84.0	525.3	83.1	164.3	9.0	-	58.3	-	57.2	6.9	1,767.2
1982	616.0	332.8	-	376.7	11.2	180.7	162.1	65.4	86.7	1.7	2.4	29.7	-	144.5	7.6	2,017.5
1983	761.2	295.8	-	55.4	6.1	172.1	106.7	74.8	38.0	-	3.3	24.0	-	191.0	-	1,728.4
1984	686.2	219.1	-	84.6	14.3	192.4	190.2	63.7	27.2	-	2.9	41.5	-	104.5	-	1,626.6
1985	588.7	104.7	104.7	115.5	28.9	168.2	283.7	58.0	23.9	-	1.0	43.9	1.7	109.9	-	1,632.8
1986	588.4	212.8	212.8	143.1	25.0	258.2	262.1	110.2	69.5	0.7	2.6	55.6	3.5	117.5	-	2,062.0
1987	391.6	188.7	-	106.1	26.0	250.7	212.7	121.5	77.5	0.1	7.5	0.3	1.3	16.8	-	1,400.8
1988	169.4	196.4	-	214.8	22.2	97.6	226.9	41.6	122.6	1.5	17.5	45.5	3.3	101.4	-	1,260.7
1989	382.0	110.3	110.3	235.6	33.0	48.1	214.4	43.2	112.3	0.5	25.0	10.1	10.4	136.1	-	1,471.3
1990	376.1	153.3	-	82.6	37.0	44.5	151.2	0.3	13.2	-	-	-	0.8	71.1	5.4	936.1

a/ Differs from Table 10.2 due to difference in sector coverage.

Source: State Statistical Office.

Table 10.5: CHANGE IN STOCKS BY SECTOR, 1979-90

(in millions of Tugriks)

	1979	1980	1981	1982	1983	1984	1985	1986	1987	1988	1989	1990
Material sphere	1071.0	18.5	316.8	546.8	574.2	280.5	839.9	1421.3	-114.9	-203.4	134.4	-237.5
Agriculture	-10.0	-7.2	126.6	84.6	32.8	55.1	62.9	147.1	90.1	92.0	61.2	-90.1
Industry	176.7	108.2	110.7	240.7	272.8	176.8	267.5	389.5	18.6	-127.8	-83.1	-261.2
Construction	122.2	-26.4	45.8	14.9	-10.9	-9.9	18.5	98.4	-7.9	45.1	6.5	-1.9
Transport	11.2	24.4	-99.4	2.1	15.4	9.4	48.9	21.6	-17.5	-2.1	7.9	-6.5
Communications	-1.6	-1.5	3.2	0.3	-0.1	0.0	3.2	3.1	-1.6	2.0	2.4	-1.5
Trade & catering	772.5	-80.0	129.9	204.2	264.2	49.1	438.9	761.6	-196.6	-212.6	139.5	123.7

Source: State Statistical Office.

Table 10.6: STOCKS AT THE END OF THE YEAR, 1978-90

(in millions of Tugriks)

	1978	1979	1980	1981	1982	1983	1984	1985	1986	1987	1988	1989	1990
Material sphere	5,473	6,544	6,563	6,880	7,427	8,001	8,281	9,121	10,542	10,428	10,224	10,359	10,121
Agriculture	1,118	1,108	1,101	1,227	1,312	1,345	1,400	1,463	1,610	1,700	1,792	1,853	1,763
Industry	876	1,052	1,161	1,271	1,512	1,785	1,962	2,229	2,619	2,637	2,509	2,426	2,165
Construction	336	458	432	478	493	482	472	491	589	581	626	633	631
Transport	183	194	218	119	121	136	146	195	216	199	197	205	198
Communications	15	13	11	15	15	15	15	18	21	20	22	24	22
Trade & catering	2,947	3,720	3,640	3,770	3,974	4,238	4,287	4,726	5,488	5,291	5,078	5,218	5,342

Source: State Statistical Office.

Table 10.7: CHANGES IN STOCK OF INCOMPLETE INVESTMENT PROJECTS, 1979-90

(in millions of Tugriks)

	1979	1980	1981	1982	1983	1984	1985	1986	1987	1988	1989	1990
Total	641.8	(439.8)	912.0	452.8	668.3	(1,072.3)	(1,273.8)	1,018.3	115.9	490.9	261.3	1,270.9
Material sphere	495.9	(368.3)	634.5	231.4	277.9	(972.7)	(1,169.7)	740.8	(177.0)	574.3	24.9	727.4
Industry	192.5	38.2	625.5	191.2	(177.5)	(1,099.2)	(783.6)	650.7	(190.8)	211.1	(221.2)	486.8
Construction	117.7	(250.1)	35.7	142.5	295.1	(157.4)	(185.2)	16.0	23.6	46.3	39.0	13.1
Agriculture	102.0	(199.1)	5.4	58.6	86.8	123.4	(268.5)	(56.9)	64.6	178.3	27.4	70.1
Transport	65.6	10.7	74.8	(174.8)	11.2	116.2	150.8	1.4	(78.0)	179.5	80.4	185.9
Communications	40.2	15.1	(103.4)	30.6	53.8	32.6	(83.6)	81.6	(46.4)	(35.2)	36.6	(23.2)
Trade & catering	(22.1)	16.9	(3.5)	(16.7)	8.5	11.7	0.4	48.0	50.0	(5.7)	62.7	(5.3)
Other material sphere	2.2	3.5	(11.0)	-	-	(0.2)	(0.1)	(0.2)	-	2.9	(1.2)	0.8
Nonmaterial sphere	145.9	(71.5)	277.5	221.4	390.4	(99.6)	(104.1)	277.5	292.9	(83.4)	236.4	543.5
Housing, communal and consumer services	185.0	(87.3)	325.1	162.2	139.5	(142.2)	(21.0)	146.9	208.0	199.3	214.4	805.4
Science & scientific services	(17.7)	(15.2)	(13.3)	(1.9)	(2.6)	(0.4)	1.6	3.7	1.3	3.2	12.5	31.1
Public health, social security, sport & tourism	7.7	17.5	(6.8)	17.7	64.7	(16.3)	(28.0)	(79.1)	(2.3)	12.4	24.0	57.9
Education, culture & arts	(21.3)	3.4	(20.4)	3.5	63.1	(27.8)	19.0	85.9	43.2	(120.5)	29.0	26.5
Other services	(7.8)	10.1	(7.1)	39.9	125.7	87.1	(75.7)	120.1	42.7	(177.8)	(43.5)	(377.4)

Source: State Statistical Office.

Table 11.1: FAMILY INCOME AND EXPENDITURES, 1975-90

		Tugrik						Percentages					
		1975	1980	1985	1988	1989	1990	1975	1980	1985	1988	1989	1990
Income													
Total	Rural /a	4,997.6	5,838.7	6,866.8	7,028.6	7,087.6	7,093.7	100.0	100.0	100.0	100.0	100.0	100.0
	Urban /b	11,822.8	12,981.5	14,039.6	14,809.8	14,980.4	15,170.0	100.0	98.7	99.2	99.3	99.1	100.0
Wages and salaries	Rural /a	3,632.4	4,369.6	5,217.4	5,313.7	5,394.8	5,375.3	72.7	74.8	76.0	75.6	76.1	75.8
	Urban /b	10,051.9	11,064.4	11,686.7	12,397.1	12,680.4	12,821.7	85.0	85.2	83.2	83.7	84.6	84.6
Social insurance, pension, allowances /c	Rural /a	392.1	533.3	600.2	394.1	436.6	499.6	7.8	9.1	8.7	5.6	6.2	7.1
	Urban /b	1,046.3	1,175.7	1,492.3	1,449.6	1,341.8	1,406.1	8.8	9.1	10.6	9.8	9.0	9.3
Extra income from household	Rural /a	752.1	722.5	830.0	1,068.1	1,012.4	930.2	15.0	12.4	12.1	15.2	14.3	13.1
	Urban /b	-	83.5	171.0	285.0	253.0	298.8	0.0	0.6	1.2	1.9	1.7	2.0
Monetary benefits received /d	Rural /a	-	135.4	139.4	154.3	157.8	195.3	0.0	2.3	2.0	2.2	2.2	2.7
	Urban /b	314.5	321.5	408.5	362.9	383.5	341.4	2.7	2.5	2.9	2.5	2.6	2.2
Other	Rural /a	221.0	77.9	79.8	98.4	86.0	93.3	4.4	1.3	1.2	1.4	1.2	1.2
	Urban /b	410.1	336.4	281.1	315.2	321.7	302.0	3.5	1.3	1.2	1.4	1.2	2.0
Foodstuff Expenditures													
Total	Rural /a	1,629.2	2,007.0	2,298.8	2,087.2	2,039.8	2,470.5	100.0	100.0	100.0	100.0	100.0	100.0
	Urban /b	5,473.9	6,112.9	6,046.1	6,058.7	6,184.2	6,294.4	100.0	100.0	100.0	100.0	100.0	100.0
Meat, meat products	Rural /a	228.0	320.9	276.3	283.0	269.0	269.1	14.0	16.0	12.0	13.6	13.2	10.9
	Urban /b	2,010.3	2,151.9	1,982.9	1,920.8	1,953.2	2,000.1	36.7	35.2	32.8	31.7	31.6	31.8
Flour and cereals	Rural /a	622.6	760.0	842.7	907.8	823.1	961.6	38.2	37.9	36.7	43.5	40.4	38.9
	Urban /b	688.5	752.9	734.4	685.5	627.1	633.7	12.6	12.3	12.1	11.3	10.1	10.1
Bakery products	Rural /a	61.6	69.5	120.1	115.8	111.6	216.9	3.8	3.5	5.2	5.5	5.5	8.8
	Urban /b	484.7	539.0	596.7	628.5	634.7	614.4	8.9	8.8	9.9	10.4	10.3	9.8
Confection and fruit	Rural /a	318.8	372.6	479.2	455.5	515.4	535.7	19.6	18.6	20.8	21.8	25.3	21.7
	Urban /b	561.8	620.8	696.0	746.0	746.1	749.8	10.3	10.2	11.5	12.3	12.1	12.2
Milk, milk products	Rural /a	27.1	35.4	23.4	56.3	33.4	54.7	1.7	1.8	1.0	2.7	1.6	2.2
	Urban /b	629.0	592.1	608.3	700.3	690.5	675.6	11.5	9.7	10.1	11.6	11.2	10.7
Potatoes and vegetables	Rural /a	5.0	5.6	22.1	25.8	19.0	39.1	0.3	0.3	1.0	1.2	0.9	1.6
	Urban /b	119.7	213.5	230.9	289.9	315.8	312.1	2.2	3.5	3.8	4.8	5.1	5.0
Tea and salt	Rural /a	155.7	161.6	191.4	169.7	148.5	199.7	9.6	8.1	8.3	8.1	7.3	8.1
	Urban /b	124.8	123.6	109.7	100.3	92.8	93.7	2.3	2.0	1.8	1.7	1.5	1.5
Cafeterias and restaurants	Rural /a	9.5	6.6	7.1	16.1	5.5	7.0	0.6	0.3	0.3	0.8	0.3	0.3
	Urban /b	266.0	340.4	374.8	441.1	461.1	417.8	4.9	5.6	6.2	7.3	7.5	6.6
Alcohol and alcoholic beverages	Rural /a	198.6	274.0	335.4	50.4	110.4	179.7	12.2	13.7	14.6	2.4	5.4	7.3
	Urban /b	556.1	740.8	614.7	342.4	476.8	583.7	10.2	12.1	10.2	5.7	7.7	9.3
Other	Rural /a	2.3	0.8	1.1	6.8	3.9	7.0	0.1	0.0	0.0	0.3	0.2	0.2
	Urban /b	33.0	37.9	97.7	203.9	186.1	203.4	0.6	0.6	1.6	3.4	3.0	3.0
Nonfood Product Expenditures													
Total	Rural /a	2,602.2	2,901.1	3,773.6	4,243.1	4,209.9	4,260.9	100.0	100.0	100.0	100.0	100.0	100.0
	Urban /b	4,022.6	4,339.1	4,747.1	4,992.8	5,051.6	5,265.3	100.0	100.0	100.0	100.0	100.0	100.0
Cotton and woolen fabrics	Rural /a	634.6	619.3	779.4	809.9	722.9	808.4	24.4	21.3	20.7	19.1	17.2	19.0
	Urban /b	467.2	442.8	373.5	280.0	304.6	310.9	11.6	10.2	7.9	5.6	6.0	5.9
Other consumer goods	Rural /a	63.2	122.3	170.4	151.3	139.5	152.7	2.4	4.2	4.5	3.6	3.3	3.6
	Urban /b	212.3	196.6	295.5	296.7	345.8	368.3	5.3	4.5	6.2	5.9	6.8	7.0

(Continued)

Table 11.1: FAMILY INCOME AND EXPENDITURES (concluded)

		Tugrik						Percentages					
		1975	1980	1985	1988	1989	1990	1975	1980	1985	1988	1989	1990
Ready-made clothes	Rural /a	235.5	385.6	551.6	621.7	661.5	689.6	9.1	13.3	14.6	14.7	15.7	16.2
	Urban /b	1,099.0	1,299.4	1,540.5	1,791.2	1,751.8	1,747.7	27.3	29.9	32.5	35.9	34.7	33.2
Footwear	Rural /a	436.2	549.7	660.2	751.2	734.7	712.6	16.8	18.9	17.5	17.7	17.5	16.7
	Urban /b	773.8	726.8	961.0	960.8	906.5	988.9	19.2	16.8	20.2	19.2	17.9	18.8
Articles of educational need /e	Rural /a	130.7	105.9	151.1	201.9	256.0	244.9	5.0	3.7	4.0	4.8	6.1	5.7
	Urban /b	250.7	287.2	273.9	418.0	377.2	416.6	6.2	6.6	5.8	8.4	7.5	7.9
Perfume and cosmetics	Rural /a	59.2	76.7	150.2	113.9	99.4	103.4	2.3	2.6	4.0	2.7	2.4	2.4
	Urban /b	253.1	293.4	232.2	258.7	294.9	307.9	6.3	6.8	4.9	5.2	5.8	5.8
Furniture	Rural /a	384.3	327.3	559.2	631.9	700.1	614.3	14.8	11.3	14.8	14.9	16.6	14.4
	Urban /b	364.8	548.4	566.3	514.4	653.1	668.4	9.1	12.6	11.9	10.3	12.9	12.7
Tobacco	Rural /a	114.2	123.7	150.1	104.3	113.2	119.2	4.4	4.3	4.0	2.5	2.7	2.8
	Urban /b	157.8	178.4	141.3	126.4	126.1	134.6	3.9	4.1	3.0	2.5	2.5	2.6
Fuel /f	Rural /a	11.7	32.2	48.3	58.2	80.6	82.6	0.4	1.1	1.3	1.4	1.9	1.9
	Urban /b	270.8	239.0	155.9	148.9	91.3	90.2	6.7	5.5	3.3	3.0	1.8	1.7
Other	Rural /a	532.6	558.4	553.1	798.8	702.0	733.2	20.5	19.2	14.7	18.8	16.7	17.3
	Urban /b	173.1	127.1	207.0	197.7	200.3	231.8	4.3	2.9	4.4	4.0	4.0	4.4
Other Expenditures													
Total	Rural /a	377.3	524.9	466.2	453.9	392.9	476.4	100.0	100.0	100.0	100.0	100.0	100.0
	Urban /b	2,330.0	2,269.2	2,903.0	3,391.4	3,641.2	3,674.5	100.0	100.0	100.0	100.0	100.0	100.0
Cinema, theater, sports	Rural /a	14.7	8.3	8.3	15.2	14.5	12.7	3.9	1.6	1.8	3.3	3.7	2.7
	Urban /b	125.9	91.4	75.9	89.5	82.4	78.3	5.4	4.0	2.6	2.6	2.3	2.1
Transport, communications	Rural /a	45.9	78.7	79.4	55.5	50.0	50.5	12.2	15.0	17.0	12.2	12.7	10.6
	Urban /b	353.8	410.8	553.7	728.7	709.2	733.1	15.2	18.1	19.1	21.5	19.5	20.0
Housing and communal services /g	Rural /a	4.2	4.4	1.7	0.9	1.3	3.2	1.1	0.8	0.4	0.2	0.3	0.7
	Urban /b	740.2	846.6	923.4	902.8	1,123.2	1,142.8	31.8	37.3	31.8	26.6	30.8	31.1
Health services	Rural /a	5.9	6.8	1.1	1.3	5.0	5.5	1.6	1.3	0.2	0.3	1.3	1.2
	Urban /b	142.3	128.1	127.0	167.4	138.9	114.6	6.1	5.6	4.4	4.9	3.8	3.1
Service repair	Rural /a	-	-	11.8	5.3	9.8	12.2	0.0	0.0	2.5	1.2	2.5	2.6
	Urban /b	-	-	125.5	166.1	172.5	157.8	0.0	0.0	4.3	4.9	4.7	4.3
All taxes	Rural /a	27.7	39.7	68.6	47.5	39.9	43.6	7.3	7.6	14.7	10.5	10.2	9.1
	Urban /b	438.0	417.3	438.7	475.3	520.1	475.8	18.8	18.4	15.1	14.0	14.3	12.9
Other	Rural /a	278.9	387.0	295.3	328.2	272.4	348.7	73.9	73.7	63.3	72.3	69.3	73.1
	Urban /b	529.8	375.0	658.8	861.6	894.9	972.0	22.7	16.5	22.7	25.4	24.6	26.5
Total Expenditures													
Total	Rural /a	4,608.7	5,433.0	6,538.6	6,784.2	6,642.6	7,207.8	100.0	100.0	100.0	100.0	100.0	100.0
	Urban /b	11,826.5	12,721.2	13,696.2	14,442.9	14,877.0	15,234.2	100.0	100.0	100.0	100.0	100.0	100.0
Foodstuff	Rural /a	1,629.2	2,007.0	2,298.8	2,087.2	2,039.8	8,470.5	35.4	36.9	35.2	30.8	30.7	34.3
	Urban /b	5,473.9	6,112.9	6,046.1	6,058.7	6,184.2	6,294.4	46.3	48.1	44.1	41.9	41.6	41.3
Nonfood products	Rural /a	2,602.2	2,901.1	3,773.6	4,243.1	4,209.9	4,260.9	56.5	53.4	57.7	62.5	63.4	59.1
	Urban /b	4,022.6	4,339.1	4,747.1	4,992.8	5,051.6	5,265.3	34.0	34.1	34.7	34.6	34.0	34.6
Other expenditures	Rural /a	377.3	524.9	466.2	453.9	392.9	476.4	8.2	9.7	7.1	6.7	5.9	6.6
	Urban /b	2,330.0	2,269.2	2,903.0	3,391.4	3,641.2	3,674.5	19.7	17.8	21.2	23.5	24.5	24.1

/a Members of agricultural producer cooperatives.
/b State employees.
/c Social funds including children and student allowances.
/d Monetary remuneration from the workplace and the municipality.
/e Includes books, pencils and notebooks.
/f Includes petroleum, coal and firewood.
/g Includes electric energy.

Source: State Statistical Office.

Table 11.2: CONSUMPTION OF FOODSTUFFS PER PERSON, 1980-90

(Kg)

	1980	1985	1988	1989	1990
Meat, meat products	92.0	91.5	89.9	93.1	97.0
Milk, milk products	99.2	110.1	118.9	120.7	120.0
Butter	2.6	3.1	3.0	3.0	3.0
Flour	100.3	108.0	109.0	105.3	83.0
Sugar	23.1	22.1	23.8	23.6	18.0
Fish	1.1	0.8	1.4	1.3	1.0
Rice (cereals)	9.6	11.6	12.5	12.4	9.3
Eggs (units)	18.3	26.6	27.4	26.9	28.0
Potatoes	15.3	27.3	28.7	27.4	27.0
Vegetables	14.8	17.0	23.1	21.5	22.0
Fruit	7.6	9.4	11.4	12.1	12.0
Vegetable oil	0.9	1.2	1.3	1.4	1.0
Animal fat	2.0	2.7	2.6	2.7	3.0

Source: State Statistical Office.

Table 11.3: PENSIONS AND ALLOWANCES, 1990

Type pensions and allowances	No. of persons covered (Thousands)	Amount spent (Tug mln)	The source of finance
Pensions			
Age pension	170.5	351.5	State budget
Disability pension	29.4	45.2	--/--
For loss of a breadwinner	37.0	60.9	--/--
Permanent pension	5.7	2.8	--/--
Subtotal	242.6	460.4	
Allowances			
For mothers of a large family	99.4	68.2	--/--
Premium of a hero-mother medal	6.0	0.7	--/--
For twins	0.6	0.4	--/--
For looking after a baby in arms	44.5	15.6	--/--
To war and revolution veterans	12.9	5.1	--/--
Others	1.0	1.9	--/--
Subtotal	164.4	91.9	
Second allowances			
Temporary disability allowance	215.4	40.9	Social insurance
Pregnancy and confinement allowance	57.4	63.7	fund
For ill person attendance	92.9	9.6	--/--
For the care of children	19.5	4.4	--/--
For funeral	4.4	0.5	--/--
Subtotal	389.6	119.1	
Total	796.6	671.4	

Source: Ministry of Labor.

Table 12.1: EDUCATION SECTOR, 1980–1991

	1980	1981	1982	1983	1984	1985	1986	1987	1988	1989	1990	1991
Primary schools												
No. of schools	113	111	103	101	103	104	97	100	95	94	96	93
No. of students ('000)	145.5	146.9	150.8	153.0	153.9	153.1	156.0	157.8	162.9	165.4	166.3	154.6
Secondary schools												
No. of schools	460	467	473	480	482	486	492	504	512	521	538	550
No. of students ('000)	226.6	232.5	237.2	245.0	252.4	262.6	268.1	272.7	275.3	281.3	274.6	257.1
Total No. of schools	573	578	576	581	585	590	591	604	607	615	634	643
Colleges and universities												
No. of schools	7	7	8	8	8	8	8	8	8	8	9	7
No. of students ('000)	23.2	24.1	25.1	26.0	25.1	24.6	23.5	22.6	20.7	19.5	17.3	17.5
Technical and vocational schools (secondary level)												
No. of schools	25	25	25	25	27	28	28	28	28	30	31	32
No. of students ('000)	18.7	19.8	20.7	21.4	21.8	23.0	23.2	23.8	22.6	20.5	18.5	15.8
Mean years of school attendance											7.0	7.0
Adult literacy rate (Percent of population above 15 years of age)											90.6	

Source: State Statistical Office.

Table 13.1: CONSTRUCTION OF HOUSING, 1980-91

		New housing completed Floor area (Thousands Square Meters)
1980		296.7
1981		214.3
1982		263.4
1983		245.0
1984		318.4
1985		257.1
1986		217.3
1987		277.3
1988		358.1
1989		348.6
1990		265.5
1991		112.0

Sources: State Statistical Office.

Table 14.1: HEALTH AND NUTRITION, 1980–91

	1980	1981	1982	1983	1984	1985	1986	1987	1988	1989	1990	1991
Life expectancy at birth (years)											62.5	
Total no. of physicians	3,686	3,881	4,070	4,234	4,371	4,595	4,870	5,192	5,485	5,715	6,180	6,318
Total no. of other medical personnel ('000)	12.6	12.9	13.6	14.1	14.6	15.2	15.7	16.4	17.2	18.0	19.4	18.7
Bed/population ratio per 10,000	108	106	108	109	110	114	113	115	115	118	126	121
Daily calorie supply (per capita)	2,394	-	-	-	-	2,486	-	-	2,529	2,621	2,538	-
Percent of required daily calories	-	-	-	-	-	117.0 a/	-	-	-	-	-	-

a/ Average for 1984–87.

Sources: Asian Development Bank and International Monetary Fund.

Table 15.1: TELECOMMUNICATIONS SYSTEM, 1940-91

	Telephones 1/ (Thousands)	Long-distance calls (Millions)	Telephones 1/ (Per hundred population)	Long-distance calls (Per thousand population)
1940	2.4	..	0.3	..
1960	5.6	0.3	0.6	326
1970	19.5	1.0	1.6	814
1980	39.8	3.6	2.4	2,227
1985	49.3	4.4	2.6	2,392
1988	58.6	6.1	2.9	3,045
1989	62.6	6.3	3.1	3,120
1990	66.4	19.6	3.1	9,443
1991	68.5	..	..	..

1/ Telephone sets of all kinds connected to the public network.

Sources: National Economy of the MPR for 70 Years (1921-1991), Anniversary Statistical Yearbook, (Several data of 1990 are preliminary), State Statistical Office of the MPR, Ulaanbaatar, 1991 (Tables 2.2, 7.9, 7.10) and staff estimates.

Table 16.1: VEHICLE FLEET, 1970-89

	1970	1980	1985	1986	1987	1988	1989
				(Units)			
Cars	3,608	5,912	5,671	5,755	5,787	5,775	5,660
Trucks	13,511	21,880	25,118	25,805	26,577	27,316	27,384
Buses	703	1,331	1,460	1,514	1,628	2,105	2,410
Special vehicles	1,015	2,863	3,335	3,399	3,322	3,962	4,072
Trailers	4,137	7,511	8,536	8,941	9,868	10,639	n.a.
Total (excl. trailers)	18,837	31,986	35,584	36,473	37,314	39,158	39,526
				(Tons)			
Average truck capacity (load)	3.14	3.84	4.35	4.35	4.42	n.a.	n.a.

Source: Ministry of Transport

Table 16.2: PASSENGER TRANSPORT, 1970–91

	1970	1980	1985	1986	1987	1988	1989	1990	1991
				('000 Passengers)					
Total	53.4	122.1	171.1	187.5	211.6	234.5	242.2	231.7	234.5
Railway	0.7	1.4	2.1	2.3	2.5	2.6	2.7	2.6	2.6
Highway	52.4	120.2	168.4	184.5	208.3	231.1	238.7	228.3	231.3
River transport	0.0	0.0	0.0	0.0	0.0	0.0	0.0	0.0	0.0
Air transport	0.2	0.4	0.6	0.7	0.8	0.8	0.8	0.8	0.6
				(Average Trip Length, km)					
Average	8.4	8.2	8.3	8.3	8.0	8.5	8.7	8.8	8.2
Railway	193.1	211.9	207.5	203.1	194.6	204.2	214.3	218.9	230.0
Highway	3.9	4.1	4.1	4.0	4.0	4.0	4.0	4.0	3.9
River transport	0.0	0.0	0.0	0.0	0.0	0.0	0.0	0.0	0.0
Air transport	531.0	533.0	490.8	460.4	459.6	655.5	709.1	704.1	680.2
				(Million Passenger—km)					
Total	477.8	1,007.1	1,418.5	1,536.5	1,692.8	1,986.8	2,102.9	2,047.2	1,919.4
Railway	135.2	296.6	435.8	467.1	486.5	531.0	578.6	569.3	598.0
Highway	206.4	497.2	688.2	747.1	838.6	923.4	957.0	914.6	913.3
River transport	0.0	0.0	0.0	0.0	0.0	0.0	0.0	0.0	0.0
Air transport	106.2	213.2	294.5	322.3	367.7	532.4	567.3	563.3	408.1

Source: Ministry of Transport.

Table 16.3: DOMESTIC FREIGHT TRANSPORT, 1970-91

	1970	1980	1985	1986	1987	1988	1989	1990	1991
					('000 Tons)				
Total	14,465.5	33,092.8	50,982.6	55,431.3	60,141.1	63,716.7	62,013.8	51,443.6	33,896.4
Railway	4,724.6	9,783.2	15,029.3	15,929.4	17,752.9	17,850.4	16,848.7	14,523.6	10,185.4
Highway	9,710.7	23,263.3	35,903.1	39,453.3	42,331.3	45,807.6	45,095.9	36,837.6	23,660.1
River transport	27.4	37.4	38.6	35.5	43.0	44.2	56.1	71.6	46.5
Air transport	2.8	8.9	11.6	13.1	13.9	14.5	13.1	10.8	4.4
					(Average Trip Length, km)				
Average	149.1	150.7	155.1	151.3	140.2	132.1	130.1	133.5	125.0
Railway	323.3	352.6	394.0	397.6	368.9	349.6	353.5	350.2	290.4
Highway	64.3	65.7	53.7	51.6	49.6	47.2	46.5	48.1	53.7
River transport	131.4	125.7	123.8	121.1	120.9	110.9	89.1	68.4	36.6
Air transport	535.7	505.6	542.0	542.0	582.7	731.0	755.7	722.2	863.6
					(Million Ton--km)				
Total	2,157.3	4,987.5	8,390.9	8,390.9	8,292.3	8,418.8	8,068.9	6,870.3	4,234.4
Railway	1,527.6	3,449.4	5,959.6	6,333.4	6,179.9	6,241.1	5,956.1	5,085.9	2,957.9
Highway	624.5	1,528.7	1,934.3	2,046.0	2,099.1	2,162.2	2,097.9	1,771.7	1,271.0
River transport	3.6	4.7	4.7	4.3	5.2	4.9	5.0	4.9	1.7
Air transport	1.5	4.5	6.5	7.1	8.1	10.6	9.9	7.8	3.8

Source: Ministry of Transport.

Table 16.4: **MAIN GOODS TRANSPORTED BY ROAD, 1970–90**
('000 tons)

	1970	1980	1985	1986	1987	1988	1989	1990
Coal	735.3	1,411.2	1,605.8	1,721.6	1,717.6	1,800.5	1,716.1	1,502.5
Metal products (steel)	0.0	246.7	309.6	277.5	592.2	555.9	398.2	383.8
Construction materials	1,654.1	9,998.1	17,979.0	21,179.3	23,805.5	27,616.2	19,584.3	21,443.5
Cement	152.5	466.8	891.0	642.6	744.6	691.7	416.4	412.5
Wheat	339.1	528.7	1,399.0	1,501.0	1,329.5	1,383.4	1,100.3	945.8
Petroleum & Gas	346.2	462.0	533.9	603.9	597.7	684.7	673.7	602.6
Fodder	96.7	323.4	630.4	686.5	769.6	589.3	494.9	630.4
Drinking Water	0.0	942.2	1,363.5	1,346.9	1,394.9	1,341.0	1,071.0	1,088.4
Food Products	69.6	102.6	196.7	271.8	307.1	125.8	222.2	134.4
Others	1,952.2	5,887.5	11,127.6	7,751.9	8,206.5	8,320.3	20,128.9	9,515.7
Total	5,345.7	20,369.2	36,036.5	35,982.1	39,465.2	43,108.8	45,806.0	36,659.6

Source: Ministry of Transport.

Distributors of World Bank Publications

ARGENTINA
Carlos Hirsch, SRL
Galeria Guemes
Florida 165, 4th Floor-Ofc. 453/465
1333 Buenos Aires

AUSTRALIA, PAPUA NEW GUINEA, FIJI, SOLOMON ISLANDS, VANUATU, AND WESTERN SAMOA
D.A. Books & Journals
648 Whitehorse Road
Mitcham 3132
Victoria

AUSTRIA
Gerold and Co.
Graben 31
A-1011 Wien

BANGLADESH
Micro Industries Development Assistance Society (MIDAS)
House 5, Road 16
Dhanmondi R/Area
Dhaka 1209

Branch offices:
156, Nur Ahmed Sarak
Chittagong 4000

76, K.D.A. Avenue
Kulna 9100

BELGIUM
Jean De Lannoy
Av. du Roi 202
1060 Brussels

CANADA
Le Diffuseur
C.P. 85, 1501B rue Ampère
Boucherville, Québec
J4B 5E6

CHINA
China Financial & Economic Publishing House
8, Da Fo Si Dong Jie
Beijing

COLOMBIA
Infoenlace Ltda.
Apartado Aereo 34270
Bogota D.E.

COTE D'IVOIRE
Centre d'Edition et de Diffusion Africaines (CEDA)
04 B.P. 541
Abidjan 04 Plateau

CYPRUS
Cyprus College Bookstore
6, Diogenes Street, Engomi
P.O. Box 2006
Nicosia

DENMARK
SamfundsLitteratur
Rosenoerns Allé 11
DK-1970 Frederiksberg C

DOMINICAN REPUBLIC
Editora Taller, C. por A.
Restauración e Isabel la Católica 309
Apartado de Correos 2190 Z-1
Santo Domingo

EGYPT, ARAB REPUBLIC OF
Al Ahram
Al Galaa Street
Cairo

The Middle East Observer
41, Sherif Street
Cairo

EL SALVADOR
Fusades
Alam Dr. Manuel Enrique Araujo #3530
Edificio SISA, 1er. Piso
San Salvador 011

FINLAND
Akateeminen Kirjakauppa
P.O. Box 128
SF-00101 Helsinki 10

FRANCE
World Bank Publications
66, avenue d'Iéna
75116 Paris

GERMANY
UNO-Verlag
Poppelsdorfer Allee 55
D-5300 Bonn 1

GUATEMALA
Librerias Piedra Santa
5a. Calle 7-55
Zona 1
Guatemala City

HONG KONG, MACAO
Asia 2000 Ltd.
46-48 Wyndham Street
Winning Centre
2nd Floor
Central Hong Kong

INDIA
Allied Publishers Private Ltd.
751 Mount Road
Madras - 600 002

Branch offices:
15 J.N. Heredia Marg
Ballard Estate
Bombay - 400 038

13/14 Asaf Ali Road
New Delhi - 110 002

17 Chittaranjan Avenue
Calcutta - 700 072

Jayadeva Hostel Building
5th Main Road Gandhinagar
Bangalore - 560 009

3-5-1129 Kachiguda Cross Road
Hyderabad - 500 027

Prarthana Flats, 2nd Floor
Near Thakore Baug, Navrangpura
Ahmedabad - 380 009

Patiala House
16-A Ashok Marg
Lucknow - 226 001

Central Bazaar Road
60 Bajaj Nagar
Nagpur 440010

INDONESIA
Pt. Indira Limited
Jl. Sam Ratulangi 37
P.O. Box 181
Jakarta Pusat

ISRAEL
Yozmot Literature Ltd.
P.O. Box 56055
Tel Aviv 61560
Israel

ITALY
Licosa Commissionaria Sansoni SPA
Via Duca Di Calabria, 1/1
Casella Postale 552
50125 Firenze

JAPAN
Eastern Book Service
Hongo 3-Chome, Bunkyo-ku 113
Tokyo

KENYA
Africa Book Service (E.A.) Ltd.
Quaran House, Mfangano Street
P.O. Box 45245
Nairobi

KOREA, REPUBLIC OF
Pan Korea Book Corporation
P.O. Box 101, Kwangwhamun
Seoul

MALAYSIA
University of Malaya Cooperative Bookshop, Limited
P.O. Box 1127, Jalan Pantai Baru
59700 Kuala Lumpur

MEXICO
INFOTEC
Apartado Postal 22-860
14060 Tlalpan, Mexico D.F.

NETHERLANDS
De Lindeboom/InOr-Publikaties
P.O. Box 202
7480 AE Haaksbergen

NEW ZEALAND
EBSCO NZ Ltd.
Private Mail Bag 99914
New Market
Auckland

NIGERIA
University Press Limited
Three Crowns Building Jericho
Private Mail Bag 5095
Ibadan

NORWAY
Narvesen Information Center
Book Department
P.O. Box 6125 Etterstad
N-0602 Oslo 6

PAKISTAN
Mirza Book Agency
65, Shahrah-e-Quaid-e-Azam
P.O. Box No. 729
Lahore 54000

PERU
Editorial Desarrollo SA
Apartado 3824
Lima 1

PHILIPPINES
International Book Center
Fifth Floor, Filipinas Life Building
Ayala Avenue, Makati
Metro Manila

POLAND
ORPAN
Palac Kultury i Nauki
00-901 Warzawa

PORTUGAL
Livraria Portugal
Rua Do Carmo 70-74
1200 Lisbon

SAUDI ARABIA, QATAR
Jarir Book Store
P.O. Box 3196
Riyadh 11471

SINGAPORE, TAIWAN, MYANMAR, BRUNEI
Information Publications Private, Ltd.
02-06 1st Fl., Pei-Fu Industrial Bldg.
24 New Industrial Road
Singapore 1953

SOUTH AFRICA, BOTSWANA
For single titles:
Oxford University Press Southern Africa
P.O. Box 1141
Cape Town 8000

For subscription orders:
International Subscription Service
P.O. Box 41095
Craighall
Johannesburg 2024

SPAIN
Mundi-Prensa Libros, S.A.
Castello 37
28001 Madrid

Librería Internacional AEDOS
Consell de Cent, 391
08009 Barcelona

SRI LANKA AND THE MALDIVES
Lake House Bookshop
P.O. Box 244
100, Sir Chittampalam A. Gardiner Mawatha
Colombo 2

SWEDEN
For single titles:
Fritzes Fackboksforetaget
Regeringsgatan 12, Box 16356
S-103 27 Stockholm

For subscription orders:
Wennergren-Williams AB
Box 30004
S-104 25 Stockholm

SWITZERLAND
For single titles:
Librairie Payot
1, rue de Bourg
CH 1002 Lausanne

For subscription orders:
Librairie Payot
Service des Abonnements
Case postale 3312
CH 1002 Lausanne

TANZANIA
Oxford University Press
P.O. Box 5299
Maktaba Road
Dar es Salaam

THAILAND
Central Department Store
306 Silom Road
Bangkok

TRINIDAD & TOBAGO, ANTIGUA BARBUDA, BARBADOS, DOMINICA, GRENADA, GUYANA, JAMAICA, MONTSERRAT, ST. KITTS & NEVIS, ST. LUCIA, ST. VINCENT & GRENADINES
Systematics Studies Unit
#9 Watts Street
Curepe
Trinidad, West Indies

UNITED KINGDOM
Microinfo Ltd.
P.O. Box 3
Alton, Hampshire GU34 2PG
England

VENEZUELA
Libreria del Este
Aptdo. 60.337
Caracas 1060-A

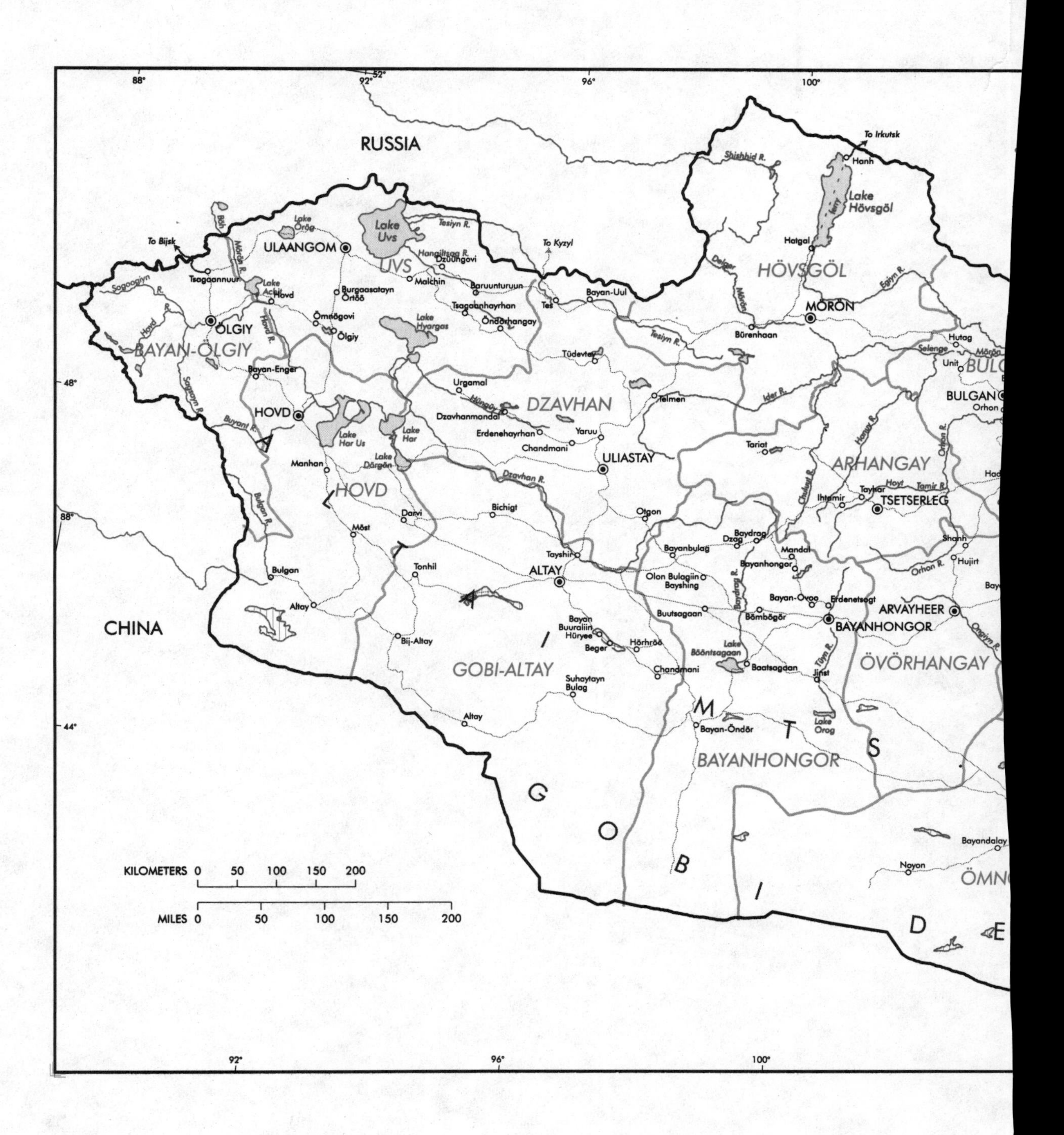

RUSSIA
CHINA
88°
92°
96°
100°
52°
48°
44°
To Irkutsk
To Biisk
To Kyzyl
Hanh
Lake Hövsgöl
Hatgal
HÖVSGÖL
MÖRÖN
Bürenhaan
ULAANGOM
Lake Uvs
UVS
Lake Achit
Tsagaannuur
Hovd
Malchin
Baruunturuun
Tsagaanhayrhan
Öndörhangay
Tes
Bayan-Uul
ÖLGIY
BAYAN-ÖLGIY
Ömnögovi
Ölgiy
Lake Hyargas
Bayan-Enger
Tüdevtey
Urgamal
Telmen
Dzavhanmandal
DZAVHAN
HOVD
Lake Har Us
Lake Har
Lake Dörgön
Erdenehayrhan
Yaruu
Chandmani
ULIASTAY
Tariat
ARHANGAY
Ihtamir
Tayhar
TSETSERLEG
Manhan
HOVD
Darvi
Bichigt
Otgon
Möst
Tayshir
Bayanbulag
Dzag
Baydrag
Mandal
Bulgan
Tonhil
ALTAY
Olon Bulagiin Bayshing
Bayanhongor
Altay
Bayan-Ovoo
Erdenetsogt
Buutsagaan
Bömbögör
BAYANHONGOR
ARVAYHEER
Bij-Altay
Bayan Buuraliin Hüryee
Beger
Hörhröö
Lake Böönstagaan
Baatsagaan
Chandmani
Jinst
GOBI-ALTAY
ÖVÖRHANGAY
Suhaytayn Bulag
Altay
Bayan-Öndör
Lake Orog
BAYANHONGOR
Hutag
Unit
BULGAN
Orhon
Shanh
Hujirt
Bayandalay
Noyon
ÖMN
A L T A Y
M T S
G O B I
D E
Selenge
Mörön
Orhon R.
Tamir R.
Hoyt
Dzavhan R.
Ider R.
Tesiyn R.
Egiyn R.
Delger
Shishhid R.
Hovd R.
Bulgan R.
Buyant R.
Tüyn R.
KILOMETERS 0 50 100 150 200
MILES 0 50 100 150 200

IBRD 24156

RUSSIA
CHINA
MONGOLIA
LAKE
BAIKAL
Lake
Hu-lun
Lake
Buyr
SELENGE
HENTIY
DORNOD
TÖV
SUKHBAATAR
DUNDGOBI
DORNOGOBI
S E R T
ULAANBAATAR
DARHAN
DZUUNMOD
ÖNDÖRHAAN
CHOIBALSAN
BARUUN-URT
MANDALGOBI
SAYNSHAND
DALANDZADGAD
To Ulan-Ude
To Borzja
To Cita
To Xilinhot
To Erenhot
To Ulan Hot
Sukhbaatar
Darhan
Binder
Ereentsav
Dashbalbar
Gurvandzagal
Onon
Halhin Gol
Tamsagbulag
Matad
Buhaiin Hashaatayn Hudag
Jargalant
Hoshuu Süme
Suhbaatar
Dzotol
Erdenetsagaan
Haldzan
Hongor
Ongon
Bayandelger
Delgereh
Delgerhet
Altanshiree
Ihhet
Buyant
Sümber
Gobi-Ugtaal
Delgertsogt
Erdenedalay
Tsagaan-Ovoo
Delgerhangay
Huld
Bayan Dobo Suma
Tsogt-Ovoo
Hanbogd
Hatanbulag
Hövsgöl
Zameen-Uud
Erliang
Erdene
Ulaan-Uul
Örgön
Dzüünbayan
Sayhandulaan
Dalanjargalan
Har-Ayrag
Darhan
Bayanmönh
Bürentsogt
Mönhhaan
Tümentsogt
Bayan-Ovoo
Berh
Bayan-Adraga
Mörön
Jargalthaan
Tsenhermandal
Delgerhaan
Bayanjargalan
Baga-Nuur
Baga-Nuur Coal Mine
Arhust
Nalayh
Bayantsogt
Altanbulag
Lün
Bayanchandmani
Bornuur
Baga Mandal
Tsogt-Öndör
Tünhel
Dzüünharaa
Bayangol
Büren
Önjüül
Delgerhaan
SEPTEMBER 1992
104°
108°
112°
116°
120°
48°
44°
52°
SELECTED TOWNS / VILLAGES
AIMAK CAPITALS
NATIONAL CAPITAL
FAIR-WEATHER ROADS, TRACKS OR TRAILS
ALL-WEATHER HARD OR LOOSE SURFACE ROADS
RAILROADS
AIRFIELDS
INTERNATIONAL AIRPORT
AIMAK BOUNDARIES
INTERNATIONAL BOUNDARIES